Health Seekers

A formula for living a healthier and longer life

"An innovative, practical approach to maximise your inherent
potential within the context of the real world."
– Dr André Sinden

by

Célène Bernstein

Health Seekers

Published by

Vivlia
Education for the Nation
Publishers & Booksellers (Pty) Ltd

1 Amanda Avenue
Lea Glen, Florida
PO Box 1040
FLORIDA HILLS
1716
RSA
Telephone: National (011) 472-3912
International + (27 11) 472-3912
Fax: (011) 472-4904

Copyright © 1997

Typesetting and Reproduction: G.L.E. Typesetting

Editing: Maggie Parsons

Cover design: Dennis Kalil

Index: Naomi Musiker

Bibliography: Prof. Reuben Musiker

Printed and bound by: ABC Printers, 21 Kinghall Avenue, Epping II, Cape Town

First Edition, Second Impression 1998

ISBN 1086867-080-5

Dedication

I dedicate this book to my loving and supportive family. Thank you Mommy, Daddy, Ivan, Martin, Tracy, Rowan, our precious grandson, Dylan, and granddaughter Carly.
Also to all my students studying the Life Science – Natural Hygiene Course throughout South Africa and abroad. You will find it a useful handbook, which will help you counsel people in their quest for a better lifestyle and improved health.

Preface

The physician should not treat the ailment but the patient who is suffering from it
MAIMONIDES

It is so sad that most people will refuse to believe or test dietary changes because they have not been "medically" or "scientifically" proven. There is thus a great reluctance on the part of so many of us to change our eating habits.

The reason for me writing this book is that I found a definite need for people to have access to health and nutritional guidance in a simple form.

I want to help those people who are unable to see me personally to start improving their health. This book guides people in the correct pattern of eating and sets out simply the reasons for eating certain foods and avoiding others.

I feel that once people have this information and guidance, it will encourage them to improve their eating patterns and lifestyle.

You will learn in the following sections that our bodies are designed to operate on a specific type of fuel and this fuel will only add to the health and life of the organism. If we use the fuel I recommend, as the mainstay of our diet, we will remain well. You will find in various sections a good many "**don'ts**" and "**no, no's**". But try not to dwell on the negative. I will inform you as to what are the worst influences on your health, and in time you will eventually be able to eliminate these foods, and work towards a healthier lifestyle.

When you go on my Maintenance Programme and you **do** make occasional exceptions to the foods and practices I recommend (and you will), do not make a big deal of it. Most importantly, don't have guilt feelings about occasional binging. Try to make sure that occasional binging does not become regular binging. Just keep coming back to the Maintenance Programme and persevere until it becomes your regular pattern of eating. It takes 21 days to break a habit. One way of breaking this yo-yo behaviour is to go to a health hydro or fasting institution. This will help you overcome both physiological and psychological desires for the wrong foods.

It is not what you do now and again that will bring on serious diseases; it is what you do daily, and habitually that will make the difference. A healthy body can cope with occasional exceptions. In order to help you overcome guilt feelings, I emphasise again that it is what you do "the day before the day of the intended indulgence and the day after" that counts. It is extremely important not to become angry with yourself, otherwise you will lose control. The scenario usually goes like this: "Well I blew it, I may as well blow it all the way", and you carry on eating. Getting angry with yourself can create a series of bad eating sprees, which may last a full week. Rather say "I made a mistake; I'll do better next time," then forget the incident. Skip a meal or two until you feel comfortable again. Do not give up. It takes years of discipline to stick rigidly to the diet I recommend and to develop a healthy lifestyle. Just keep on trying.

Do not concentrate on what you will be giving up, but on what you will be gaining – you have to be willing and eager to make changes in your lifestyle.

Certain people involved in the Natural Health industry may criticise the fact that I don't totally condemn the eating of certain foods. Because I do not advocate that everyone follow the Natural Hygiene way rigidly, these people may misunderstand my work. The target readership of this book is the ordinary person in the street and not the "converted". I want to enrol millions of people in the quest for better health who would otherwise be left out. Everyone can choose the level he or she would like to attain. I really believe that very few people in this country are ready to live on a totally raw food, vegetarian diet. I am offering major improvements, without insisting on being totally radical, which can often put people off.

My belief in the principles of Natural Hygiene will remain with me forever, but the practice of Natural Hygiene has to change because of the kind of environment we live in and the stress we are subjected to in the 20th century.

A health-supporting diet is unfamiliar to many of us because we are so used to eating processed foods which are so cleverly advertised by the food and health industries. Social changes have contributed to the increasing demand for convenience foods (processed foods). They can be prepared quickly, have a long shelf life and allow housewives to shop less frequently. It is important for us to realise, however, that what we enjoy eating and what we believe to be the correct nutrition for our bodies, is solely a result of previous conditioning and it therefore **can** and **must** be changed. Taking care of yourself is not an act of extravagance. It is a personal responsibility. You can make changes towards improving your health at your own pace. **You** must decide what you want to accomplish.

Eating is a social activity and I am aware that we sometimes have psychological problems with regard to the eating of certain foods. There may be particular reasons rooted in childhood or automatic habits that we carry with us during our lifetime. Remember, eating correctly is an ongoing process and every small improvement takes us a step further down the path to healthy eating. Everyone is psychologically different and even small dietary changes can have profound cognitive and emotional effects.

You can make better food available for your family, but don't try to force them to eat in a particular way. Once you start choosing the right foods, your understanding and application of correct eating habits/patterns and your enjoyment of a better lifestyle will become increasingly synchronised. You will find it easier today than yesterday; easier tomorrow than today. Remember, if you expect a significant difference to occur in your health, you must make a significant change. It is hard to quit old dietary habits and switch to a healthier diet overnight.

From my counselling sessions I have observed that people find it easier to stop eating meat and other animal products, but find it psychologically more difficult to give up ice cream, chips and popcorn etc. I cannot expect people to change overnight. I am just creating the conditions for change by encouraging you, by being there for you, supporting and showing you by my good example, how wonderful it is to be healthy and happy. I really believe that you should not put off healthful living for another day. Another day may just be too late.

Nutritional Counsellor
Célène Bernstein

The Promise of This Book

Health Seekers:

- contains detailed information on how to develop a better lifestyle, and a correct eating plan which is so different from everything you have been taught.

- serves as a guideline for establishing eating habits which will keep your body at its best and preserve health.

- gives step by step instructions on how to make simple changes without being too radical.

- offers guidelines for losing weight, increased energy, and improved vision and thinking.

- stresses not only the importance of the types of food you eat but how and when you eat these foods.

- encourages a 20% change in lifestyle and eating habits which should bring about an 80% improvement in health.

- contains scrumptious menus and recipes which can really help to ease your transition to more healthful foods.

- contains everything you need to know regarding what to eat and what to avoid in the case of certain diseases, such as asthma, eczema, yuppie flu, osteoporosis, arthritis etc. Read the book; find out all the answers to your questions and institute a plan of action. **This book is designed to provide educational information and does not replace the expertise of a physician.** It also provides you and your health care professional with a more natural approach to healing, which may be used in conjunction with your current medical treatment.

Statement of Responsibility

The author does not offer medical advice either directly or indirectly or prescribe the use of a diet as a form of treatment for sickness without the approval of a medical doctor. Dieticians and other experts in the field of health hold widely varying viewpoints regarding eating patterns. It is not the intent of the author to diagnose or prescribe.

The sole purpose of this book is to offer health information to help readers co-operate with their doctors in their mutual quest for health. Not every reader will be ready for every message presented by the author.

The information in this book is of a general nature, and should not be taken as medical advice for specific health problems.

The author and publisher cannot be held responsible for persons who use the information in this book without first obtaining their medical doctor's approval.

About the Author

Célène Bernstein has been interested in the field of alternative health for 25 years. She has a BA degree in remedial teaching from the University of the Witwatersrand, Johannesburg and taught retarded children for many years. Subsequently, she taught normal children in the local government schools where she came across many learning problems which might have been overlooked but for her experience with retarded children. She began reading books by Adele Davis and realised the great urgency to change the eating patterns of these children.

Célène pursued her knowledge by studying Health and Nutritional Science at the American College of Health Science, known as the Life Science Institute in Austin, Texas, USA.

She is the principal in South Africa of the same Health and Nutritional Science Correspondence Course, and has over 120 students. She was awarded a professorship by the Life Science Institute because of a thesis she wrote on "How the body acts on the food we eat". The thesis maintains that the body is a highly intelligent organism which, if given the right conditions, is able to maintain the individual in a continual state of good health.

She works in conjunction with medical doctors, where she is first and foremost a teacher who assists in the re-evaluation of an individual's eating patterns and lifestyle.

Célène is a regular guest on the 702 Radio programme, Alternative Thinking. She also lectures and gives cookery demonstrations every week at Hoogland Hydro, just outside Pretoria.

In addition, she gives lectures and runs seminars on health-related educational issues at various institutions.

When you read her book, you will realise you are being given a personal consultation in the comfort of your own home, with easy guidelines to follow.

Make your commitment to health by reading all that Célène Bernstein has to offer.

Acknowledgements

Much of the information in this book has been learned from the Feeling Fit . . . For Life Nutritional Course.

I am also greatly indebted to the many authors cited in this book, who are also fully acknowledged throughout the text and in the Select Bibliography.

I wish to express my deep gratitude to my husband, Ivan, for his patience and guidance, and the lonely nights he spent while I was so involved in putting the book together.

Heartfelt thanks also to my son, Martin, for his expertise in running our health shop "Health Seekers" and the support and encouragement he gives to all those people seeking health.

To Elizabeth, thank you for rewriting the manuscript neatly for Tracy, Lesley, Judy and René to type. Without all of you, I would never have been able to complete this lifelong desire, a handbook for retarding the ageing process.

Finally, a big thank you to all of you out there who put your trust and faith in me to bring about positive changes in your eating patterns and lifestyle. You are all my badges of recognition.

Contents

PART 1

The Philosophy of Natural Hygiene and the Elements of Health

Introduction

The health of human beings depends more on what they put into their mouths, than it does on any other single factor.

There are 3 basic factors that can lead to disease:

- Inherent weaknesses that we are born with,
- Toxic materials we have accumulated in our bodies, either from junk foods, pollution, chemicals added to foods and drugs taken over the years, and
- The lack of certain basic nutritional elements needed by the body.

The kind of foods I am going to encourage you to eat are designed to help the body overcome these weaknesses.

You have to realise that health is not a pill you take from a bottle. It's a lifestyle programme which has to be learned and you have to understand that the speed with which you can overcome a chronic disease, rests with you and the way you approach the nutritional advice given. *Dr Edward A. Taub* insists that his patients keep asking themselves the following three questions:

"What are the real roots of my problem?
What can I do in general to aid my recovery?
What can I do specifically, that medicine, surgery and physicians cannot?"
(Source: Taub, Edward A. – The Wellness Rx)

Remember, the choice is yours, through the food you eat and the way you live.

We have five elimination channels which have to be continually taken care of more than any other body organs. These elimination organs are the bowels, the lungs, the skin, the liver and the kidneys. If there is an overload of toxins (poisons) in the bloodstream and they have not been eliminated through the normal channels on a daily basis, then we can expect a breakdown of every other organ in the body and as a result, some form of disease will manifest itself. Through my counselling and the results I have achieved, I have realised that only **we** can create the conditions for the body to do the healing. A healthy body is vital in getting rid of poisons in the bloodstream on a daily basis. We have to carry our body around with us from the cradle to the grave, so we have to see that it runs more efficiently and with fewer repairs.

Every one of us has a built-in blueprint for good health, vitality, wellbeing and resistance to diseases of all kinds, but we spend most of our lives tearing up this blueprint with deadly living and eating patterns. One of the commandments of eating is "Thou shalt not poison thyself".

We all unknowingly commit 20 – 30 poisoning acts daily by smoking, drinking alcohol, taking in caffeine (coffee, tea, chocolates and cola drinks), adding extra salt to our food, eating an excess amount of animal products (meat and dairy which incorporate excess protein), and resorting to junk foods for convenience.

Unfortunately all these acts are poisonous, carcinogenic (cancer causing) and habit forming. It is these kinds of food and drink that eventually overload the bloodstream with toxins (poisons) and put stress on our elimination organs causing them to function inefficiently.

I support *Dr Edward A. Taub's* view that our health is much too important to be unscientific about, but it is also much too important to leave only up to medical science.

We have to re-examine the existing incorrect diehard teachings of eating patterns, lifestyle, why we become ill and why no cures have yet been found for terminal illnesses.

I want to make all of you aware that there has to be *"a positive shift in attitude towards proper nutrition, total fitness and correct lifestyle".*
(Source: Diamond, Harvey and Marilyn – Fit for Life)

The information I am offering contains both truth and simplicity. It does not involve taking pills, and the side effects you will experience are all positive. It is called . . .

Natural Hygiene

Natural Hygiene offers us a blueprint for living that can help us maximise our health at any age

SUSAN TAYLOR

Natural Hygiene is an age-old science.

It is a formula for people who are well and for people who are sick and tired of being "sick and tired!" Throughout my counselling sessions I have followed the Natural Hygiene formula and have helped people improve their eating patterns and lifestyles, bringing about a dramatic improvement in their health.

According to the concept of Natural Hygiene, the body is a highly intelligent organism that is self-programming, self-repairing and self-healing provided that its needs are met in accordance with our biological adaptations (we have to look at the way our body is designed physiologically).

Natural Hygiene holds that exuberant and radiant health is normal and natural and that disease and suffering are abnormal, unnatural and unnecessary. The medical world views disease as inevitable, unless prevented. Natural Hygiene concludes that disease does not have to be prevented, because it will not happen unless caused. Years of insufficient exercise, poor spiritual nurturing and the eating of processed foods in abundance have caused our bodies to stop performing as they should. You have to stop indulging in the causes of disease and start instituting the conditions of health. In order to realise why we become sick, you have to understand . . .

The Nature and Purpose of Disease

Disease enters through the mouth

CHINESE PROVERB

Let food be thy medicine

HIPPOCRATES

Amongst wild animals health is the rule and disease the exception. Disease is evidence of the body's attempt to purify, cleanse and repair itself and to restore body balance (homeostasis).

Diseases are due to one cause only – poisons (toxins) in the bloodstream. Diseases will not occur if you follow a healthy lifestyle with occasional fasting. (Do not attempt to fast for longer than 3 days without consulting a nutritional counsellor.)

If you want to remain well, you have to continuously cleanse the body of its toxic waste and never allow toxic waste to build up to an unacceptable level. If you continue to follow an improper diet and lifestyle, not only will discomforts continue, but they will develop into serious diseases. You should therefore not suppress symptoms with drugs (medication) on a continual basis, as this does not remove the poisonous overload in the bloodstream. You have to remove the causes of disease to prevent more serious illnesses developing.

I will explain to you very simply how degenerative diseases develop.

A simple cold is merely an expression of the body's effort to do some house cleaning. It is a temporary end point of our ability to carry toxins (poisons). Each time you get a cold and you suppress it with medication, these toxins will be reabsorbed back into the bloodstream, only to be stored somewhere else. After a period of time, you may notice you no longer get your usual cold, but instead you catch flu. Again, you suppress the flu with medication and again the toxins are reabsorbed into the bloodstream. As time goes on you notice that you no longer get flu, but suffer from bronchial infections.

Again, if you "treat" this infection with medication, you will be driving the toxins back into the bloodstream to be stored elsewhere in the body, along with the medication. As time goes on, you notice that you no longer get bronchial infections, or colds. You seem to be fine for a number of years and then one day you really feel awful and don't know why.

You then visit your doctor and he diagnoses one of the degenerative diseases eg diabetes, heart disease, arthritis etc.

Once you understand this explanation of the progression of disease, you will be more aware of why there is an urgency to change your original eating patterns and to look at your lifestyle. If you follow what I recommend in this book, you will be doing something for yourself today that definitely will spare you misery in the future. It is a

5

mistake to assume that the body can digest and assimilate everything that passes between our teeth and that food which is doing no harm now, will not eventually cause problems.

For many years you can eat the wrong kind of foods and show no clinical signs of illness, but sooner or later, depending on your constitution, inherited genes and the extent of body abuse through incorrect eating, latent degeneration turns into serious illness.

Day and night, each function and activity of your system, physical, mental and spiritual, is dependent on the attention you give it. The type and quality of food you put into your body is of vital importance to every phase of your existence.

The elimination of undigested food and other waste products is equally important. When you fail to effectively eliminate these waste products from the body, they ferment and putrefy in the colon. The neglected accumulation of such waste can cause a lot of problems.

The kind of food you put into your body has a direct link with your colon. If you continually eat processed, fried, highly refined foods and add enormous amounts of salt to your food, your colon cannot possibly be effective in eliminating the poisons from your bloodstream. In order to remain in good health, the human body must be nourished with food which has life-giving properties whose function is to cleanse and remove used up cells and tissues and send this waste matter to the colon to be evacuated (a bowel motion).

A diet of fresh fruits, raw vegetables, nuts, seeds, whole grains and legumes allows the body's own rejuvenating powers to work, often with surprising results. The body will never give up on us. It is such an intelligent organism. The only way we are made aware of what is going on inside our body, is by the recurring, warning signals that we keep receiving, such as continual headaches, constipation, colds, infections etc. What do we do about these signals? We either ignore them, or if they do get out of hand, we resort to medication in our quest for a quick fix. Medication suppresses the symptoms, but does not address the underlying cause of the disease.

We do at times need the expertise of medical doctors, and traditional medical treatments can be life-saving in emergency situations, such as accidents, or in the case of broken limbs etc.

We have to start removing the obstacles to healing and give the body the opportunity to use its capacity to heal – **IT CAN!**

Now in order to realise why degenerative diseases are not inevitable but rather caused, we have to understand the chemical functioning of the body which is dependent on . . .

Acid-Alkaline Balance

The regulation of hydrogen ion concentration (pH or acid-alkaline balance), is one of the most important aspects of homeostasis

ARTHUR GUYTON

In order to have optimum health and ward off degenerative diseases, the body must be in homeostasis (a state of equilibrium).

The body functions best with an internal chemistry which is slightly alkaline. Nature's way of replenishing alkalinity in the body is by means of natural food.

All foods are either acid or alkaline based. These foods could either leave an acid or alkaline ash in the body. Foods typically consumed by the majority of people are predominantly acid forming. Foods with a high protein or fat content, and highly refined foods produce very high levels of acidity. The average South African diet consists of 20% alkaline-forming foods and 80% acid-forming foods. There has to be a change to 80% alkaline-forming foods and 20% acid-forming foods. It is not unusual for the average South African to go 7 – 14 days without eating any alkaline-forming foods whatsoever.

If alkaline-forming foods are eaten **but** not consumed at the right time, nor in the right combinations, acidity will also result.

The foods we are accustomed to eating ie the acid-forming foods seem to be short of the elements listed in the table.

Real foods (alkaline-forming foods) provided by nature, contain everything the body requires for their proper digestion. If any of these elements are lacking in a food when it is eaten, the body must make an effort to supply the missing elements, and this exacts a price. The body now borrows the missing elements from its reserves eg organs, glands, muscles, bones etc. These reserves are really intended for short-term, emergency situations, and not for use on a continual basis. They eventually become depleted due to continuous borrowing.

This continual action of borrowing results in the body slowing down. We begin to feel out of sorts. Our joints are always sore, we start losing calcium from our bones, we always feel tired and get continual infections. Our cells become weaker and progressively diseased. These are all signs of an acid build-up in the body.

Our alkaline reserves (buffer salts) eg calcium are used to neutralise the acid build-up in the body, and to render the acid by-products left by acid-forming foods less harmful to the body. This means, however,

---

ELEMENTS NEEDED TO SUSTAIN LIFE		
Glucose	–	energy (fuel)
Protein	–	building/repairing
Fatty acids	–	building component of body tissues
Minerals	–	catalysts and building components
Enzymes (Vitamins)	–	increase efficiency (catalysts)
Water	–	medium for chemical processes.

(Source: Robbins, Joel – Eating for Health and Wellness)

that we are continually losing calcium and other alkaline minerals.

DO WE NEED EXTRA CALCIUM IN THE FORM OF SUPPLEMENTS?

You should not take extra calcium in the form of supplements because the body cannot utilise calcium in this form. In addition, this results in serious consequences. The excess is not just eliminated from the body. It is picked up by the blood and deposited in the soft tissues ie blood vessels, skin, eyes, joints and internal organs. Excess calcium combines with fats and cholesterol in the blood vessels to cause hardening of the arteries.

The calcium that ends up in the skin causes wrinkling; in the joints it crystallises and forms very painful arthritic deposits; in the eyes it takes the form of cataracts; in the kidneys it forms hard deposits known as kidney stones.

My advice to you is, **change** your eating pattern. Eat more raw fruit, raw vegetables, raw nuts, seeds and avocado pears. These kinds of foods are our source of live, alkaline, healing foods. Eat less meat, fish, chicken, dairy products etc. Some foods which qualify as real foods eg brown rice, whole-wheat bread, and legumes do however have an acid reaction, but this is nature's way of keeping a balance, so that the individual eating real food (nature's food) does not have a body chemistry which is too alkaline.

The acid content of these acid ash real foods is still very low and contains valuable nutrients which can be utilised by the body.

THE BREAKDOWN OF FOODS INTO ACID ASH AND ALKALINE ASH CATEGORIES

ACID ASH: Foods listed in order of least acid to most acid

Raw nuts – (except almonds which are alkaline)

Raw seeds – sesame, pumpkin, sunflower

Some raw fruits and vegetables eg *cranberries, *blueberries, *prunes, *plums, *squash

Whole grains (except millet which is alkaline)

Overcooked fruits/vegetables

Legumes

Dairy products – cheese, eggs, milk

Sugar and refined grains

White meats   – fish, fowl
                     raw
                     rare
                     well done

Fried fruits/vegetables

Fried pastries

Red meats   – beef, pork, mutton
                     rare
                     well done

ALKALINE ASH: Foods listed in order of most alkaline to least alkaline

Raw fruits (note *exceptions in acid ash column)

Dried fruits

Raw vegetables

Frozen fruits/vegetables

Lightly steamed fruits and vegetables

Almonds

ACID ASH (CONTINUED)	ALKALINE ASH (CONTINUED)

Herbs, spices, condiments, spicy foods
      – garlic, hot peppers, onions,
        horseradish etc
Fried meats
Coffee and tea
Salt
Alcohol
Drugs/medications
Tobacco	

(Source: Robbins, Joel – Eating for Health and Wellness)

So how are we going to remain well? Not only by eating the right foods, but also by developing a . . .

Correct Lifestyle

Early to bed, early to rise. In addition to that, some exercise
UNKNOWN

Nature has provided us with all the means to build the body from birth to old age and to maintain it in a state of vibrant health. These basic means are physically present in our natural foods. The answer to achieving a full life lies not only in proper nourishment, but also in non-nutritive factors, such as adequate rest, emotional wellbeing etc. This lifestyle is absolutely necessary for the maintenance of health and the prevention of disease. This is the plan of action to incorporate into your daily life.

EXERCISE
Regular exercise is absolutely essential for a healthy lifestyle as well as the restoration of wellbeing (muscles atrophy when not used). Our bones and muscles are designed to be used. You have to do some form of physical activity regularly, involving all parts of the body. This physical activity must be sufficient to keep the pulse elevated for at least 20 minutes, 5 or more times weekly.

Swimming, aqua-aerobics, strength and endurance weight training, brisk walking, cycling and aerobics are all excellent forms of exercise. Tennis, squash and bowling etc are substantially less beneficial because they are stop-start exercises.

Choose exercises you enjoy and do them regularly. Remember, the key essentials to exercise are stretching, toning and increasing cardiovascular fitness.

The benefits of exercise are manifold:

• Exercise improves the tone and quality of every tissue in the body.

• Exercise accelerates the assimilation of nutrients, and excretion (bowel movements) by stimulating the peristaltic action of the intestines. This minimises any carcinogenic waste materials which would otherwise collect in the colon.

• Exercise also improves the bone structure and increases bone mass. You must do resistance exercises such as push ups, circuit and weight lifting. These kinds of exercises put a demand on the body to cope with the load. This is how bones and muscles develop.

• Exercise helps everyone handle stress more effectively. Ten minutes of vigorous exercise triggers an increase in the production of the body's own cortisone by the adrenal glands.

(The drug cortisone damages the adrenals, so they atrophy, and do not function optimally.)

My advice to you is, do not eat heavy meals before exercising, as this interferes with digestion. You must wait at least $2^1/_2$ hours after eating before undertaking vigorous exercise. (I feel that the early morning is the best time to exercise.)

It is important not to underestimate the role of activity in maintaining health and wellbeing.

HOW IMPORTANT IS ADEQUATE REST AND SLEEP?

It is imperative to get enough rest and sleep daily. You have to rest when tired (even if it's for just 10 minutes per day but preferably longer).

I have found that when my clients are tired they reach out for stimulative foods such as chocolate, soft drinks, tobacco, alcohol, and vitamins, instead of listening to their body and resting.

Food is best taken after, and not before a period of sleep. During the hours of sleep all the organs of the body are given an opportunity to rest and relax. Repair and healing takes place while we are sleeping. If you are not feeling well, or recovering from an illness, it is advisable to get as much sleep as possible and eat foods that are not highly concentrated, eg fresh fruit and raw vegetables.

DO NOT BE AFRAID OF SUNSHINE!

Regular exposure of the body to sunlight is a prerequisite for superior health. Like plants we humans need sun energy to grow and to keep our organs functioning efficiently. Without sufficient sun energy, we soon become weak and anaemic.

The best time to get the most benefit without harmful effects, is before 9.30 in the morning and after 3.30 in the afternoon. You must try to absorb approximately 20 minutes to an hour of sunshine daily. When sunshine interacts with the skin, vitamin D is manufactured in the tissues. Vitamin D regulates the calcium and phosphorus metabolism of the body, thus the body is better able to absorb calcium and iron to build bones and teeth.

Warmth is essential to wellbeing. We should avoid chilling the body. Invalids and the elderly should be especially careful to keep their hands and feet warm at all times.

10

THE BENEFITS OF FRESH AIR

We have to breathe in clean, fresh air daily which furnishes the oxygen necessary for life's processes. It is therefore important to spend time out of doors on a daily basis. We should all sleep in rooms with the windows always open, whether it be summer or winter. If it is very cold and if you are concerned about your safety, leave a fan light open. Without fresh oxygen, every function of the body is minimised and the fluids and tissues of the body cannot operate effectively.

POSITIVE PLUSES IN LIFE

Included in this plan of action are all the things that make us happy, secure, give us emotional mental poise and a sense of purpose in life.

I refer to such things as a happy marriage, congenial surroundings, a desirable occupation, a loving and supportive family, a pleasing hobby, convivial companions and friends, financial security etc.

When we lack these psychological pluses, then life becomes drab and meaningless. We have to be positive in our thoughts and make life worth living.

The above are all absolute essentials of health which should improve our lifestyle and reduce stress.

There is however also a vital need for a dietary intake that will not pollute or present problems to the body. We have to make . . .

Proper Food Choices

The way to a man's heart is through his stomach. To care for that heart, follow the same route
UNKNOWN

Our bodies are designed physiologically to operate on a specific fuel. Much of the fuel we give our bodies comes directly from the things we eat. Every animal has a class of food to which it is naturally adapted. Humans are no different; they are unique in the animal kingdom, but are remarkably similar, both physiologically and in temperament to primates, who are frugivores (fruit eaters). *Dr Alan Walker*, an anthropologist of Johns Hopkins University in Maryland, has done research showing that humans were once exclusively fruit eaters. The essence of Walker's research is that though humans have adopted omnivorous eating practices, our anatomy and physiology has not changed; we remain biologically, a species of fruit eaters. This is indicated, for example, by the structure of our teeth and the length and structure of our digestive system. Moreover, if we compare the human anatomy and digestive system to those of the primates who are natural frugivores, we find they are virtually identical. Man, however, eats all types of food.

Are we natural meat eaters, or are we natural vegetarians?

In any standard biology textbook you will find humans listed as primates.

"Most primates are essentially vegetarian and their digestive systems cannot handle raw meat well."

(Source: The First Men – Time Life Books, NY, 1973, p 28)

11

A Comparative Anatomy and Physiology Chart

THE CARNIVORE	THE HERBIVORE	THE FRUGIVORE
4-footed with claws	4-footed with hooves	Two hands and two feet
Goes on all fours	Goes on all fours	Walks upright
Teeth adapted to tearing flesh (including pointed molar teeth)	Teeth adapted for grinding grasses and stalks	Teeth adapted for biting into fruits and chewing fruits (including blunt molar teeth)
Small salivary glands	Well-developed salivary glands	Well-developed salivary glands
Acid reaction of saliva and urine	Alkaline reaction of saliva and urine	Alkaline reaction of saliva and urine
Highly concentrated hydrochloric acid secreted by the stomach	Weakly concentrated hydrochloric acid secreted by the stomach	Very weak hydrochloric acid secreted by the stomach
Secretes enzyme uricase, which breaks down uric acid eg meat	Does not secrete enzyme uricase	Does not secrete enzyme uricase
Stomach simple and roundish	3 to 4 stomach compartments	Stomach with duodenum
Intestinal canal 3 times body length	Intestinal canal usually 20 times body length	Intestinal canal 12 times body length
Smooth colon	Intestinal canal both smooth and convoluted	Convoluted colon
Lives on flesh	Lives on grass and plants	Lives on fruits

(Source: Fry, T.C. – Correspondence Course: Natural Hygiene, Nutrition and Health Sciences)

It is thus obvious that the food we eat must be suited to our digestive system. The foods I suggest will definitely keep you in good health.

WHAT IS THE PROPER DIET OF MAN?

Originally man's diet consisted of seed bearing plants, which included fruit and nuts, cucumbers, green / red sweet peppers, tomatoes, avocados, squash, etc. Over the centuries man's tastes became more sophisticated and he wanted a more varied diet. Taste and palatability became more and more important and eating became an integral part of social life. "Eat to live" became "live to eat".

The problem is that many of the essential nutrients which people should be consuming are lacking in today's diet. We should be eating **more** fresh fruits, raw vegetables and cooked whole grains, and fewer animal proteins.

EXAMPLE OF A DIET MAN IS BIOLOGICALLY ADAPTED TO EAT

Breakfast

1 peach	(200 g)
1 apple	(200 g)
2 pears	(400 g)

Lunch

romaine lettuce	(400 g)
collard (a kind of cabbage)	(100 g)
celery	(200 g)
tomato	(300 g)
alfalfa sprouts	(100 g)
almonds	(60 g)
sunflower seeds	(50 g)

Supper

romaine lettuce	(400 g)
cucumber	(200 g)
mung bean sprouts	(100 g)
parsley	(50 g)
broccoli	(100 g)
1 baked sweet potato	(500 g)

THIS DIET PROVIDES THE FOLLOWING NUTRIENTS

	DIET	USA RDAs (Recommended Daily Allowances)
CALORIES	2 ,266	2 800
FIBRE	29,9 g	10 g
PROTEIN	69 g	70 g
CALCIUM	1 531 mg	800 mg
IRON	10 – 30 mg	35,7 mg
PHOSPHORUS	1 531 mg	800 mg
POTASSIUM	8,819 mg	2 000 mg
SODIUM	503 mg	300 mg
IODINE	,34 mg	0,15 mg
VITAMIN A	37,911 IUs	6 000 IUs
VITAMIN B-1	2,87 mg	1,7 mg
NIACIN (B-3)	24 mg	18 mg
VITAMIN B-12	trace	5 mcg
VITAMIN C	727 mg	60 mg

(Source: Robbins, Joel – Eating for Health and Wellness)

This pattern of eating is made up of "real foods" which come to us from nature as "complete packages". This means they have everything in them necessary for the body to process and assimilate. They contain vitamins, minerals, hydrocarbons, water, enzymes, amino acids and fats. It is these nutrients that allow us to sustain life, by providing us with the basic materials our body needs to carry on its daily functions. Thus it is physiologically and biochemically possible for humans to properly nourish themselves on a diet free of animal products. You need not become a vegetarian overnight, but you definitely have to reduce the amount of animal protein you are consuming. When man is placed on a diet for which he is not naturally adapted, this places unnatural stress on his organs of purification and elimination.

This causes great harm to the body, impairing its normal functions. The problem with most of us is that we do not get what we need from our modern diet. Even if you are not sick you may not necessarily be healthy. It simply means you are not yet showing any overt symptoms of illness.

WHAT HAPPENS TO THE BODY WHEN YOU CONSUME FOODS YOU ARE NOT BIOLOGICALLY ADAPTED TO EAT

Man's liver is smaller than that of a carnivore (meat eater) and because of this we cannot detoxify the poisonous products inherent in animal foods very easily. Our kidneys are also small and become diseased from overwork caused by a diet high in animal protein. A carnivore's gastric juice is highly acidic, to prevent putrefaction, while flesh undergoes digestion. Man secretes a much less concentrated and less abundant quantity of hydrochloric acid, thus he is unable to stop

the bacterial decomposition of flesh – a process that begins at the animal's moment of death. About 5% of the flesh of all animals consists of waste material called uric acid which is normally eliminated by the kidneys of an animal. Uric acid is a poison to humans, because it is non-metabolisable (can't be broken down).

All carnivores (animals) secrete the enzyme uricase which breaks down uric acid so it can be readily eliminated. We humans do not generate this enzyme, but instead absorb uric acid when meat is eaten. As a result calcium urate crystals form and become concentrated in the joints, feet and lower back. These deposits lead to arthritis, gout, rheumatism, bursitis and lower back pain.

Thus 3 balanced vegan meals daily, based upon whole grains, legumes, vegetables, fruit, nuts, avocados and seeds will definitely provide ample amounts of all nutrients for adults and growing children without draining the alkaline reserves from the skeletal structure.

In order to make the proper food choices we have to look at . . .

The Criteria of Ideal Foods

We have become so accustomed to the practice of dividing food stuffs into their various nutritive factors – protein, carbohydrates, fats, minerals, vitamins etc, that we often miss the importance of wholefoods

HERBERT M. SHELTON

By understanding the principles of nutrition and knowing which nutrients we need, we can improve the state of our health, stave off disease and maintain a harmonious balance in the way nature intended. Food must contain certain qualities which will render it nutritious. There are 12 criteria which we must always look for.

1 Ideal foods must supply our caloric (glucose) needs

Man's greatest need from foods is fuel (energy). Raw fresh fruits have the highest glucose content, followed by fresh raw vegetables. They are superior to starch as a source of carbohydrates. Certain fruits and vegetables contain phytochemicals (they fight free radicals) which act as inhibitors to cholesterol and some cancers.

Fruit and vegetables, known as **primary plant foods**, can provide approximately 2 300 calories per day.

WHY FRUIT IS SO GOOD FOR YOU

Fruit is easy to eat and easy to digest. It has natural sugars for instant energy. The body does not have to convert the starch to fructose (this involves energy), because it is already converted while ripening under the sun.

All fruit contains fibre, vitamins, minerals and enzymes. These elements provide a rich source of calcium, phosphorus, sulphur, iron and magnesium. The phosphoric acid is in the most soluble form, while the iron in the fruit is more easily taken into the blood than iron from any other source. The vitamin C found in fruits is an infection fighter and protects us against pollutants like lead, mercury and food additives. A shortage of vitamin C may result in dental problems with the possibility of tooth decay and gum disease as well as the failure of wounds to heal.

Fruit helps you deal with stress, boosts energy and is a natural antihistamine to help your body fight allergic reactions, eg hayfever.

RULES TO OBSERVE WHEN EATING FRUIT

- Only eat fresh fruits in season.
- Avoid fresh fruits kept in cold storage. Much of the vitamins and minerals are lost.
- Be aware that all fruit and vegetables lose some of their nutritional value when they are cut, sliced, blended or juiced. Do not peel fruit and vegetables long before eating them as they will lose some of their flavour and undergo oxidation.
- *Dr William L. Esser* insists that when oranges or other citrus fruits form a regular part of the diet, you should rinse your mouth after eating them, because the citric acid contained in these fruits can cause erosion of the dental enamel. Nevertheless

15

oranges are rich in lime and other alkaline salts. They furnish twice our protein needs, 10 times our iron needs, 100 times our vitamin C needs, and 9 times our calcium needs.

- A word of caution: If **only** fruit is eaten throughout the day for a couple of days (no other foods with it) a cleansing crisis may occur, ie you may have flu-like symptoms. Don't suppress these symptoms with any medication. I feel that you should not live on fruit only, for very long periods, because it is not as high in minerals and certain vitamins as raw, green leafy vegetables. Raw vegetables are very important for the maintenance of our mineral balance. However, a diet of fresh fruit only is sometimes advisable, especially as a temporary elimination diet (cleansing diet).

  I have found that adding lettuce and/or celery to any fruit, except the melon family, slows down the metabolism of the sugar and thus reduces that uncomfortable or light-headed feeling.

  Lettuce and celery are neutral foods; they will not interfere with the digestion of fruits, and will also ensure a high mineral intake (calcium) etc.

- Do not eat unripened or overripened fruit. Unripened fruit is highly indigestible and quite unpalatable. It contains starch and other carbohydrate substances that are unwholesome. Overripened fruit is in the process of fermentation and is not suitable as a food. The sugar in the fruit has changed into carbon dioxide, alcohol and acetic acid and the fruit is no longer wholesome.

- If fruit is not sweet to the taste, leave it alone. You cannot add any form of sweetener to get rid of the sour taste.

- Always eat fruit in correct combinations with other fruit.

- Fruit must be your first food of the day, even it you don't eat any food until lunch time. After eating the fruit, wait 1 hour and then choose any other foods in the correct combinations.

- Never cook or heat fruits. They will change from alkaline-forming to acid-forming foods, and this upsets our pH acid/alkaline balance.

- Always wash fresh fruit and vegetables carefully in purified water before eating them. It is best to peel fruit, unless organically grown.

- Avoid canned (tinned) fruits or vegetables as they are acid forming. They also contain excess sugar and are high in sodium.

- Believe it or not, certain fruits should not be eaten on a regular basis or in excessive amounts.

  Be wary of plums; they contain an excess of benzoic acid. Do not eat rhubarb and cranberries as they contain an excess of oxalic acid (a calcium antagonist).

- Dried fruit is the next best food other than fresh raw fruit, especially during the winter months, when a selection of fruit is not always available. Dried fruit should not be bleached with sulphur dioxide, which is a preservative used to enhance its colour and shelf life. Washing the dried fruit does not get rid of the sulphur dioxide completely.

- If you are following my programme of eating, I suggest that you don't eat fruit and refined sugar or any refined flour products within a short time of each other, because within an hour or two fermentation sets in and causes discomfort. Once you change to a more healthful pattern of eating, the body will no longer tolerate refined foods so readily.

IMPORTANT FACTS ABOUT CERTAIN FRUITS

I would like to mention some fruits in detail, but remember that **all** fruits contain all the necessary vitamins and minerals.

Fruit contains:
- 90% glucose/fructose
- 5% amino acids (protein)
- 2 – 3% minerals
- 1 – 2% essential fatty acids

DATES are richer in protein than most fruit; the protein content varies from 1,3% to over 2%.

The mineral content in FIGS closely resembles that of mother's milk.

My favourite fruit is the BANANA. It is the king of all fruit and is available all year round. Buy bananas unripe (green or yellow without freckles) unless you plan to eat them right away. If that is the case, the skins must be speckled brown, otherwise the carbohydrate doesn't dextrinise (convert) into sugar and the banana is difficult to digest.

A fully ripened banana is about equal in protein value to nuts. It contains the 8 essential amino acids which form a complete protein. It is rich in vitamins A, B, and D and high in potassium.

There is little doubt that an adult could live for some time on bananas alone, without any appreciable decrease in strength or health. If bananas are soft, don't despair. You haven't wasted your money. You can make the most delicious banana ice cream. Bananas **can** be mucus forming, so never eat them when you have a cold. I have found that when my clients follow the eating pattern I suggest, many have an insatiable craving for salt, because I have either reduced or cut salt out of their diet. My advice in this particular instance is to eat either bananas, watermelon or celery in the correct combinations and the craving for salt will be satisfied.

Bananas contain cobalamin which enables the bacteria in our intestinal tract to synthesise more vitamin B_{12} than we need; and each banana contains 20 mg of iron. If concerned about losing weight, eat only 2 bananas a day.

The PAPAYA (papino, pawpaw) has a high vitamin content per 100 grams. It contains 2 500 units of vitamin A, 33 units of vitamin B and 70 units of vitamin C.

Dr David P. van Velden, a doctor at the Department of Family Medicine and Primary Care at Tygerberg Hospital in Cape Town, has this to say about GRAPES *"After analysing grapes it was found that this particular fruit had amongst other nutrients, 3 – 4 potent combinations of antioxidants, that play an important role in the prevention of cancer.*

Grapes were also found to have micro-nutrients that help to prevent disease and promote healing. People on the 'grape diet' showed no deficiency diseases after several weeks. Whatever the reason, there is no doubt that a monodiet, eg the grape diet, seems to have a beneficial effect. At the very least, it purifies the body and there are health benefits.

Grapes may well correct abnormal biochemistry, caused by nutritional and environmental imbalances. Following the 'grape diet' for short periods could alleviate a variety of disorders, not only by eliminating impurities, but also by creating a longer term commitment towards a healthier lifestyle.

Our diet which has been referred to as the 'western way of death' is pushing our natural defence mechanisms to the limits. Nutrition could be the future of medicine. I endorse the 5 fruits and vegetables per day concept."

(Source: Personal Communication with author, 14th January 1997)

I would like to encourage you to eat

AVOCADOS, also known as "Alligator Pears."

They are not recognised as "true fruits" but can be eaten with subacid or acid fruits. Avocados contain considerable amounts of amino acids. They are rich in potassium, high in iron, magnesium, folic acid, vitamins B_2, B_6 and niacin. They contain monounsaturated fat and are high in essential fatty acids, which aid our hormonal system to function properly.

Avocados definitely help in reducing cholesterol and uric acid levels in our blood. They are not fattening, but don't eat more than 1 per day. Eat either 1 small or $1/_2$ a medium avocado if you want to lose weight. Never heat avocados – they will taste bitter.

Avocados can be ripened at room temperature or wrapped in newspaper, and packed in airtight containers to hasten ripening.

When ripe, store in the refrigerator. Avocados are not readily available from December to the middle of March.

Eating an abundance of fresh fruit in the correct combinations, will satisfy your craving for sweet foods and definitely reduce your desire to eat chocolates and cakes.

WHY YOU HAVE TO EAT RAW VEGETABLES ON A DAILY BASIS

Fresh vegetables, preferably raw, could help reduce the risk of cancer. Raw, green leafy vegetables are the richest source of minerals. They have a rich supply of sodium, calcium, alkaline organic salts, and vitamins A and C. They are the best source of chlorophyll and are also a source of small quantities of the highest grade of protein and trace minerals, all in the proper proportions and balance for the body to use in the making of "replacement parts" (cells). The green outer leaves of lettuce, celery and cabbage contain more vitamins and minerals than the white inner leaves.

Anaemic conditions will dramatically improve if you increase your intake of raw leafy vegetables. Raw vegetables can be eaten in the form of a tossed salad, or as vegetable sticks, but you must eat a substantial quantity. Keep your salads simple, 3 – 4 vegetables at a time, but eat a variety of raw vegetables daily.

Don't leave your vegetables soaking in water for long periods, because minerals and vitamins are leached from them and this reduces their nutritional content. Eating vegetable salads does not have to be boring. Many combinations are possible. Invent your own.

Certain vegetables should not be eaten in abundance because of the concentration of undesirable substances they contain, ie onions, garlic, radishes, watercress and mustard greens. These foods are less harmful, however, after they have been cooked.

Vegetables that grow above the ground, in the sun, eg lettuce, pumpkin and beans, tend to contain more vitamins and minerals than those vegetables that grow under the ground. Steaming vegetables is preferable to just boiling them, as fewer nutrients are lost and fibre is retained. Don't overcook them; they must still be crispy.

VEGETABLE STEAMING CHART

You can, however, also bake vegetables eg butternut, potatoes, sweet potatoes etc. These vegetables take much longer to cook.

	Approximate Time (in minutes) per 500 g
beans, string	12 – 15
broccoli	10
Brussels sprouts	10
cabbage (green or red) 1 head	10 – 15
celery	10
chard	5
collards	5
eggplant, sliced, 1 large	5 – 10
fennel	5 – 8
kale	5 – 8
kohlrabi	10 – 15
okra	5
parsnips, sliced	10
peas, pods (snow)	5
peppers, 4 large, preferably red, yellow or black peppers	5 – 8
spinach	5
courgettes (zucchini, baby marrows)	15 – 20

I have always insisted that my clients eat a raw vegetable salad first, before any cooked and processed foods, eg bread etc. There is no waiting after the salad, before eating the cooked meal. If you are really not excited about eating the salad, you need only have a side plate size, but it must be eaten first.

WHY?

Jennifer Meek claims that all processed food, and this includes cooked wholefoods, requires your immune army to defend your gut, and many white blood cells are lost.

Raw foods, however, do not cause this loss of white blood cells. Thus the raw salad, taken before cooked food, reduces the depletion of white blood cells and this saves you the energy used in the defence, repair and replacement of these cells.

Not many people are fond of a plain salad. You can add an oil and lemon dressing.

You must be aware of the drawbacks of COMMERCIAL SALAD DRESSINGS. Read the labels and note the ingredients. They frequently have a mineral oil base, which is a coal tar derivative. This mineral oil base coats the digestive tract, thus blocking the absorption of necessary nutritive elements.

Always use cold-pressed oils with fresh lemon juice when making salad dressings. Most salad dressings contain vinegar. Vinegar inhibits the effect of the digestive enzymes, which are essential for good digestion.

IMPORTANT FACTS ABOUT CERTAIN VEGETABLES

Remember, all raw vegetables contain all the right nutrients. I am giving you extra information on some vegetables.

ARTICHOKES: Artichokes are very tasty vegetables, which contain natural insulin.

BROCCOLI: This has a high vitamin A content, besides being rich in potassium, phosphorus and sulphur. Broccoli and cauliflower contain specific elements which could protect us against mammary and stomach tumours.

CABBAGE: Always use a young, sweet cabbage. A mature cabbage is often bitter and high in oxalic acid (a calcium antagonist). People with thyroid problems should avoid cabbage. Flatulence is often experienced when eating cabbage and this is due to improper chewing. When cabbage is cooked, it is also difficult to digest. So eat it raw and chew it very well. It is high in potassium and iodine.

CARROTS: These are very high in vitamin A (6 000 units of vitamin A are found in a 15 cm carrot). Carrot juice should not be taken more than 3 times a week. When juicing fruit and vegetables, you are getting the best live enzymes in a concentrated organic form, which the body uses quite comfortably. Carrots are high in sodium, calcium, magnesium, manganese and iron. Never peel your carrots, just scrub them well. The tiny hairs on the carrots contain vitamin B_{12}.

CELERY: This provides an excellent source of sodium and potassium. The green leaves contain a valuable hormone, insulin, which is needed by diabetics. When cooking a meal, add celery stalks as well as the leaves for natural seasoning. They do not contain the harmful substances that salt and other condiments do.

CUCUMBERS: These are rich in iron, potassium, magnesium, calcium and vitamin C. They are natural diuretics. Always peel cucumbers if they are waxed.

COS (ROMAINE) AND BUTTER LETTUCE: These are much higher in nutritional value than your so-called crispy lettuce (iceberg, head lettuce). Lettuce stimulates the metabolism and is high in calcium, magnesium, iron, iodine, potassium and natural sodium.

GREEN PEAS: These are neutral vegetables when eaten fresh, when dried they are classified as legumes.

MUSHROOMS: Although not really toxic, mushrooms are indigestible. My advice to you is chew them very well. When animal products are removed from the diet, add lots of big brown mushrooms. They seem to have the same texture as meat, so you will not feel totally deprived.

POTATOES (alkaline food): We cannot eat this vegetable raw because the starch content is too complex for our digestive system to break down. However, when cooked, the starchy molecules are broken down. The best way to bake a potato is to steam it first for 30 minutes and then bake it uncovered (no foil) at 350 °C until done. Cooking it this way cuts down on high temperature cooking time, thus retaining more nutrients. Always eat potatoes in their skins, which are highly nutritious. Please watch out for greenish areas on the potato. These contain a bitter poisonous alkaloid called solanine, which causes stomach upsets. Sprouts on potatoes also contain solanine. Don't be tempted to buy potatoes that have been treated with a sprout retardant (ask your greengrocer all these questions). Always keep potatoes in a brown paper bag to prevent exposure to daylight.

SPINACH, BEET GREENS, SWISS CHARD, COLLARD, ENDIVE AND PARSLEY: These vegetables are high in oxalic acid (a calcium antagonist) which tends to bind calcium, preventing this mineral from being assimilated into the blood. This occurs largely when the leaves are older and larger, and taste bitter and gritty. My advice is, do not eat these vegetables cooked on a regular basis.

You can however use baby raw spinach sparingly, provided the leaves are small and succulent.

SPROUTS: Sprouts are a live food full of live enzymes, and are a wonderful addition to any salad. The most popular and best tasting are the alfalfa and mung bean sprouts.

SWEET PEPPERS (BELL PEPPERS): Rather eat red, yellow or black peppers than green peppers, which are not ripe and thus very indigestible. Peppers are high in vitamin C, sweet and very tasty when eaten with steamed vegetables. Hot peppers (chilies) are irritants to the intestines, kidneys and bladder. If you do enjoy them, try not to eat them on a regular basis. People with haemorrhoids should definitely avoid chilies.

SWEET POTATOES: These vegetables can be eaten raw in a fresh raw vegetable salad or steamed in their skins.

TOMATOES: Tomatoes contain both vitamins A and C and are high in alkaline elements. They can be used freely in salads and are not acid forming in the bloodstream. They must be firm and red. Don't eat tomatoes if you have an ulcer. Never cook tomatoes as this renders them acidic.

YELLOW MEALIES: These should be eaten ideally in their raw state (just cut them off the cob) or steamed for just 1 minute in boiling water. Chewing carefully is of great importance as this assists in digesting the starch content of the food.

Fresh raw vegetables are also a rich source of natural fibre. They speed up the digestive process and decrease the overall time it takes for food to pass through the intestinal tract. Thus there is less time for intestinal bacteria to convert bile acids into carcinogenic compounds.

HOW DO YOU REALLY GET THE BEST OF ALL THE NUTRIENTS IN A PLANT-BASED DIET?

As there are different nutrients in different parts of plants, try to make sure you are eating from each part of the plant to get the full spectrum of health-giving nutrients. Each nutrient performs its own special function in the body, but no nutrient acts independently of others.

All the nutrients should be present in the diet, in varying quantities, for the body to stay healthy.

One way to do this, is to visualise a whole plant while making your food selections.

THE NEW CENTURY GARDEN GUIDE – PLANT PARTS AND THEIR NUTRIENTS		
Plant Part	**Sources**	**Rich In**
Roots	Beets, potatoes, carrots	Caratenoids, vitamin C, carbohydrates
Leaves	Lettuce, spinach, kale, cabbage	Tocopherol, caratenoids, folate, vitamin C, vitamin K
Fruits	Apples, bananas, oranges, tomatoes	Vitamin C, carbohydrates
Flowers	Brussels sprouts, broccoli, cauliflower	Folate, vitamin C, vitamin K

(Source: Campbell, T. Colin – New Century Nutrition, June 1996)

To put it very simply: fresh fruits act more as the cleansers of the body, while raw vegetables are builders of the cells and tissues of the body. It is therefore equally important to incorporate both in your daily food intake.

LIST OF SEASONAL FRUITS
SUMMER FRUITS:

Apricots	Cherries
Grapes	Watermelons
Mangoes	Nectarines
Prickly Pears	Peaches
Plums	Fresh Prunes
Strawberries	Lychees

WINTER FRUITS:

Persimmon	Oranges
Pears	Naartjies
Pawpaw (papinos)	Minneolas
Guavas	Grapefruit
Apples – all kinds	

ALL YEAR ROUND:

Bananas	Melons
Pineapples	Lemons
Spanspek	

If you want to find out more about other fruits and vegetables please read the following books:

Foods That Heal – Bernard Jensen
The Healing Power of Natural Foods – May Bethel
Dictionary of Natural Foods – William L. Esser

2 Ideal foods must have protein adequacy

A varied diet consisting of fresh fruits, vegetables, nuts (unsalted and unroasted), seeds, avocados, sprouts, legumes and unrefined grains furnishes us with the highest quality of protein in a form that is readily digested and assimilated by the body along with all the other nutrients we need. Protein in this form does not sabotage our health with poisons.

The most commonly asked question concerning a fruitarian/vegetarian diet is "are we getting enough protein eating this way?" We are told that we need 70 – 100 grams of protein daily. This is definitely far in excess of the body's needs and is the source of much trouble. Much of this protein comes from the eating of animal products. The countries which consume the largest amounts of animal protein are the sickest nations in the world. Meat and dairy products have too much protein for human consumption and our whole system becomes overcharged with the poisonous by-products of protein metabolism, which cannot be eliminated, thus resulting in gout, arthritis and other degenerative diseases, such as atherosclerosis, osteoporosis, accelerated ageing and obesity. In the case of obesity, excess protein is converted to fat and stored.

PROTEIN CONTENT IN CERTAIN FOODS

Protein Source	% protein
Mother's milk	1,6%
Meat	18 – 24%
Dairy products	12 – 18%
Fruit and vegetables	0,5 – 6%
Nuts and seeds (vegetable source)	up to 12%

During the first 6 months of a baby's life it will double its birth weight. This it achieves on mother's milk (breast milk) which has 1,6% protein. From the age of 6 months it continues to grow, but not as rapidly. When it becomes an adult it stops growing and the protein requirement decreases.

Every day we break down millions of cells and replace them. The body retains two thirds of the protein from these broken down cells and recycles it.

A big bull grows to his size on a vegetable source of protein, and so does the gorilla, the strongest animal per body weight.

HOW MUCH PROTEIN DO WE NEED?

The body really needs only 25 – 30 grams of protein daily. This is equivalent to 1 gram per 2 kg of body weight, for example: if you weigh 50 kg you need 25 grams of protein. This is adequate and should be derived from raw, unprocessed food. You need to eat only half a cup (100 g) of nuts/seeds three times per week.

We need protein for healthy tissue, growth and repair and not as a fuel source. Humans cannot use "protein" as such. We must laboriously digest it into amino acids before we can absorb and use it. Amino acids are the chemical units or the "building blocks" as they are popularly called, that make up protein.

Protein cannot exist without the proper combination of amino acids. Fruits, however, have their protein complement reduced to amino acids during the ripening process. Amino acids aid in the balance and functioning of the adrenal glands, in maintaining the condition of the skin and hair, and in the structure and functioning of the reproductive organs.

You must be aware that protein needs are somewhat greater for growing children, during pregnancy, lactation and recovery from a debilitating disease, weight training and after a prolonged fast.

In the above circumstances you can thus increase your protein needs to 35 grams. Remember, there is a small amount of protein in all fruits and vegetables and if you are eating a varied diet, you are meeting the body's requirements.

COMPLETE PROTEINS – ESSENTIAL AMINO ACIDS

The argument I keep getting is that vegetarian food does not provide complete proteins. Protein is composed of 23 amino acids. Of these 23 amino acids, 8 are termed essential amino acids. These 8 cannot be manufactured by the body, and so must be supplied directly to the body via food. A complete protein is a food that contains all 8 of the essential amino acids. According to popular thinking, a food that contains only some of the 8 essential amino acids is known as an incomplete protein food. According to conventional thinking, only meat, dairy products, eggs, soya beans and nuts are complete protein foods and fruit and vegetables are accepted as incomplete protein foods.

You must be aware that with animal protein comes cholesterol. No fruit or vegetable has the ability to manufacture cholesterol, therefore no plant food contains cholesterol. *Dr Joel Robbins* (Eating for Health and Wellness) says *"all 8 essential amino acids may be obtained from a varied diet of fruits, vegetables, nuts, seeds, and sprouts. It is not necessary for one food, or one meal, or one day's intake of food to contain all 8 essential amino acids.*
We thus do not need to eat only meat, cheese or soya beans to obtain complete protein, nor do we need to mix grains and beans or milk and cereals, to get a complete protein."

THE AMINO ACID POOL

According to *Guyton's Physiology* we have an AMINO ACID POOL, which stores amino acids, so that as the body needs them to manufacture protein, they are available. This amino acid pool is located in the liver and the bloodstream. The amino acid pool is like a bank that is open 24 hours a day.

"If our breakfast contains only 3 of the essential amino acids – not enough to make a complete protein, these 3 are put into the amino acid pool. During the next meal, we may eat 2 additional of the essential amino acids. These too are sent to the amino acid pool. Then at supper we may eat another variety of fresh fruit, which will make up the missing 3 essential amino acids. Now the body can draw from the amino acid pool all that it needs to make up a complete protein."

(Source: Robbins, Joel – Eating for Health and Wellness)

If you are really concerned about eating a food that has all 8 essential amino acids, which are in a form easily used by the body and not difficult to digest, I suggest you eat some of the following wholesome foods.

FOODS CONTAINING 8 ESSENTIAL AMINO ACIDS

Fruits: Bananas, Tomatoes, Dates.

Nuts: (Raw and Unsalted) Almonds, Coconuts, Hazelnuts, Sunflower seeds, Walnuts, Brazil nuts, Pecans, Pumpkin seeds, Pistachio nuts, Pine nuts and Cashew nuts.

Vegetables: Alfalfa sprouts, Bean sprouts, Carrots, Eggplant, Sweet potatoes, Broccoli, Cabbage, Corn and Squashes, Leafy green vegetables.

RULES TO OBSERVE WHEN EATING NUTS AND SEEDS

- The best protein to eat is unsalted, unroasted nuts and seeds correctly combined.
- Nuts and seeds should be bought fresh and stored in the freezer or refrigerator. Nuts that are not fresh contain rancid oils which are harmful to the stomach. They retard pancreatic enzymes and destroy vitamins.
- Although there is a greater need for nuts and seeds in winter than in summer, you should not consume an excess of these foods.
- It is not necessary to eat nuts or any other form of protein every single day to obtain your protein needs, provided you are eating a varied diet of fresh fruit and vegetables daily.
- People whose digestion has been impaired by incorrect eating in the past, may have difficulty digesting nuts and seeds. This will manifest in stomach distention, possible pain and a bloated feeling. My suggestion here is that a fast should be undertaken under supervision to improve the digestion.
- You should not eat nuts and seeds with starch meals. Nuts and seeds being high in fat, should not be eaten together in the same meal as avocados, or on the same day.
- For better digestion, it is best to eat only one kind of nut or seed, or only one other kind of protein, at a given meal. You must chew your nuts very well. If you have impaired digestion, grind your nuts.
- Never snack on nuts and seeds between meals. This will encourage thirst. Nuts and seeds should always be eaten together with high water content foods such as fruit or raw vegetables.
- Food combining rules are of major importance in the consumption of protein foods.

THE HEALTH BENEFITS OF EATING NUTS AND SEEDS

Nuts, especially almonds, are thought to be invaluable in the fight against osteoporosis, as they are a valuable source of the trace mineral boron. Research shows that women on low boron diets are more likely to lose magnesium and calcium, two very important minerals for strong, healthy bones. All nuts are free from the uric acid and waste poisons found in all flesh foods. They are very rich in phosphorus and magnesium.

I would like to mention the following nuts and seeds:

NUTS

PECANS: Easy to chew.

ALMONDS: The most alkaline of the nuts. Babies can be given almond milk but this should not replace formula.

SEEDS

These are excellent sources of protein, essential fatty acids, vitamins, minerals and trace elements. They are also rich in magnesium and calcium, which aid in the building of strong bones.

SUNFLOWER SEEDS: These are high in vitamin D, rich in B complex vitamins and contain liberal amounts of vitamins E and K, calcium, phosphorus, silicon, magnesium, fluorine, lecithin and trace minerals.

PUMPKIN SEEDS: Besides being rich in essential fatty acids, pumpkin seeds contain iron, phosphorus, calcium, and vitamins A and B complex. These seeds with all their good properties build healthy red blood cells.

SESAME SEEDS: Use the ones that are brown in colour. They are a good source of minerals, especially calcium and B complex vitamins. Tahini sauce (also called tachina or tachini) is made from pulped sesame seeds. You can use tahini sauce as a dressing or a dip for vegetables.

SEED AND NUT MILKS can be used instead of cream or milk.

WHAT ABOUT COCONUTS AND PEANUTS?

COCONUTS: If you enjoy eating coconut, my advice to you is to always put the coconut in your freezer for an hour or so before cracking. It will then come away from the shell more easily. Coconut is acceptable with sweet fruits but never with acid fruits. You can also add coconut to cereals. Although coconut is high in fat, when eaten raw, it is easier to digest. Eat in small quantities if trying to lose weight.

PEANUTS: These are not true nuts. They belong to the legume family and should be sprouted. If you enjoy peanut butter choose the "raw one", which is available at health shops. It is neither salted nor hydrogenated. "Ordinary" peanut butter is very high in cholesterol.

As pointed out, we simply are not anatomically and physiologically made to deal with or make use of any kind of meat. *Dr T. Colin Campbell*, American co-ordinator of the China Study of Cornell University, concludes that we're basically a vegetarian species and should be eating a wide variety of plant foods and minimising our intake of animal foods. A high animal protein diet overworks the liver and the elimination of the toxins this diet causes places a heavy strain on the adrenal glands and kidneys. All available evidence indicates that a low protein diet composed of plant foods, ie a varied diet of fresh fruits, vegetables, nuts, seeds, sprouts, avocados, legumes and cooked whole grains, is most conducive to good health.

The problem isn't how to get enough protein, but how to avoid getting too much.

Chart 1   Protein content of various foods

* The Better Choice

* NUTS AND SEEDS (RAW AND UNSALTED)

Almond	18,6%	Chestnut	2,9%	Pecan	9,2%
Beechnut	19,4%	Coconut	3,5%	Pistachio	19,3%
Brazil Nut	14,3%	Filbert	12,6%	Black Walnut	20,5%
Butternut	23,7%	Hickory	13,2%	English Walnut	14,8%
Cashew	17,2%	Macadamia	7,8%	Sunflower Seed	24,0%
Pumpkin and		Dried Coconut	7,0%	Coconut Milk	3,0%
Squash seeds	24,0%	Sesame Seed	18,6%		

ANIMAL PRODUCTS

Cooked Beef	18,0%	Milk	3,0%	Dry Cottage Cheese	17,0%
Cooked Fowl	25,0%	Dried Milk	27,0%	Brick Cheese	25,0%
Cooked Fish	16,0% – 20,0%	Dried Skim Milk	37,0%	Eggs	12,0%

LEGUMES

Peanuts (not really a nut)	26,0%	*Dried Chick Peas	20,0%	*Fresh Green Peas	6,0%
* Dried Soybeans	34,0%	*Edible Podded Peas	3,0%	*Dried Green Peas	24,0%
* Fresh Soybeans	11,0%	*Dried White or		*Green Lima Beans	8,0%
* Soybean Sprouts	6,0%	Red Beans	22,0%	*Dried Lima Beans	20,0%
* Dried Mung Beans	24,0%	*Dried Lentils	25,0%		
* Mung Bean Sprouts	4,0%	*Dried Pinto Beans	23,0%		

* VEGETABLES

Artichoke, Globe	3,0%	Carrot	1,0%	Lettuce	1,0%
Artichoke, Jerusalem	2,0%	Cauliflower	3,0%	Kale leaves	6,0%
Broccoli	4,0%	Celery	1,0%	Okra	2,0%
Brussels Sprouts	5,0%	Collard leaves	5,0%	Potato with skin	2,0%
Cabbage, Chinese	1,0%	Corn, Sweet	4,0%	Yam	2,0%
Cabbage, Green	1,0%	Eggplant	1,0%	Squash	1,0%
Cabbage, Red	2,0%	Greens (Turnip,		Green Beans	2,0%
Cabbage, Savoy	2,0%	Mustard, Dandelion)	3,0%	Turnips	1,0%
Beets	2,0%	Asparagus	3,0%		

* FRUITS

Apples (Dried)	1,0%	Cherries	1,0%	Papayas	1,0%
Apricot (Dried)	5,0%	Dates (Dried)	3,0%	Peaches (Dried)	3,0%
Apricot (Fresh)	1,0%	Figs (Fresh)	1,0%	Pears (Dried)	3,0%
Avocados (Calif.)	2,0%	Grapes	1,0%	Prunes	2,0%
Avocados (Fla.)	1,0%	Olives	1,0%	Strawberries	1,0%
Bananas (Fresh)	1,0%	Oranges	1,0%	Melon	1,0%
Bananas (Dried)	4,0%	Tomatoes	1,0%	Water Chestnuts	1,0%

(Source: Allen, Hannah - The Happy Truth About Protein)

Chart 2 Composition & Nutritive Value of Nuts: (Per 100 g Portion)

NUT	WATER	PROTEIN	FAT	CARBOHYDRATES TOTAL	FIBRE	ASH	CALCIUM	PHOSPHORUS	IRON	SODIUM
	%	g	g	g	g	g	mg	mg	mg	mg
ALMOND	4,7	18,6	54,2	19,5	2,6	3,0	234	504	4,7	4
BRAZIL	4,6	14,3	66,9	10,9	3,1	3,3	186	693	3,4	1
CASHEW	5,12	17,2	45,7	29,3	1,4	2,6	38	373	3,8	15
CHESTNUT	52,5	2,9	1,9	42,1	1,1	1,0	27	88	1,7	6
HAZELNUT	5,8	12,6	62,4	16,7	3,0	2,5	209	337	3,4	2
MACADAMIA	3,0	7,8	71,6	15,9	2,5	1,7	48	161	2,0	–
PECAN	3,4	9,2	71,2	14,6	2,3	1,6	73	289	2,4	Trace
PINE NUT	5,6	31,1	47,4	11,6	0,9	4,3	12	604	5,2	–
PISTACHIO	5,3	19,3	53,7	19,0	1,9	2,7	131	500	7,3	–
WALNUT	3,5	14,8	64,0	15,8	2,1	1,9	99	380	3,1	2

NUT	POTASSIUM	VITAMIN A VALUE IU	MAGNESIUM	THIAMIN	RIBOFLAVIN	NIACIN	ASCORBIC ACID mg	FUEL VALUE Cal
	mg		mg	mg	mg	mg		
ALMOND	773	0	270	0,24	0,92	3,5	TRACE	598
BRAZIL	715	TRACE	225	0,96	0,12	1,6	–	654
CASHEW	464	100	–	0,43	0,25	1,8	–	561
CHESTNUT	454	–	41	0,22	0,22	0,6	–	194
HAZELNUT	704	–	184	0,46	–	0,9	TRACE	634
MACADAMIA	264	0	–	0,34	0,11	1,3	0	691
PECAN	603	130	142	0,86	0,13	0,9	2	687
PINE NUT	–	30	–	1,28	0,23	4,5	TRACE	552
PISTACHIO	972	230	158	0,67	–	1,4	30	594
WALNUT	450	30	131	0,33	0,13	0,9	2	651

– not measured

Chart 3

Amino Acids

AMINO ACIDS

FOOD SOURCE

Name	Vegetables	Fruits	Nuts
Alanine	Alfalfa Carrot Celery Kale Lettuce Cucumber Turnip Sweet Pepper	Apple Apricot Avocado Grapes Olive Oranges Strawberry	Almond
Arginine (Considered Essential by Some Authorities)	Alfalfa Green Vegetables Carrot Beet Cucumber Celery Potato Parsnip	Bananas Oranges	
Aspartic	Carrot Celery Cucumber Turnip Greens	Tomato Grapefruit Apple Apricot Pineapple Watermelon	Almond
Cystine	Alfalfa Carrot Beet Cabbage Cauliflower Kale Brussels Sprouts	Apple Currant Pineapple Raspberry	Brazil Nut Filbert

Chart 3　　Amino Acids (continued)

AMINO ACIDS　　　　　　　　　　　　　　FOOD SOURCE

Name	Vegetables	Fruits	Nuts
Glutamic	Snap Beans Brussels Sprouts Carrot Celery Kale Lettuce	Papaya	
Glycine	Carrot Kale Celery Alfalfa Okra Potato	Fig Orange *Huckleberry Raspberry Pomegranate Watermelon	Almond
Histidine (Considered Essential by Some Authorities)	Carrot Beet Celery Cucumber Kale Turnip Greens Alfalfa	Apple Pineapple Pomegranate Papaya Bananas Oranges	Most Nuts
Hydroxyglutamic	Carrot Celery Lettuce Tomato	Grapes *Huckleberry Raspberry Plum	
Hydroxyproline	Carrot Beet Kale Lettuce Turnip Greens Cucumber	Apricot Cherry Fig Raisin Grapes Oranges Olive Avocado Pineapple	Almond Brazil Nut Coconut

*Huckleberry – like a Blueberry, but darker in colour with larger seeds

Chart 3   Amino Acids (continued)

AMINO ACIDS   FOOD SOURCE

Name	Vegetables	Fruits	Nuts
Iodogorgoic	Carrot Celery Tomato Lettuce	Pineapple	
Isoleucine (Essential)	Carrot Kale Cabbage Most Green Vegetables	Bananas Papaya Avocado Oranges	Coconut All Nuts (Except Cashew and Chestnut)
Leucine (Essential)	Same as for Isoleucine		
Lysine (Essential)	Cabbage Carrot Beet Cucumber Celery Kale Turnip Greens Alfalfa Soya Bean Sprouts	Papaya Apple Apricot Pear Grapes Bananas Oranges	Most Nuts
Methionine (Essential)	Brussels Sprouts Cabbage Cauliflower Kale	Pineapple Apple Bananas Oranges	Brazil Nuts Filbert
Norleucine	No Reported Plant Sources – Helps Leucine Function, Synthesised If Needed		
Phenylalanine	Most Green Vegetables Carrot Beet	Pineapple Apple Bananas Oranges Tomato	Most Nuts

Chart 3   Amino Acids (continued)

AMINO ACIDS   FOOD SOURCE

Name	Vegetables	Fruits	Nuts
Proline	Carrot Beet Lettuce Kale Turnip Cucumber	Apricot Cherry Avocado Fig Raisins Grapes Olive Oranges Pineapple	Coconut Almond Brazil Nuts
Serine	Carrot Beet Celery Cucumber Cabbage Alfalfa	Papaya Apple Pineapple	
Threonine (Essential)	Carrot Alfalfa Green Leafy Vegetables	Papaya Bananas Oranges	Most Nuts
Thyroxine	Carrot Celery Lettuce Turnip	Pineapple Tomato	
Tryptophan (Essential)	Cabbage Carrot Beet Celery Kale Snap Beans Brussels Sprouts Alfalfa Turnips	Bananas Oranges	Most Nuts

Chart 3   Amino Acids (continued)

AMINO ACIDS   FOOD SOURCE

Name	Vegetables	Fruits	Nuts
Tyrosine	Alfalfa Carrot Beet Cucumber Lettuce Kale Parsnip Asparagus Sweet Pepper	Strawberry Apricot Cherry Apple Watermelon Fig	Almond
Valine (Essential)	Carrot Turnip Kale Lettuce Parsnip Squash Celery Beet Okra	Apple Pomegranate Bananas Oranges Tomato	Almond

(Source: Fry, T.C. – Correspondence Course: Natural Hygiene, Nutrition and Health Sciences)

3 Foods must be adequate in minerals

Minerals are essential to life. They are needed for proper utilisation of vitamins and proteins and for the digestion of food. Mineral salts are found chiefly in the ash constituents of plants. Our only real source of minerals is from the food we eat and they are contained in the purest form in fresh fruit, a variety of leafy green vegetables, nuts, seeds, sprouts, avocados, legumes and whole grains. This kind of live food assures us of receiving a totally adequate supply of organic minerals in a form the body can assimilate and use. Organic minerals are necessary to build the bones and teeth as well as to ensure healthy blood and sound nutrition.

All other minerals taken into the body, whether from mineral supplements, mineral waters or processed, concentrated foods (dairy products etc), cannot be used by the body and do not promote good health as they are in an inorganic form. Any form of processing, pasteurisation or adding preservatives to foods results in denatured food.

33

Minerals fall into 2 groups:

MACROMINERALS: These include calcium, magnesium, sodium, potassium and phosphorus. These minerals are needed in larger amounts than Microminerals (trace minerals).

MICROMINERALS: These include zinc, iron, copper, manganese, chromium, selenium and iodine. Minerals are stored primarily in the body's bone and muscle tissue. You should not overdose on mineral supplements as this could affect the absorption of other minerals, for example: if too much calcium is taken in, in the form of supplements, it can affect magnesium absorption. Thus minerals are not isolated food factors but part of the nutritional whole. I will only discuss a few minerals in detail.

MACROMINERALS

CALCIUM is vital in the formation of strong bones and teeth. It is therefore the most abundant mineral in the body. You should be aware that calcium is metabolised under the influence of vitamin D which is obtained through sunlight. The calcium requirements for a vegetarian diet, especially when there is a high intake of fresh fruit and raw vegetables, are significantly less than the calcium requirements for a diet high in animal protein.

YOUR CALCIUM INHIBITORS

- Recent scientific studies show that the more animal protein you consume (meat, fish, eggs, chicken and dairy products) the more calcium is lost via the urine.
- Laxatives can lower the absorption of calcium.
- Sugar disturbs the calcium/phosphorus balance, eg soft drinks.
- Preservatives also reduce the levels of calcium in the body.
- Alcohol, coffee, tea and chocolates are among the worst offenders in destroying calcium. Mothers want their children to have strong bones, yet give them hot chocolate drinks, and this of course defeats the purpose.
- Over the counter sedatives, tranquillisers, antibiotics, steroids, cholesterol-reducing agents, diuretics and chemotherapy are all directly related to a subclinical calcium deficiency.
- Smoking causes calcium to be drawn from the bones and teeth to neutralise the acid from the nicotine.
- Tap water contains chemicals, such as cadmium and mercury, which hinder the absorption of calcium.
- Vinegar leaches calcium from the bones.
- Excessive intake of salt drives calcium from the bones.
- Wheat and gluten contain phytic acid (a phosphorus-like compound) which prevents the absorption of calcium. Phytic acid is found primarily in the husks of grains. There are high levels of phytic acid in bran. Gluten is found in wheat, oats, rye, barley and breakfast cereals.
- Some leafy vegetables contain oxalic acid which forms an insoluble compound (calcium oxalate) in the intestines. This insoluble compound lessens the absorption and utilisation of some of the calcium present in the body.

Consumption of such foods in moderation should not pose a problem, but overindulgence will inhibit the absorption of calcium.

CALCIUM is found in all foods that grow from the ground. Plants absorb calcium from the soil and incorporate it into their structure.

Animals such as cows consume plants and in this way absorb calcium.

FOODS HIGH IN CALCIUM:

Sesame seeds	Broccoli
Most nuts	Almonds
Dates	Most seeds
Pawpaws (papinos)	Oranges
Leafy green vegetables	Apricots
Most vegetables	Figs
Sunflower seeds	Most fruits
Strawberries	

CALCIUM CONTENT IN CERTAIN FOODS

FOOD	PORTION/SERVING (g)	CALCIUM (mg)
Cow's milk (lowest because milk is pasteurised)	100	120
Collard (like a cabbage)	100	304
Kale	100	249
Chickpeas	100	150
Almonds	100	290
Tofu	100	150
Oats	120	170

Recommended Daily Allowance (RDA) for calcium

Adult males	1 000 – 1 200 mg
Adult females	1 500 mg
Pregnant and lactating women	1 900 mg
Infants	60 – 70 mg

If you eat a variety of the foods I suggest you will be able to achieve these recommended allowances.

MAGNESIUM gives flexibility to the bones and elasticity to the muscles. A lack of magnesium is a contributory cause of nervous conditions and irritability, digestive disorders, poor complexion, heartbeat acceleration and soft bones.

Studies show that magnesium is essential for strong bones. Magnesium and calcium have a natural affinity for each other. A high protein diet increases the need for magnesium. If either calcium or magnesium is consumed in excess (supplementation), it drives the other from the body.

Magnesium is also eliminated from the body by harsh laxatives. Alcohol stimulates the kidneys causing excessive elimination of magnesium. Diuretics (water pills) taken to

FOODS HIGH IN MAGNESIUM

The best food sources are **nuts**, especially **almonds,** and **pumpkin** seeds.

Whole grains	Cherries
Dates	Leafy green vegetables
Bananas	Beets
Walnuts	Avocados
Sesame seeds	Tofu
Raisins	Pears
Mangoes	Broccoli
Melons	Millet

Recommended Daily Allowance (RDA) for magnesium

Infants		60 – 70 mg
Children	(1 – 4 years)	150 mg
	(5 – 6 years)	200 mg
	(7 – 10 years)	250 mg
Males	(11 – 14 years)	350 mg
	(15 – 18 years)	400 mg
	(19 and older)	350 mg
Females		300 mg
Pregnant and lactating women		450 mg

alleviate water retention or reduce high blood pressure can precariously lower the levels of magnesium.

Large amounts of fat, cod liver oil and protein also decrease magnesium absorption as well as foods high in oxalic acid.

PHOSPHORUS is used together with calcium in the building of bones and teeth. The largest amount of phosphorus is found in the bones. A lack of this mineral can result in fatigue and a feeling of depression.

FOODS HIGH IN PHOSPHORUS

Coconuts	Apples
Peaches	Pears
Apricots	Avocados
Broccoli	Green vegetable leaves
Figs	Carrots
Dates	Mung bean sprouts
Cabbage	Beets
Squash	Persimmons
Corn	Legumes
Whole grains	
All seeds	
All nuts	

SODIUM is needed for the maintenance of water balance and blood pH.

Although a sodium deficiency is rare, its symptoms include confusion, low blood sugar, dehydration and heart palpitations. Because a balance of potassium and sodium is necessary for good health and most people overindulge in sodium, potassium is typically needed in greater amounts.

Excess sodium intake results in oedema, high blood pressure, potassium deficiency, and liver and kidney disease. Sodium may lead to heart disease when not properly balanced with potassium. Here I am talking

FOOD HIGH IN NATURAL SODIUM

Strawberries	Sunflower seeds
Celery	Broccoli
Carrots	Melons
Raisins	Cabbage
Kale	Lettuce
Beets	Peaches
Sesame seeds	Cucumber
Tomatoes	
Pumpkin	

about processed, tinned and frozen foods that have an unnaturally high sodium content.

Excessive use of inorganic sodium (bicarbonate of soda, sodium chloride (common table salt)) tends to cause hardening of the arteries and Bright's disease.

POTASSIUM is important for a healthy nervous system and a regular heart rhythm. It works with sodium to control the body's water balance and aids in maintaining

FOODS HIGH IN POTASSIUM

Apricots	Green leafy vegetables
Sunflower seeds	Tomatoes
Peaches	Bananas
Almonds	Carrots
Raisins	Beets
Dates	Nectarines
Figs	Cabbage
Avocados	Lettuce
Pecans	Most fruits
Pawpaws	Most vegetables
Melons	Brown rice
Grapes	Sweet potatoes
Baked potatoes (with skin)	

normal blood pressure. In addition, it regulates the transfer of nutrients to the cells. The use of diuretics and laxatives, kidney disorders, excessive salt intake and diarrhoea all disrupt potassium levels.

A potassium deficiency can also result in liver ailments, acne and the slow healing of sores.

MICROMINERALS

IRON is essential for the production of haemoglobin and the oxygenation of red blood cells. Iron deficiency symptoms include brittle hair and nails, hair loss, fatigue, dizziness and anaemia. Iron deficiency is more prevalent in those suffering from candidiasis and chronic herpes infections.

Certain food factors are essential for iron utilisation in the blood. If the B vitamins found in the foods I recommend are under-supplied, the stomach is unable to secrete sufficient hydrochloric acid to dissolve iron, hence it can't be absorbed. If you take laxatives regularly you will not readily absorb iron.

The greatest loss of iron occurs through menstruation, bleeding piles, stomach ulcers and regular blood donations.

If you drink lots of tea, add vinegar and/or raw onions to your salads, and use antacid tablets, you will definitely cause poor iron absorption. Folic acid, a constituent of the vitamin B complex, thought to be useful in treating anaemia which is associated with low iron, is definitely destroyed when foods are cooked at very high temperatures. Oral contraceptives increase the need for folic acid. On a varied raw fruit and vegetable diet, some cooked whole grains, legumes, nuts, seeds, avocados and sprouts, you consume an average of 30 – 40 mg of iron daily.

Do not resort to iron supplements, as they furnish inorganic iron which the body cannot use.

There seems to be an abundance of all the minerals mentioned in the variety of foods I recommend. If you make these foods an essential part of your diet, you will not need supplementation. Remember, the mineral salts in organically grown raw fruit and vegetables are colloidal, which means they are in a state of such extreme suspension, that they can easily be absorbed by the human

FOODS HIGH IN IRON	
Raisins	Walnuts
Figs	Sesame seeds
Apricots	Dates
Broccoli	Prunes
Wheat germ	Beets
Peaches	Most fruits
Gooseberries	Most vegetables
Cherries	Berries
Dark green leafy vegetables	
Whole grains - brown rice	

Recommended Daily Allowance (RDA) for iron:	
Adult males	10 mg
Menstruating women	18 mg
Pregnant and lactating women	30 mg

organism.

If food is not organically grown it is often lacking in essential minerals and trace elements. I have found a wonderful food supplement with ionised (electrically charged) essential minerals and trace elements if you are unable to find organically grown food. It is made from finely ground coral harvested from the ocean floor. No living coral is harmed. By drinking OCEAN MILK and ALKA-MINE you are continually oxygenating your cells and flushing acidic wastes from your body. Coral calcium is naturally ionised making it significantly more bioavailable to people of all ages.

This form of calcium is easily absorbed and therefore prevents osteoporosis.

4 Foods must supply our needs for essential fatty acids

There are 3 essential fatty acids which the body requires, but cannot synthesise (the body cannot make these fatty acids). The most essential of the fatty acids is linoleic acid. It is found in fruits, nuts, seeds, avocados and plant-based foods. These essential fatty acids aid the body to manufacture hormones. They are also known as unsaturated fats; they promote thin blood and render high energy levels.

The oils (except cold pressed) that you add to salad dressings or use to fry foods are the very ones that are harmful to your health. They are called free oils. Free oils are those fats and oils which have been separated from the foodstuffs in which they naturally occur. It is the overheating and the re-use of these oils that promote rancidity in the body, resulting in those free radicals that age us. Heated fats are carcinogenic, ie capable of causing cancer. Free oils in our conventional diet are made up of vegetable, animal and synthetic oils.

VEGETABLE OILS

The most commonly used are olive oil, corn oil, sunflower oil, peanut oil, flaxseed (linseed) oil and other generic oils. The majority of vegetable oils are processed by heating a number of times, under intense pressure and at high temperatures to extract the oil from the seed, as well as being hydrogenated. These processes change the chemical structure of the oil and it cannot be used by the body. These oils are cheaper and easier to spread, as in margarine compared to butter. If you are going to use vegetable oils, they must be **cold pressed**. The cold-pressed method is a slower physical method (no heating involved) which takes time and is far

more costly. These cold-pressed oils are more expensive than ordinary oils, but remember, our health is more important to us. Use cold-pressed oil as a salad dressing sparingly – everything in moderation. Oils in nature's foods are in the correct proportion and concentration for human needs, for example, avocados, nuts and seeds.

ANIMAL OILS

These oils are composed of saturated fats, for example, lard and butter. Be aware that animals store pesticides, chemicals, additives and injected hormones in their fat cells. Butter is usually coloured and salted. If you want to use butter, rather buy unsalted butter from a health shop where you know that the animals have not been injected with hormones or antibiotics. Butter is also a dairy product and can cause mucus build-up. I regard it as an acceptable "transitional" food, but it must be used sparingly and correctly, ie never cook with oil or butter.

You can let it melt over steamed vegetables and baked potatoes **after** they are cooked. You can spread butter on bread. Butter is better than margarine. Margarine is a processed fat and is extremely acid in the bloodstream. It contributes more to cholesterol problems than butter. Always store unsalted butter in cut-up portions in the freezer. Keep a cut-up portion in the fridge, ready for use.

SYNTHETIC OILS

These synthetic oils are made totally from petroleum by-products. You will find synthetic oils in ice cream, artificial coffee creamers and artificial butter. You must read your labels. These oils are very harmful to the body. If the body has no use for a substance and cannot effectively eliminate it from the system, then it stores that substance where it can do the least harm, or walls it off by creating a tumour around it. These synthetic oils may have a worse effect on the body than the animal products people are avoiding, in order to remain well.

The diet which I recommend contains all the right fats (essential fatty acids). There is no nutritional need for animal fats, cooked fats, extracted oils or high fat foods in your diet.

LINOLEIC ACID CONTENT IN CERTAIN FOODS	
FOOD	% Linoleic Acid
Sunflower seeds	30
Sesame seeds	22
Pumpkin seeds	20
Walnuts	40
Brazil nuts	17
Pecans	14
Almonds	11
Hazelnuts	10
Pistachios	10
Cashew nuts	3
Avocados	2
Coconuts	1
Raw sweet corn	1

(Source: Fry, T.C. – Correspondence Course: Natural Hygiene, Nutrition and Health Sciences)

You should have 25 calories of unsaturated fatty acids daily. All fresh fruits contain between 0,5% and 1% unsaturated fat. Some fruits are higher in fat (avocado contains 15 – 22% fat). Thus, if only fruits were consumed, we would still meet the RDA of 1% unsaturated fats in our diet.

The right fats are very satisfying, and they keep the sensation of hunger away for a longer period of time than some fruits or vegetables.

The rule of thumb is: no fats should be eaten that will leave an oily film on a bowl or plate that will not wash off with water alone (no soap or detergent).

5 Foods must have vitamin adequacy

Vitamins are essential to life. They are considered micronutrients because the body needs them in relatively small amounts, compared to other nutrients, such as carbohydrates, proteins, fats and water.

Ample amounts of fresh fruit, fresh raw garden salads, steamed green and yellow vegetables, a moderate amount of nuts, seeds, avocados, sprouts, legumes and cooked whole grains supply us with all the necessary vitamins and minerals in the best form for healing and health. These foods hold the key to our vitamin insurance.

We require 2 main types of vitamins: Water soluble and Fat soluble vitamins.

WATER SOLUBLE VITAMINS must be taken into the body daily as they cannot be stored, and are excreted within 1 – 4 days. They are vitamin C and the B complex vitamins.

FAT SOLUBLE VITAMINS can be stored for longer periods of time in the body's fatty tissues and the liver. They are vitamins A D E and K.

Study the following table and discover the abundance of vitamins in wholefoods.

VITAMINS

WATER SOLUBLE
(Not stored – needed daily)

FAT SOLUBLE
(Stored in liver – needed 3 – 5 times per week)

The "B Complex":
B-1 (Thiamine)
B-2 (Riboflavin)
B-6 (Pyridoxine)
Choline
Biotin
Folic Acid
Others of "B Complex"
Vitamin C
Found in:

Vitamin A
Vitamin E
Essential Fatty Acids
(EFAs)

FRUITS
Melons – cantelope, honeydew, etc (also contain Vitamin A)
Citrus – oranges, grapefruit etc (for Vitamin C)

Found in:

GREEN VEGETABLES
Alfalfa Sprouts
Avocados
Beans (green)
Broccoli
Brussels sprouts
Cabbage family
Collards
Cucumbers, Endive
Kale, Leeks
Mustard greens
Romaine Lettuce
Spinach
Sprouts
(mung beans, etc)
Swiss Chard
Turnip Greens
Nutritional yeast (Vit B-12) if needed

YELLOW VEGETABLES AND OIL-RICH FOODS
Carrots
Corn
Pumpkin
Butternut
Hubbard Squash
Sweet potatoes
Almonds
Corn Oil
Flaxseed oil (EFAs)
Safflower oil
Sesame (Tahini)
Sunflower seeds
Whole grains

(Source: Klaper, Michael – Vegan Nutrition: Pure and Simple)

I do agree that the soil in which fruit and vegetables were grown in years past, definitely had fewer chemicals, fertilisers and pesticides added to it. Unfortunately, today, fruit and vegetables do not compare in nutrient value to those of years ago, **but** fresh fruit and vegetables are live foods and contain live enzymes which the body needs on a daily basis to maintain health. We eat far too much cooked food and nutrients are definitely lost through this process.

WHAT HAPPENS TO THE BODY WHEN YOU TAKE VITAMIN SUPPLEMENTS?

You cannot just take a handful of vitamins and hope to get well. That is wishful thinking. Scientific research has proven that an excess of an isolated vitamin or mineral can produce the same symptoms as a deficiency of that vitamin or mineral. In addition, there are certain substances that block the absorption and effects of vitamins, for example, the absorption of vitamin C is greatly reduced when you take antibiotics.

Synthetic vitamins are produced in a laboratory and cannot be used at all by the body. Our need for vitamin supplements has been grossly exaggerated by certain commercial interests, and as a result there are many uninformed people who take a number of different supplements every single day, perhaps even in megavitamin doses. This places an unnecessary burden upon all the organs, especially the liver, which tries to rid the body of the toxic waste. The easiest and quickest way to get rid of excess vitamins is to evacuate them from the body via the bladder; this makes your urine a very expensive secretion. When you take vitamin supplements, the body is stimulated and shifts into "high gear"; metabolic activity is increased. The stimulation which results from taking vitamin supplements makes the individual feel good (have more energy); and it is for this reason that the need for this kind of stimulation can become habitual. When you use any form of stimulants, you feel good. It is like "whipping a dead horse". The individual maintains he has to keep taking more and more supplements to feel as good as he did when he first started taking them.

Many people feel that by taking vitamin supplements they are compensating for the lack of nutrients in their normal diet. The missing elements in these foods cannot be replaced by a dried and crystallised tablet. Nature's foods come as complete packages, with the whole gamut of nutrients, ie they contain the full spectrum of nutritional co-factors. Vitamins cannot work in isolation. When you eat a variety of the foods I suggest, you don't have to be concerned about "am I getting enough vitamins and minerals?"

When we rely on one particular mineral or vitamin via supplementation, we create imbalances at great cost to the body. All vitamin and mineral supplements are inorganic, acidic and dead, because they have been chopped, crushed and subjected to heat. Any food that is heated above a certain temperature – 44 °C (112 °F) is acid in the bloodstream and puts the body under stress.

HOW THE BODY REACTS TO MEGAVITAMINS IN THE FORM OF SUPPLEMENTS
VITAMIN B_3 (NIACIN)
RDA:

Infants and children	5 – 10 mg per day
Adults	15 – 20 mg per day

Excess niacin can cause liver damage, abnormally high levels of blood sugar, unsafe levels of uric acid and gastrointestinal diseases. Vitamin B_3 should be used with caution by women and people who suffer from gout, peptic ulcers, glaucoma, liver disease and diabetes. Natural sources of vitamin B_3 are found in: broccoli, carrots, potatoes, tomatoes and whole-wheat foods.

VITAMIN C
RDA: 100 mg per day
As the body cannot manufacture vitamin C it must be obtained from the diet. Vitamin C acts as an antioxidant (has the ability to ward off free radicals).

I do agree that people who smoke, take large quantities of pain killers and sedatives, and those women using oral contraceptives need more vitamin C than other individuals, but it is not necessary to take it in the form of supplements. The side effects of too much vitamin C in supplement form are frightening. It has been reported in scientific literature that there is a breakdown of red blood cells, irritation of the intestinal lining and kidney stone formation. If you take large amounts of vitamin C over a period of at least several months, your body will increase its level of elimination of vitamin C (evidence that your body doesn't need it). If you then decide to suddenly stop taking vitamin C, you will become deficient in this vitamin because it takes a period of time (many weeks sometimes) for your body to lower its level of elimination of vitamin C.

The best way of getting the right amount of vitamin C without overdosing is to eat a variety of fresh raw fruit and vegetables in season. Those foods particularly high in vitamin C are: asparagus, avocados, broccoli, Brussels sprouts, currants, grapefruit, kale, lemons, mangoes, oranges, papinos and green peas. It is no good using canned fruit and canned vegetables because they have a low vitamin C content as a result of the high temperatures used in the canning process.

Vitamin C found in fresh raw fruit and vegetables, facilitates the absorption of iron and calcium, increases the body's resistance to infection, and speeds up the healing of wounds.

High doses of vitamin C can interfere with tests for sugar in urine (diabetes) and for blood in the stool (a test for cancer of the large intestine). Does this sound safe? Just remember, a cold is actually a detoxification process (healing crisis) that should be left alone. Change your pattern of eating and you won't need vitamin C in tablet form.

VITAMINS A, D, E AND K are known as fat soluble vitamins. If these vitamins are taken in excess they can be harmful to your health because they stay in the body much longer than other vitamins.

VITAMIN E
RDA: 15 IUs per day
An intake exceeding 100 IUs per day has been found to cause deposits of cholesterol in blood vessels; elevation of blood fat levels; interference with the blood clotting process; increased growth of lung tumours; interference with the absorption of vitamin A and iron; gastrointestinal disturbances; skin rashes and interference with the functioning of the thyroid gland.

VITAMIN A
RDA:

Male adults:	5 000 IUs
Female adults:	4 000 IUs
Pregnant and lactating women:	5 000 IUs

Infants: 1/10 of the male adult requirement
Excessive supplementation of vitamin A causes: fatigue, a generalised feeling of sickness, stomach discomfort, bone and/or

joint pain, severe headaches, insomnia and restlessness, night sweating, loss of body hair, brittle nails, constipation, irregular menstruation, emotional irritability, dry scalp and rough skin.

VITAMIN D
RDA: 400 IUs per day
Vitamin D is required for calcium and phosphorus absorption and utilisation. It is especially important for normal growth and development of bones and teeth.

Excessive vitamin D supplementation can cause: nausea, diarrhoea, unnecessary weight loss, kidney damage and other problems. Vitamin D is not really a vitamin at all, but a hormone made within our bodies through the action of sunlight upon substances within our skin. Vitamin D utilisation is more efficient on a proper diet of mostly raw fruits and vegetables.

PLANT FOODS IN WHICH VITAMIN B_{12} HAS BEEN ISOLATED	
Whole-wheat bread	Green beans
Green vegetables	Dates
Bananas	Oats
Soya beans	Beetroot
Sunflower seeds	Tofu
Peas	Sprouts

VITAMIN B_{12} (CYANOCOBALAMIN)
This seems to be of major concern to vegetarians who consume no animal foods. It has been stated that you can only get vitamin B_{12} from animal products. According to *Dr Joel Robbins* (Eating for Health and Wellness) this statement is unfounded and inaccurate. While it is true that animal products seem to be good sources of vitamin B_{12}, it is also true

that many fruits and vegetables do contain vitamin B_{12}. The dangers of eating animal products far outweigh the so-called lack of vitamin B_{12} in fruit and vegetables.

Although plant foods contain only small amounts of B_{12}, our daily need for vitamin B_{12} is very small. We need less than 1 mcg (a millionth of a gram per day). We also have in our intestinal tract a vitamin B_{12} factory. Vitamin B_{12} is manufactured by micro-organisms (friendly bacteria).

FACTS TO CONSIDER REGARDING VITAMIN B_{12}
When you overload the digestive system with incorrect food combinations on a regular basis, you create impaired digestion. Food then breaks down through putrefaction instead of digestion. This destroys the friendly flora and in time leads to a vitamin B_{12} deficiency. An excess of concentrated protein foods and foods high in fat destroys our friendly flora. These friendly flora are also destroyed by chemical additives, drugs such as neomycin, oral contraceptives, emotional stress and tobacco.

Where do cows get their vitamin B_{12} from? – they don't eat meat. The friendly flora in their intestines is responsible for the manufacture of vitamin B_{12}. Vitamin B_{12} is recycled in the body and stored in the liver. I have to stress, however, that impairment of the ability to synthesise and absorb vitamin B_{12} is a primary cause of vitamin B_{12} deficiency. Study after study has shown that the deficiency of vitamin B_{12} is due to the failure to absorb this vitamin from the intestinal tract because of the absence of the "intrinsic factor" (a chemical which is normally present in the gastric juices in the stomach).

Certain diseases can also interfere with the production of the intrinsic factor, for example, stomach, intestinal, kidney or liver disease. Anti-gout medications, anticoagulant drugs and potassium supplements may also block the absorption of vitamin B_{12} in the digestive tract. Malabsorption is most common in the elderly and in individuals suffering from digestive disorders.

The blood and nerve cells suffer the most when vitamin B_{12} is in short supply. Vitamin B_{12} was discovered in the 1950s. A great deal is known about vitamin B_{12} today and there could be a vitamin B_{12} deficiency on a purely vegetarian diet especially if you do not eat a variety of foods. Please discuss this with a nutritional counsellor. Vitamin B_{12} is very important especially during pregnancy, lactation and childhood.

"A baby should be given from birth (unless breast fed) $1/8 - 1/4$ teaspoon daily of Bifidobacterium Infantis. This provides a natural antibiotic, helps with the assimilation of nutrients, and manufactures the B vitamins, including B_{12}."

(Source: Robbins, Joel – Health and Wellness Clinic, Inc.)

Adults can also take Probiotics. Enquire from a nutritional counsellor.

Dr T. Colin Campbell has reached the following somewhat unorthodox conclusions and observations.

"Contrary to the most recent US Dietary Guidelines, B_{12} can be found in plants.

Organically grown plants contain higher levels of B_{12} than plants grown non-organically with chemical fertilisers."

(Source: Campbell, T. Colin – New Century Nutrition, November 1996)

In order to put your mind at ease regarding the vitamin and mineral content of various foods, see the Nutrient Composition table for selected fruits and vegetables.

Chart 4 Nutrient Composition for Selected Fruits and Vegetables (Per 100 g Portion)

	Protein (g)	Fat (g)	Carbohydrates (g)	Calcium (mg)	Phosphorus (mg)	Iron (mg)	Sodium (mg)	Potassium (mg)	Vitamin A (mg)	Thiamine, Vit B₁ (mg)	Riboflavin, Vit B₂ (mg)	Niacin (mg)	Ascorbic Acid (mg)
Apples	0,2	0,6	14,5	7	10	0,3	1	110	90	0,03	0,02	0,1	4
Apricots	1,0	0,2	12,8	17	23	0,5	1	281	2 700	0,03	0,04	0,6	10
Artichokes	2,0	0,2	10,6	51	88	1,3	43	430	160	0,08	0,05	1,0	12
Asparagus	2,5	0,2	5,0	22	62	1,0	2	278	900	0,18	0,20	1,5	33
Avocados	2,1	16,4	6,3	10	42	0,6	4	604	290	0,11	0,20	1,6	14
Bananas	1,1	0,2	22,2	8	26	0,7	1	370	190	0,05	0,06	0,7	10
Beans (White)	22,3	1,6	61,3	144	425	7,8	19	1196	–	0,65	0,22	2,4	–
Beans (Pinto)	22,9	1,2	63,7	135	457	6,4	10	984	–	0,84	0,21	2,2	–
Beans (Lima)	8,4	0,5	22,1	52	142	2,8	2	650	290	0,24	0,12	1,4	29
Beans (Mung)	24,2	1,3	60,3	118	340	7,7	6	1028	80	0,38	0,21	2,6	–
Beans (Snap)	1,9	0,2	7,1	56	44	0,8	7	243	600	0,08	0,11	0,5	19
Beans (Mung Sprouts)	3,8	0,2	6,6	19	64	1,3	5	223	20	0,13	0,13	0,8	19
Beet (Red)	1,6	0,1	9,9	16	33	0,7	60	335	20	0,03	0,05	0,4	10
Beet (Greens)	2,2	0,3	4,6	119	40	3,3	130	570	6 100	0,10	0,22	0,4	30
Blackberries	1,2	0,9	12,9	32	19	0,9	1	170	200	0,03	0,04	0,4	21
Blueberries	0,7	0,5	15,3	15	13	1,0	1	81	100	0,03	0,06	0,5	14
Breadfruit	1,7	0,3	26,2	33	32	1,2	15	439	40	0,11	0,03	0,9	29
Cabbage	1,3	0,2	5,4	49	29	0,4	20	233	130	0,05	0,05	0,3	47
Carrots	1,1	0,2	9,7	37	36	0,7	47	341	1 100	0,06	0,05	0,6	8
Cauliflower	2,7	0,2	5,2	25	56	1,1	13	295	60	0,11	0,10	0,7	78
Celery	0,9	0,1	3,9	39	28	0,3	126	341	240	0,03	0,03	0,3	9
Chard (Swiss)	2,4	0,3	4,6	88	39	3,2	147	550	6 500	0,06	0,17	0,5	32
Cherries (Sweet)	1,3	0,3	17,4	22	19	0,4	2	191	110	0,05	0,06	0,4	10
Chives	1,8	0,3	5,8	69	44	1,7	–	250	5 800	0,08	0,13	0,5	56
Collards	4,8	0,8	7,5	250	82	1,5	–	450	9 300	0,16	0,31	1,7	152

Chart 4 Nutrient Composition for Selected Fruits and Vegetables (Per 100 g Portion) (Continued)

	Protein (g)	Fat (g)	Carbohydrates (g)	Calcium (mg)	Phosphorus (mg)	Iron (mg)	Sodium (mg)	Potassium (mg)	Vitamin A (mg)	Thiamine, Vit B₁ (mg)	Riboflavin, Vit B₂ (mg)	Niacin (mg)	Ascorbic Acid (mg)
Corn (Field)	8,9	3,9	72,2	22	268	2,1	1,0	284	490	0,37	0,12	2,2	–
Corn (Sweet)	3,5	1,0	22,1	3	111	0,7	Trace	280	400	0,15	0,12	1,7	12
Crabapples	0,4	0,3	17,8	6	13	0,3	1	110	40	0,03	0,02	0,1	8
Eggplant	1,2	0,2	5,6	12	26	0,7	2	214	10	0,05	0,50	0,6	5
Elderberries	2,6	0,5	16,4	38	28	1,6	–	300	600	0,07	0,60	0,5	36
Endive	1,7	0,1	4,1	81	54	1,7	14	294	3 300	0,07	0,14	0,5	10
Figs	1,2	0,3	20,3	35	22	0,6	2	194	80	0,06	0,05	0,4	2
Garlic	6,2	0,2	30,8	29	202	1,5	19	529	Trace	0,25	0,08	0,5	15
Gooseberries	0,8	0,2	9,7	18	15	0,5	1	155	290	–	–	–	33
Grapefruit	0,5	0,1	10,6	16	16	0,4	1	135	80	0,04	0,02	0,2	38
Grapes	1,3	0,1	15,7	16	12	0,4	3	158	100	0,05	0,03	0,3	4
Guavas	0,8	0,6	15,0	23	42	0,9	4	289	280	0,05	0,05	1,2	242
Kale	6,0	0,8	9,0	249	93	2,7	75	378	10 000	0,16	0,26	2,1	186
Kumquats	0,9	0,1	17,1	63	23	0,4	7	236	600	0,08	0,10	–	36
Leeks	2,2	0,3	11,2	52	50	1,1	5	347	40	0,11	0,06	0,5	17
Lemons	1,1	0,3	8,2	26	16	0,6	2	138	20	0,04	0,02	0,1	53
Lentils	24,7	1,1	60,1	79	377	6,8	30	790	60	0,37	0,22	2,0	–
Lettuce	1,2	0,2	2,5	35	26	2,0	9	264	970	0,06	0,06	0,3	8
Mushrooms	2,7	0,3	4,4	6	116	0,8	15	414	Trace	0,10	0,46	4,2	3
Muskmelons	0,7	0,1	7,5	14	16	0,4	12	251	3 400	0,04	0,03	0,6	33
Mustard greens	3,0	0,5	5,6	183	50	3,0	32	377	7 000	0,11	0,22	0,8	97
Nectarines	0,6	Trace	17,1	4	24	0,5	6	294	1 650	–	–	–	13
Okra	2,4	0,3	7,6	92	51	0,6	3	249	520	0,17	0,21	1,0	31
Onions (Dry)	1,5	0,1	8,7	27	36	0,5	10	157	40	0,03	0,04	0,2	10
Onions (Green)	1,5	0,2	8,2	51	39	1,0	5	231	2 000	0,05	0,05	0,4	32
Oranges	1,0	0,2	12,2	41	20	0,4	1	200	200	0,10	0,04	0,4	50
Papayas	0,6	0,1	10,0	20	16	0,3	3	234	1 750	0,04	0,04	0,3	56
Parsley	3,6	0,6	8,5	203	63	6,2	45	727	8 500	0,12	0,26	1,2	172

Chart 4 Nutrient Composition for Selected Fruits and Vegetables (Per 100 g Portion) (Continued)

	Protein (g)	Fat (g)	Carbohydrates (g)	Calcium (mg)	Phosphorus (mg)	Iron (mg)	Sodium (mg)	Potassium (mg)	Vitamin A (mg)	Thiamine, Vit B₁ (mg)	Riboflavin, Vit B₂ (mg)	Niacin (mg)	Ascorbic Acid (mg)
Parsnips	1,7	0,5	17,5	50	77	0,7	12	541	30	0,08	0,09	0,2	16
Peaches	0,6	0,1	9,7	9	19	0,5	1	202	1 330	0,02	0,05	1,0	7
Pears	0,7	0,4	15,3	8	11	0,3	2	130	20	0,02	0,04	0,1	4
Peas (Edible pod)	3,4	0,2	12,0	62	90	0,7	–	170	680	0,28	0,12	–	21
Peas (Green)	6,3	0,4	14,4	26	116	1,9	2	316	640	0,35	0,14	2,9	27
Peppers (Hot red)	3,7	2,3	18,1	29	78	1,2	–	–	21 600	0,22	0,36	4,4	369
Peppers (Sweet green)	1,2	0,2	4,8	9	22	0,7	13	213	420	0,08	0,08	0,5	128
Persimmons	0,7	0,4	19,7	6	26	0,3	6	174	2 700	0,03	0,02	0,1	11
Pineapples	0,4	0,2	13,7	17	8	0,5	1	146	70	0,09	0,03	0,2	17
Plums	0,5	Trace	17,8	18	17	0,5	2	299	300	0,08	0,03	0,5	–
Pomegranates	0,5	0,3	16,4	3	8	0,3	3	259	Trace	0,03	0,03	0,3	4
Potatoes	2,1	0,1	17,1	7	53	0,6	3	407	Trace	0,10	0,04	1,5	20
Rhubarb	0,6	0,1	3,7	96	18	0,8	2	251	100	0,03	0,07	0,3	9
Spinach	3,2	0,3	4,3	93	51	3,1	71	470	8 100	0,10	0,20	0,6	51
Squash	1,1	0,1	4,2	28	29	0,4	1	202	410	0,05	0,09	1,0	22
Strawberries	0,7	0,5	8,4	21	21	1,0	1	164	60	0,03	0,07	0,6	59
Sweet potatoes	1,7	0,4	26,3	32	47	0,7	10	243	8 800	0,10	0,06	0,6	21
Tangerines	0,8	0,2	11,6	40	18	0,4	2	126	420	0,06	0,02	0,1	31
Tomatoes	1,1	0,2	4,7	13	27	0,5	3	244	900	0,06	0,04	0,7	23
Turnips	1,0	0,2	6,6	39	30	0,5	49	268	Trace	0,04	0,07	0,6	36
Turnip (Greens)	3,0	0,3	5,0	246	58	1,8	–	–	7 600	0,21	0,39	0,8	139
Watercress	2,2	0,3	3,0	151	54	1,7	52	282	4 900	0,08	0,16	0,9	79
Watermelon	0,5	0,2	6,4	7	10	0,5	1	100	590	0,03	0,03	0,2	7

(Source: US Department of Agriculture, Agricultural Handbook No. 8, Composition of Foods, Washington Reprinted 1975)

6 Foods must be water sufficient

Fresh fruits and vegetables meet our water needs. The purest water is found in fresh fruits and raw vegetables which are 75 – 95% water in an uncooked form. There is no need to drink an excessive amount of fluids. Special circumstances however do encourage the need for extra fluids. You should take in extra fluids if:

- you work outdoors and do a lot of physical exercise
- you are taking drugs, medication and/or smoking
- you drink an excessive amount of cold drinks, coffee, tea and alcohol
- you are fasting (purified water aids in the healing crisis)
- you are eating frozen, cooked and canned foods
- you are eating foods containing excess salt, spices and preservatives.

As our water systems are filled with industrial waste, inorganic minerals and chemicals, you should really not drink ordinary tap water. Additional fluid intake should really be distilled or purified water. There are a number of water purification devices on the market; ask your health store for further information. You can also drink fresh raw fruit and vegetable juices. Do not mix fruit and vegetables together because the digestion times differ. The only vegetables you can mix with fruit (except melons) are lettuce and celery. The popular belief is that drinking 8 – 10 glasses of water daily is beneficial. This is totally unnecessary if you are eating high water content food such as fresh raw fruit and vegetables. Most people don't eat like this, so drinking all this water represents a "cop out" for people who eat mainly cooked, and junk food. If you drink in excess of the body's needs, you will cause the kidneys to age and degenerate long before they should. When tissues are overfilled with fluid other than the water content of fruit and vegetables, they become flat, lose firmness, and age more rapidly.

RULES TO OBSERVE WHEN DRINKING LIQUIDS

- Drink only when thirsty. Listen to your body.
- Never drink with your meals. It has been shown that drinking with meals dilutes the digestive juices, which consequently retards digestion.

WHEN TO TAKE FLUIDS

Fluids, preferably water, are best taken:

- 20 – 30 minutes before a meal (fruit and vegetable juices are best taken $1^1/_2$ hours before a meal)
- 1 hour after a fruit meal
- 2 hours after a starch meal
- 3 – 4 hours after a protein meal.

7 Foods must be alkaline in metabolic reaction

The human body has what may be called an alkaline body condition. We can help the body to maintain an alkaline body condition by eating foods which have a predominance of alkaline-forming elements. When food is metabolised, either an alkaline or acid residue is left in the body, depending on which mineral elements are dominant. The acid-forming minerals are sulphur, phosphorus and chlorine. The alkaline-forming minerals are sodium, potassium, calcium, magnesium and iron. All flesh foods, eggs, cheese, legumes, grains (except millet), nuts (except almonds) and seeds are acid forming. All fruit, vegetables and sprouts are alkaline forming. I would like to point out that citrus fruits are not acid forming. They are acid to the taste but when metabolised are alkaline in the bloodstream, because of the predominance of alkaline elements. Raw milk is slightly alkaline, but because it is pasteurised it is acid forming. If your diet consists of predominantly acid-forming foods, then the body uses its alkaline reserves, especially calcium, to maintain its pH balance.

As a result the kidneys and lungs are overworked in order to rid the body of the excess acids. To maintain a proper acid/ alkaline ratio, your diet should consist of 80% alkaline-forming foods and no more than 20% acid-forming foods.

When eating acid-forming foods, eat them with a large amount of raw fresh vegetables. This balances the meal by maintaining the alkaline mineral reserves in the tissues.

8 Foods must be nontoxic (must contain no preservatives or additives)

For the past 25 years, food additives and preservatives have been the subject of many books and articles which warn of their dangers. The addition of chemicals to foods, more than any other single factor, negatively affects the nutrient content and life-sustaining energy in our foods. The effect of these additives on our bodies, and hence our health, can be immediate or long term. They increase the rate of oxidation reactions and this in turn creates stress in our bodies.

Virtually every bit of food you eat has been treated with some chemical somewhere along the line. These chemicals include dyes, bleaches, emulsifiers, antioxidants, preservatives, flavourants, thickeners, sweeteners, hydrolisers, hydrogenators and many others. Chemicals hide the true nature of the food.

Additives are used to enhance the appearance, colour, aroma, texture and flavour of both prepared and natural foods. Yes, natural foods too. In some salad bars lettuce is sprayed with bisulphate, so it won't wilt.

Chemical additives have been linked conclusively to many diseases ranging from allergies to cancer, as well as blurred vision, aching backs, and hyperactivity in children.

Preserving foods with irradiation also appears to cause a lot more problems than it solves. It could affect our energy, child-bearing capacity and the likelihood of our getting cancer. The body cannot use such substances as they are poisonous and detrimental to the organism. When the body takes in toxins, it attempts to eliminate them by revving up the metabolism.

You have to read your food product labels to know what you are taking into your body. A product always contains more of the ingredients mentioned first than those mentioned last. Our safest course of action would be to reduce our intake of processed foods in favour of fresh produce, ie fresh fruit and raw vegetables.

Boxed, tinned or canned foods contain more fat and more salt than you might otherwise eat, as well as a host of preservatives, colourants and chemicals, which enhance their shelf life.

We should insist that the labels on our foodstuffs give us more information. Marketing buzz words like "lite" should be defined and standardised.

"Additives which can cause reactions in allergy sufferers are not always indicated on the packaging of food stuffs and often they are disguised by unpronounceable scientific names which only confuse the consumer further."
(Source: O'Donoghue, Clare – Woman's Value: Food for Thought, July 1992, p 67)

WELL KNOWN ADDITIVES AND PRE-SERVATIVES

ANTIOXIDANTS   eg BHA (Butylated Hydroxyanisole) and BHT (Butylated Hydroxytoluene) prevent food from spoiling. They are often added to oils and fats because they retard the process of rancidity, thereby extending the shelf life of the products.

Antioxidants/BHA and BHT are found in crisps, margarine and other fat-containing foods.

These antioxidants can trigger hyperactive symptoms, especially in children. They can also result in urticaria (skin rash). BHA and BHT are not permitted in baby foods and have been effectively banned from food in Japan. They can be carcinogenic.

ARTIFICIAL SWEETENERS   are substances other than sugar used to sweeten foods. There has been a great deal of debate regarding artificial sweeteners, but the fact still remains they are not ideal.

Recent research shows that there is the possibility of them being carcinogenic. They are prohibited from use in any baby foods. Artificial sweeteners destroy vitamin C and can cause liver damage.

Artificial sweeteners are found in no fewer than 125 different products, but are mainly confined to soft drinks, soft drink mixes and low caloric yoghurts. Some sweeteners have been categorised as "non-nutritive" sweeteners.

A recent study showed that people who use artificial sweeteners in high doses may experience increased appetite, as well as neuroendocrine disorders. *Professor Richard Wurtman* (of the Massachusetts Institute of Technology) has clinical evidence that high amounts of aspartame, especially in combination with carbohydrates, can provoke epileptic seizures. *Professor John Olney*, of the same institute, concludes that aspartame can cause chronic brain damage, especially when consumed in combination with Monosodium Glutamate (MSG).

AZO DYES   are a group of chemicals that add colour to food. They are identified on labels as "certified colour or artificial colour" or by a specific name, for example tartrazine. Tartrazine is a bright yellow coal tar dye, often used with other colourants, such as amaranth and sunset yellow. It is used to colour many soft drinks, boiled sweets, pastries, jellies, ice lollies, smoked fish, canned vegetables, dessert mixes, marzipan, chewing gum, brown sauces and shells of medicinal capsules.

It is generally recognised to be responsible for a wide range of allergic and intolerance symptoms, including child hyperactivity, asthma, rhinitis (running nose), migraine and skin rashes (eczema).

People who are particularly sensitive to natural salicylates in wine or tomatoes or in their synthetic form in ice cream, sweets, aspirin and soft drinks are liable to be intolerant of tartrazine as well. Asthmatics can be allergic to salicylates, and this will manifest in a tight chest and wheezing.

It has been suggested that tartrazine in fruit cordials may be responsible for wakefulness in small children at night. Tartrazine is prohibited in Norway and Finland and restricted in Sweden.

ANNATTO   is a natural yellow colouring, extracted from the annatto tree. It gives cheese and butter their bright yellow colour. The dairy board claims it is totally harmless. There is evidence, however, that it could provoke symptoms of intolerance in people that are susceptible to urticaria and angio-neurotic oedema (fluid around the heart).

EMULSIFIERS AND STABILISERS prevent the separation of various ingredients, eg oil and water. They are used in salad dressings and mayonnaise. Soya is also used as an emulsifier and, as some people are allergic to milk protein, so others are allergic to soya.

ALUMINIUM is used as a silver colourant. It is a pliable heavy metal, which leaches into acidic food eg meat, fish, and chicken, leaving deposits in the kidneys, brain and intestines. There is evidence that this metal is associated with Alzheimer- and Parkinson-type diseases. Several reports suggest that a high aluminium intake may have adverse effects on the metabolism of phosphorus and calcium in the human body, and may induce or intensify skeletal abnormalities. It is found in tea (not herbal teas), some medications, antacids, commercial salt, baking powder, anti-perspirants, toothpastes and aluminium cookware. Aluminium pots oxidise and con-taminate food during the cooking process, and this can be absorbed into the body. Avoid using aluminium foil for cooking, reheating or wrapping foods.

MONOSODIUM GLUTAMATE (MSG) This additive is used to enhance the taste, flavour or smell of food without imparting any flavour of its own. It is known as the "Chinese Restaurant Syndrome".

MSG is found in soya sauce, pork pies, Chinese food, packet soups, soup cubes, canned soups, gravy mixes and certain spices. It also sneaks into many processed and packaged foods and is often not labelled as MSG.

FOOD ADDITIVES THAT ALWAYS CONTAIN MSG:

Monosodium glutamate	Yeast nutrient
	Autolyzed yeast
Hydrolyzed vegetable protein	
	Textured vegetable protein
Sodium caseinate	Calcium caseinate
Yeast extract	Yeast food
Hydrolyzed oat flour	

FOOD ADDITIVES THAT OFTEN CONTAIN MSG:

Malt extract	Malt flavoring
Bouillon	Natural flavoring
Barley malt	Natural beef flavoring
Broth	Natural chicken flavoring
Stock	Natural pork flavoring
Flavoring	Seasonings

(*Source: Fuhrman, Joel – Fasting and Eating for Health*)

Reactions usually occur half an hour after a person has eaten more than the body can tolerate. Symptoms include heart palpita-tions, headaches, dizziness, muscle tighten-ing, nausea, weakness of the upper arms, pins and needles, shortness of breath and a feeling of being disassociated from oneself. MSG can cause delayed reactions in asthmatics after about 6 – 12 hours, manifesting in a tight chest.

SULPHUR DIOXIDE is found in sausage meat, wine, beer, biltong, dried fruit, candied peel, sauces, soups, flour, dehydrated vege-tables (including mashed potatoes in packets), glucose syrup and cider vinegar.

This preservative could cause bronchiospasms and coughing fits especially in asthmatics. It is also known to reduce levels of calcium in the body, making teeth and bones brittle.

It may also cause gastric irritation, nausea, headaches, eczema, hypertension and ulcers. Foods containing this preservative should be avoided by hyperactive children.

SODIUM BENZOATE is used to preserve fruit juices and fruit products. It is found in some carbonated and other soft drinks, bottled sauces (eg barbecue, mexican and taco), margarines, cheesecake mixes, mayonnaise and pickled cucumbers. Reactions are similar to those experienced with sulphur dioxide. Sodium benzoate could also cause foetal damage, hyperactivity, asthma and urticaria.

SODIUM NITRITES AND NITRATES are used extensively in the food industry. They are used as preservatives in processed meat to inhibit botulism. They impart a red colour to meat and are used as a curing salt. Sodium nitrites and nitrates are found in all red meats, sausages, bacon, ham, salami, pâtés, corned meat, smoked fish and frozen pizza. Nitrates convert to nitrites in the stomach and have been shown to cause deoxygenation of the blood, especially in babies (banned from baby foods). Nitrites and Nitrates react with amines (basic chemicals found in foods) to form nitrosamines and these can be potentially carcinogenic (cancer forming). These preservatives can also cause gastroenteritis accompanied by severe abdominal pain, irregular pulse, vertigo and muscular weakness, bronchiospasms and urticaria. They can also exacerbate eczema.

SODIUM SULPHITE is found mainly in fruit juices, fruit pie mixes, wine, beer, shellfish, and frozen fried potato products.

Ingestion of sulphites may cause gastric irritation, nausea, and diarrhoea. It may also trigger an asthmatic attack. People with impaired kidneys and/or liver, should avoid all foods containing sulphites.

ACETIC ACID is the main ingredient in vinegar and is one of the oldest known preservatives and food additives. It is found in many pickles, savoury and fruit sauces, and ketchup. Processed cheese preparations, tinned tomatoes, tinned sardines, and horseradish cream also contain acetic acid. It not only irritates the tissues, but can also damage the central nervous system and the kidneys. It can eventually cause liver damage.

CALCIUM PROPIONATE is found in all types of breads ranging from white loaves to whole-wheat and rye bread. It is also found in Christmas puddings, some processed cheeses and in flour confectionery. It can cause migraines as well as gastrointestinal problems, with symptoms similar to a gall bladder attack. If you are concerned about getting enough calcium, avoid shop bread, because calcium propionate destroys the enzyme that enables us to assimilate calcium.

SALT (sodium chloride) is used as a preservative or flavouring in cheeses, processed meats, canned vegetables, ketchup, snacks such as salted nuts and potato chips – who would have thought that these foods could be injurious to the body?

Additional sources of salt are found in baked products because of the sodium bicarbonate in the leavening. High salt intake interferes with the body's ability to clear fats from the bloodstream. Excess sodium is a contributing cause in kidney problems, water retention, hypertension, cardiovascular disease, and possibly stomach cancer and migraine headaches.

PIMARICIN   is used in fruit juices and soft cheeses. It can cause skin irritations and stomach cramps in sensitive people.

If the kind of preservatives used in food and the way the body reacts to them scare you, I think it is wise to reduce the percentage of processed foods in your diet and eat more natural foods.

This is by no means a complete list of additives or preservatives.

If you want to find out more about preservatives refer to the select bibliography.

9 Foods must have aesthetic or sensory appeal

Foods in their natural state must be pleasing to our five senses. Fresh raw fruit, raw vegetables, nuts, seeds, and avocados definitely meet these criteria, if prepared attractively. If you have to disguise a food flavour because it doesn't taste good in its natural state, then it really should not be eaten.

10 Foods must be edible in the raw state

The highest quality foods are natural raw foods. Fresh raw fruit and raw vegetables contain all the nutrients necessary for good health, growth, maintenance and repair. These kinds of foods do not cause or support degenerative diseases.

Existing research shows that a predominantly raw diet retards the rate at which we age, brings boundless energy, reduces the amount of sleep we require, and improves our emotional outlook.

WHAT IS WRONG WITH THE "NORMAL" DIET?

Virtually everything! It is a well-known scientific fact that all heating and cooking destroys vital enzymes, vitamins and minerals in the food. When animals eat the meat of other animals, they eat it raw. When you cook your meat, chicken and fish, it looses all the enzymes and nutritional value. The "normal" diet contains processed foods, junk foods, overcooked foods full of added fats, refined flour and sugar. Eggs are mass-produced by drug-injected chickens, and the red-looking meat in the shop window, injected to keep it looking red. This and so much more is what is wrong with the "normal" diet. Food from animals is already dead. Anything dead will begin to decompose immediately. Cooked foods are often tasteless and you only like them because of the condiments which are added (salt, pepper, spices). Have you ever tried a cooked meal, meat, chicken or fish without anything added to it? Try it and I guarantee that you will find it distasteful. Hence, you only eat "normal" foods because of the many condiments added to them.

WHY SHOULD YOU EAT RAW FOODS?

Raw foods are made up of organic enzymes. According to *Dr Joel Robbins,* enzymes are catalysts which help the body work more efficiently in assimilating food for life-maintaining purposes.

We deprive the body of live enzymes when we eat cooked food which is heated above 44 °C. Most enzymes are destroyed at this temperature. Foods that have been processed or irradiated have no live enzymes. The body must then produce its own enzymes to digest the food. If this is done on a continual basis the body is taxed to produce not only digestive enzymes, but also enzymes needed for other biochemical reactions. The body thus becomes weakened and vulnerable to disease. Raw foods provide more body energy because much less energy is wasted on the elimination of the toxins found in processed foods. Fresh raw fruit and vegetables are 2 – 3 times more efficiently utilised by the body than processed and overcooked foods, and yield more energy.

Raw fresh fruit and vegetables, a moderate amount of raw nuts, seeds, avocados and sprouts definitely build a strong immune system. *Dr Douglass*, in a 1985 study in the Southern Medical Journal, found that a diet containing 40 – 63% raw foods, helped 32 patients lose weight and control their hypertension (high blood pressure).

THE BENEFITS OF A PREDOMINANTLY RAW DIET

- The body's elimination organs (the lungs, bowels, kidneys, skin and liver) are able to expel accumulated wastes and toxins more efficiently.
- The optimal sodium-potassium and acid-alkaline balances are restored more quickly.
- Raw foods improve the body's use of oxygen so that both muscles and brain are energised.
- Raw foods are also high in fibre, which does not irritate the lining of the digestive tract.
- When most of your food is eaten raw you'll find you eat less! Raw foods do not overstimulate your tastebuds and thus prevent you from overeating.
- Raw foods are easily digested within 24 hours, compared to 48 – 72 hours (2 – 3 days) for cooked foods depending on what

has been eaten. For example, red meat takes 72 hours to pass through the gastro-intestinal tract. According to *Dr Edward A. Taub* you should not eat any form of animal products for 3 days after eating red meat ie no fish or chicken or cheese etc.

For those who find it difficult to eat raw fruit and vegetables in abundance, there is an alternative: juice in a capsule called Juice Plus+®

Juice Plus+® is a wholefood that comes in capsules for adults and chewable tablets for children – 17 fresh vegetables, fruits and grains have been reduced to a powder through an unusual and gradual drying process. This removes the water and waste, and leaves behind intact the nutrition, vitamins, minerals, phytochemicals, fibre, and most important of all, the enzymes. Juice Plus+® isn't intended to replace the recommended 5 servings of raw vegetables and fruits in your daily diet. I feel Juice Plus+® is just good live nutrition in an easily digested and assimilated form which the body can use effectively and easily.

WHAT HAPPENS TO FOOD WHEN IT IS COOKED?

The most important ingredient in raw food is its life force (live enzymes). These are destroyed if the food is cooked at a temperature of over 44 °C, either by boiling, roasting, frying or baking. When food is processed or preserved, live enzymes are also destroyed. Digestion of cooked food involves a great deal of energy on the part of the body. If only cooked foods are eaten with no added raw foods, this leads to enervation (tiredness), toxins in the bloodstream, and finally chronic degenerative diseases. Depending on the length of time and the amount of heat used to cook food, most of the protein, minerals, vitamins and enzymes are destroyed. For example, when you cook fats they become saturated. These fats are attracted to the linings of the artery walls where they attach and harden. The result is hardening of the arteries.

"In 1930 Dr Paul Kouchakoff, a Russian scientist prepared a paper on his experiments regarding the phenomenon called 'leucocytosis' entitled 'The Influence of Food Cooking on the Blood Formula of Man'. He discovered that when cooked food was eaten, a tremendous proliferation of white blood cells appeared in the bloodstream, exceeding 2 – 4 times the normal count.

He concluded that this phenomenon was pathological. Conversely, when raw food was eaten there was no substantial increase in the number of white blood cells. (Prior to these experiments leucocytosis had been regarded as a normal physiological process.)"

(Source: Nelson, Dennis – Maximizing Your Nutrition)

Cooked foods thus set up a bodily alarm state to fight the invasion of a foreign and poisonous pathogen and it is for this reason that I encourage the eating of a raw salad before a cooked meal.

Another significant project was undertaken by an American physician, *Dr Francis M. Pottenger Jr.* It was an experiment conducted on the adrenal glands of cats. *Pottenger* noticed that when the cats were fed on scraps of raw meat, the animals were much healthier. They were also far less likely to die from surgery, than those fed on cooked meat. Controlled studies were then conducted to explore this phenomenon. *Dr Pottenger* used 2 groups of cats.

EXPERIMENT – "POTTENGER'S AMAZING CATS" (COOKED VERSUS RAW FOOD)

The Cooked Food Group were fed $2/3$ cooked meat, $1/3$ pasteurised milk and cod liver oil.
The Raw Food Group were fed $2/3$ raw meat, $1/3$ raw milk and cod liver oil.

RESULTS:

The Cooked Food Group of cats reproduced unhealthy kittens. Miscarriage in these cats was common: 25% miscarriages occurred in the 1st generation and 70% in the second. These cats were also irritable and experienced a high incidence of allergies, sickness and skeletal deformities. The kittens of the 3rd generation were so degenerate, that none of them survived the 6th month of life.

He also noted that the 1st generation cats of the cooked food group developed diseases near the end of the life span – the sort of diseases we commonly experience today, for example cancer, diabetes etc.

The 2nd generation cats developed the same diseases in the middle of their life span. The 3rd generation cats developed diseases when they were born or in a matter of weeks, years etc. Today children are being diagnosed with diseases which were once typically old peoples' diseases, eg juvenile arthritis, juvenile diabetes etc. The number one killer disease of children under 10 years of age is cancer. In the past, you had to be very sick and run down for a long time to get cancer – but not any more.

The Raw Food Group of cats reproduced healthy kittens from one generation to the next. Miscarriage was uncommon. They had good skeletal structure and were normal in their behaviour. *Dr Pottenger* thus concluded, that the life-damaging effects of eating cooked foods are passed on from generation to generation. He discovered that inherited damage, induced by eating cooked foods, required a full four generations of animals nourished on raw foods, in order to regenerate significantly.

(Source: Pottenger, Francis M. Jr – Pottenger's Cats: A Study in Nutrition)

"No doubt, a predominantly cooked food diet has similar effects on humans. Since the enzymes are destroyed, the body must work harder to digest the food."
(Source: Nelson, Dennis – Maximizing Your Nutrition)

What is happening now is that in each generation the enzyme pool in the newborn is becoming smaller and smaller. The more we process a food, the less nutrient value it retains. *Dr Joel Robbins* has drawn up a hierarchy of food preparation, starting at the top with no preparation (raw foods), leaving the food with its full living nutrient content, and ending at the bottom with the most processed, rendering the food dead and useless to the body, with little or no nutrient value retained.

HIERARCHY OF FOOD PREPARATION

RAW and WHOLE
- JUICED and consumed immediately once the skin of fruits or vegetables is broken, oxygen combines with the enzymes and kills them (this process is called "oxidation")

DEHYDRATED or DRIED
- loses 2 – 5% of nutrient value
  dried without chemicals or additives
  commercial brands of dried fruit contain sulphur dioxide (exception: raisins)

FROZEN
- freshly picked and frozen immediately - loses 5 – 30% of nutrient value

STEAMED
- loses 15 – 60% of nutrient value
- steamed means the green bean is still a bit crisp (if it's limp, it's cooked)

LEFTOVERS of raw foods
- these are subject to oxidation due to the breaking of the skin of the fruit or vegetable

For example, a salad prepared the night before, stored in the fridge, even in a sealed container

COOKED
- baked, broiled, boiled, grilled, steamed too long, home canned
- the green bean is limp
- loses 40 – 100% of nutrient value, depending on how long it is cooked

COOKED LEFTOVERS
- food loses 60 – 100% of nutrient value

MICROWAVED
- loses 90 - 99% of nutrient value

COMMERCIALLY CANNED FOODS

FRIED FOODS

FOODS WITH ADDITIVES
- these not only lose 100% of their nutrient value, but have toxins added to them
(Source: Robbins, Joel – Eating for Health and Wellness)

In order to gain the best nutrient value from foods, you should eat more fresh raw fruit and vegetables and occasionally some cooked foods.

11 Foods must be digested and utilised in the most efficient way

The digestion of modern processed food involves a great deal of energy on the part of the body. This is detrimental to the health of the body because the digestive enzymes have difficulty in processing the foreign ingredients in processed food. Simple foods such as fresh raw fruit and vegetables are far easier to digest and assimilate, and our digestive system is especially designed to process these types of food.

FOODS THAT UPSET DIGESTION
You might not be aware of these effects for a long time, nor connect them with digestive problems.

- **Fat and sugar combined** cause problems in our intestinal tract. For example, sugar on cereals with milk or cream causes rapid fermentation. Fruit (natural sugar) should be eaten on an empty stomach and not combined with anything else.
- **Sugar causes yeast to ferment** and even the tiniest amount added to food causes it to bubble away in your stomach, eg sugared buns.
- **Fruit kept in cold storage** develops acids and other substances which can make your life a misery as far as digestion is concerned. Only eat fruits in season.
- **Cooked fats** are indigestible. Oil, margarine and cheese are "cooked" during processing and if you then bake or fry with them, the structure of the fat changes, making it even more indigestible. When

you add sugar to cooked fat, eg chutney or a sweet marinade over chicken, meat etc you will experience terrible indigestion. Rather combine sauces which are high in fat, for example mayonnaise or cheese sauces with greens and not with meat or potatoes etc.

If you want to improve your digestion go easy on processed foods such as yellow cheese, margarine, sausages, ready to eat custard, instant sauces, pizzas, convenience foods for the microwave and coated frozen fish etc.

I have found through my counselling sessions that stomachaches, a bloated feeling, constipation and headaches seem to be related to poor digestion. Incorrect food combinations interfere with good digestion. We thus seem to bring on poor digestion through our poor lifestyle and incorrect eating habits.

12 Foods must be easily digested when eaten alone or in proper combinations

Correct food combining is just as important as the selection of food and is one of the most important ways of securing optimal nutrition. Following the rules of correct food combining enhances digestion, promotes weight loss and improves health. A lack of discomfort when digesting foods should not be taken as an indication that food is being properly assimilated, and that no digestive problems will occur in the future.

GUIDELINES FOR BETTER DIGESTION
Do not overeat.   Eat only until satisfied – listen to your body.

Eat only when hungry.   Don't eat just because it is meal time. You must learn to differentiate between hunger and appetite.

Chew food very well.   This stimulates the

salivary glands and also gives you a full feeling on less food. It should take you 20 – 30 minutes to eat a meal. You must pace yourself. My suggestion is to use an egg timer, and to place your spoon, fork and knife down in between bites. Eat only after the previous mouthful has been chewed properly and swallowed.

Always eat on an empty stomach. Allow sufficient time between meals for proper digestion of the previous meal before eating again. This way of eating will not overload the digestive system. By snacking in between meals you do not give your digestive system a rest.

Wait the following times before eating again.
• 1 hour after a fruit meal
• 2 – 3 hours after vegetable and starch meals
• 3 – 4 hours after protein meals.

Do not eat more than one type of concentrated food at a meal.
You should only eat one type of protein food or one type of starch food at a meal. For example, do not eat potatoes and mealies, or nuts and chicken at the same meal.

Do not drink with your meals. Liquids dilute the digestive juices in the food when drunk with meals, and this retards digestion.

Never eat:
• when in pain, running a fever, or feeling ill
• immediately before or after physical exercise – rather drink purified water
• when under emotional stress
• just before or during an exam
• when extremely exhausted.

WHAT IS CORRECT FOOD COMBINING?
Correct food combining means that you should digest together only those foods that digest in the same length of time or that require the same acid or alkaline medium for digestion.

For example:
• fruits with fruits
• vegetables with vegetables
• nuts, seeds, meat, fish, chicken, cheese etc with non-starchy vegetables.

Although I do not encourage the eating of flesh foods or dairy products as part of a healthy diet, they are included for the benefit of those who still want to eat them.

Certain foods require different environments for digestion:

Protein foods (nuts, seeds, fish, etc) require hydrochloric acid and therefore an acid environment.

Starchy foods (potatoes, rice, pasta etc) require an alkaline environment. The stomach cannot possibly be acid and alkaline at the same time.

Drs William Howard Hay and Herbert Shelton observed how the human body worked most efficiently in carrying out the processes of digestion through correct food combining.

Raw fruit and vegetables digest much more quickly than animal foods. Animal products can stay in the stomach for 4 – 5 hours before moving to the intestines, and it is during this waiting time that they putrefy and cause problems. Also, we humans do not secrete a sufficient amount of hydrochloric acid as do carnivores (meat-eating animals). Hydrochloric acid assists in rapidly breaking down the fats and complex proteins in meat into lipids and amino acids so they can be used by the body most efficiently, before they putrefy.

WHAT HAPPENS TO THE BODY WHEN FOODS ARE NOT COMBINED CORRECTLY?
When other foods are eaten together with fruit, which is a quickly digested food, the fruit is held up in the stomach and starts

fermenting and putrefying. This creates by-products of bacterial decomposition, such as alcohol, acetic acid and ammonia which are poisonous to the body. These toxic by-products irritate the tissues, and waste the energy the body requires to pass them through the alimentary canal. These poisons eventually end up in the bloodstream and manifest in various allergies, gas, wind, acid indigestion, flatulence and heartburn. Ant-acids are then taken to neutralise the acids in the stomach. Continual use of antacids could in time ulcerate the stomach.

Deficiencies of certain vitamins and minerals also result when foods are not combined correctly. As the food is not broken down completely, the maximum amount of nutrients are not absorbed. When foods are eaten in correct combinations, no toxins (poisons) are produced in the body and maximum nutrients are absorbed, preventing deficiencies. There is an urgent need for people with impaired digestion to adopt the practice of correct food combining.

FOOD COMBINING RULES

FRUITS are divided into 3 groups: acid, subacid and sweet fruits.

- Do not mix sweet fruits or dried fruits with acid fruits.
- Subacid fruits can be mixed with either the sweet or subacid group.
- If you don't want to mix the fruits, you can choose from one group only and eat as much as you like.
- If you want a fruit from a group that doesn't combine well with a fruit you have just eaten, then you must wait at least 1 hour before eating that particular fruit.
- For those with digestive problems, limit your intake to 2 or 3 kinds of fruit at any one meal.

- All melons belong to a group of their own. They must not be eaten with any other fruit group, but can be mixed with fruit belonging to the melon family. Melons are more than 90% liquid and leave the stomach very quickly. They should therefore not be delayed in the stomach by other foods or other fruit groups, because they decompose rapidly. This causes a great deal of gastric distress, for example: eating watermelons with nuts can be quite troublesome.

STARCH AND ACID-TASTING FOODS

Many Natural Hygienists avoid eating starch and acid-tasting foods during the same meal, eg potatoes with tomatoes or lemon juice in a salad with rice etc. This could be quite radical for those people changing to the pattern of eating I recommend.

If, however, you do experience digestive problems, I do suggest you avoid the above combinations. You should also not mix oranges and grapefruit with other fruit groups because citrus fruit can aggravate digestive problems.

FRUITS AND VEGETABLES

Never combine fruits with vegetables. The only vegetables that combine with any fruit, except the melon family, are lettuce and celery. When adding these vegetables to fruit, you actually enhance digestion because these foods require little gastric digestion. Lettuce and celery are high in water and fibre content. This makes them an excellent combination with more concentrated foods which have a lower water content such as nuts, seeds or dried fruit. Lettuce and celery help dilute the fruit sugar, especially in dates and other dried fruit, and prevent overeating. Lettuce and

59

celery also slow down the metabolising of the sugar in fruit, and they are a good addition if you are hypoglycaemic or feel bloated when eating fruit initially. Apples, however, have been found to be an acceptable addition to raw vegetable salad, provided you have no digestive problems.

FRUITS AND STARCHES
Fruits should not be eaten with starches. There are exceptions to this rule, especially for those just beginning this new programme of eating.

DRIED FRUIT
All dried fruit falls under the sweet fruit group.

Don't overeat on dried fruit as it is very high in sugar and low in water content. Use only a $1/4 - 1/2$ cup of dried fruit per day. If you want to lose weight, eat only a $1/4$ cup in the afternoon as a snack.

Men, however, can eat up to 1 cup of dried fruit per day. You should only eat 1 type of dried fruit at a time and remember to combine it correctly with high water content food. Lettuce and celery are quite delicious with dried fruit. You can also soak the dried fruit in distilled or purified water overnight. This aids digestion, as well as reconstituting the missing water content. Dried fruit must be sulphur dioxide free.

ACID FRUITS AND PROTEIN MEALS
Acid fruits combine well with a protein meal, for example, oranges with nuts or cheese, or yoghurt with pineapple. There are, however, problems when eating dairy products.

I have found that if cheese is eaten in the evening and melons are eaten the following morning, many people feel bloated and uncomfortable. If this has happened to you avoid eating melons and rather choose other fruits.

AVOCADOS – FRUITS – STARCH MEALS
Avocados go well with subacid or acid fruits only, as well as with starch meals eg, bread or potatoes.

However, exceptions can be made especially when feeding babies and children. You can, for example, mix avocado pear with bananas – quite delicious! I do not recommend food combining rules for young children.

This combination is not advisable for adults, because when avocado is eaten with sweet fruits, the high sugar content of the fruit interferes with the digestion of the protein even if the protein content is low, as in the case of the avocado. This combination will result in fermentation.

Lettuce and celery should be added to avocados with your recommended fruits. The reason for this is that fats take longer to digest than fruits and raw vegetables and by adding the lettuce and celery, you dilute the fats (avocado) and sugars (fruit), thus preventing the delay of the emptying time of the stomach. If you have a weak stomach with poor muscle tone, then I would advise you to eat avocados only with raw vegetable salads and not with fruit.

You must avoid eating avocados with protein meals such as nuts, fish, chicken etc as fats inhibit protein digestion.

TOMATOES
Tomatoes are considered as acid fruits, without the sugar content of other acid fruits. They should, however, never be combined with any fruit.

Tomatoes can be combined with either avocados, a raw vegetable salad, nuts, seeds, meat, fish, chicken, or dairy products. If you have digestive problems, do not eat starchy food with tomatoes. Again, I do suggest you eat lots of raw tomatoes when eating meat, fish, chicken, eggs and dairy products etc. This aids digestion of the acid-forming foods.

MILK
Always take milk alone because of its high protein and fat (cream) content. It combines poorly with all other foods. Combining milk and fruit is worse than combining milk with meat or vegetables, because fruit takes much less time to digest than any other food. The fruit is held up in the stomach awaiting the more lengthy digestive time required by the milk.

SOUPS
Soups are really liquids and should be consumed 20 – 30 minutes before a meal. You must have something raw before a cooked meal, so drink a fresh vegetable juice before the soup. I suggest you make a thick soup – add rice or pasta to it and make a "meal" of it. If you are still hungry, add a plate of steamed vegetables to the meal. Add only neutral vegetables (no starch vegetables) to lentil soup. Do not use packet soups or bouillon cubes, as they are very high in salt and contain monosodium glutamate. Commercial soups are processed and contain additives. Rather prepare your own vegetable soup by using raw vegetables cooked in purified water, and brown some onions in water as a form of added seasoning. Enquire from health stores regarding stock powders and soup cubes.

Remember, optimal nutrition will come from eating 75% raw fruit and vegetables correctly combined.

The food Combination Charts which follow are guidelines to streamline digestion, thus giving your body more energy. Adopt these principles at your own pace, continually striving for improvement.

If you eat foods containing all 12 criteria you will definitely be assured of better health, prevention of disease and a great zest for living.

Chart 5   Fruit Combinations

ACID FRUIT	SUBACID FRUIT	SWEET FRUIT
Goes well with subacid fruits	Goes well with acid fruits and sweet fruits	Goes well with subacid fruits
Oranges	Apples	Bananas
Grapefruit	Pears	Fresh Figs
Naartjies	Peaches	Fresh Prunes
Pineapples	Cherries	Pawpaws (Papinos)
Strawberries	Nectarines	Persimmons
Lemons	Lychees	All Dried Fruit
Limes	Grapes	
Minneolas	Mangoes	
Granadillas	Prickly Pears	
Gooseberries	Loquats	
Granny Smith Apples	Berries	
Pomegranates	Plums	
Kiwi Fruit		
Guavas		

- ALL MELONS are best eaten alone. Wait 40 – 60 minutes before eating another kind of fruit
- AVOCADOS are a fair combination with subacid or acid fruit.
- LETTUCE and CELERY combine well with any fruit, except melons.
- NUTS (not peanuts) can be mixed with acid fruit.

FOR THOSE JUST STARTING OUT ON THIS PROGRAMME I HAVE ALLOWED FOR THE FOLLOWING EXCEPTIONS:

- Macadamia Nuts (low in protein) can be mixed with subacid or sweet fruit.
- Sweet fruit can be combined with a starch meal, eg oats can be eaten with dried fruit and bananas.

    +   =   Good
    +   =   combination   +   =   Poor combination

Chart 6   Protein, Starch and Fat Combinations

PROTEIN	NEUTRAL / GREEN VEGETABLES	STARCH	FATS
All Nuts (except peanuts) All Seeds (Sunflower, Pumpkin etc) • Unprocessed cheese • Yoghurt, Legumes, Beans, Lentils etc • Eggs • Dairy Products • Fish, Seafood • Poultry •• Meat •• Milk	**Beetroot**, Broccoli, Artichokes, Asparagus, Brinjals (eggplant), Brussels sprouts, Baby marrows (zucchini), **Butternut, Pumpkin,** Cabbages, **Carrots,** Cauliflowers, Celery, Cucumbers, Fennel, Gem Squash, Green beans, Leeks, Lettuce, Marrows, Mushrooms, Olives, Onions, Parsley, **Peas** (fresh), Peppers (green, red and yellow), Radishes, Spinach, Spring onions, Sprouts, Tomatoes, Turnips, Watercress, Kohlrabi	Bread, Barley, Potatoes, Sweet potatoes, Corn, Mealies, Brown rice, Millet, Buckwheat, Bulgur wheat, Oats, Couscous, Rye, Wheat, Rice cakes Cereals, Pasta	Eat in small quantities with starch and neutral / green vegetables

- Always start a starch or protein meal with a raw vegetable salad.
- Never mix protein with starch or fat.
- Non-starchy vegetables combine well with proteins, starches and fats.
- Wait at least 3 – 4 hours after eating these foods before eating fruit again.
- Foods marked • can be eaten (if you must) twice a week, but no more than 90 – 120 grams in total.
- Foods marked •• should be eaten sparingly. Have no more than 90 – 120 grams once a week.
- Legumes (beans and peanuts) are both high in protein and starch and are well known to cause flatulence etc. Cook them correctly and eat only with neutral non-starchy vegetables to aid digestion.

Mildly starchy vegetables such as carrots, beets, butternut, pumpkin and peas should not be eaten with starchy vegetables, if you have a weight problem. Eat only 1 type of mildly starchy or starchy vegetable with neutral vegetables.

Protein + Neutral/Green Vegetables	=	Good combination
Starch + Neutral/Green Vegetables	=	
Neutral/Green Vegetables + Fat	=	

Protein + Fat	=	Poor combination
Protein + Starch	=	

63

PART 2

Information about the Foods and Drinks You Consume Daily

Secondary Plant Foods

Grains are most often associated with food allergies, especially wheat and corn
DENNIS NELSON
Sprouts are a rich source of chlorophyll which is contained in the embryo of the seeds
CARYL VAUGHAN SCOTT

In the previous section I discussed in detail our primary plant foods – fresh raw fruit, vegetables, nuts and seeds.

Our secondary plant foods are made up of GRAINS and LEGUMES.

GRAINS

These are made up of oats, rye, barley, bulgur wheat, rice, pumpernickel, millet, corn, maize meal (also known as polenta), and couscous. Although buckwheat groats are regarded as grains they are not really "true grains" as they do not belong to the grass family. They are, however, ideal for those who are gluten intolerant.

The products made from grains include cereals, flours, pastas and breads. All grains are acid forming in the bloodstream except for millet which is alkaline forming. Some people have difficulty digesting grains, even in their unprocessed, unrefined state. A healthier way to consume grains is to sprout them. They then become alkaline-forming foods, which the body is able to use much more easily.

Dr Herbert M. Shelton, a notable 20th century hygienist, advises against giving babies cereals before the age of two or before they have all their teeth, as they haven't enough of the enzyme ptyalin to digest the starch adequately. The intestinal substances required for the digestion of the starch are not secreted until a baby is about a year old. I have found through my counselling sessions when dealing with mothers with infants, that cooked cereals with milk cause mucus build-up, which often results in enlarged tonsils and adenoids, colds and gastritis.

REASONS WHY YOU SHOULD NOT EAT GRAINS ON A DAILY BASIS

- Grains always seem to be eaten and cooked with fat, sugar and/or salt. This makes them fattening. If you do eat grains, always add health salt, cold-pressed oil or unsalted butter, **after** they have been cooked.
- **Gluten**, the protein component contained in wheat, oats, rye and barley, found in breakfast cereals, some cakes and pastries, canned soups, postum, coffee substitutes, whole-wheat bread and some pastas, is not well digested by humans. We haven't the enzymes to break it down.
- People don't chew their food properly. Bread especially has to be masticated very well to prevent indigestion. I suggest that you toast bread that contains yeast. This changes the starch into dextrin, which makes for easier digestion.
- Grains can create mucus by clogging the lymphatic nodes, lungs, bronchial tubes and nasal passages, if there is an inherited

tendency. Ingesting wheat could be one of the causes of colds, as well as a contributing cause of eczema, urticaria, migraines and headaches.

- Rheumatism, arthritis and polyneuritis are aggravated by eating grains and grain products in abundance. You must vary your intake of foods in general; include more raw fruit and vegetables, steamed vegetables, potatoes, sweet potatoes, avocados, nuts, seeds, sprouts and legumes.
- A toxic component found in the husks of grains is phytic acid, a phosphorus-like compound. This substance prevents the absorption of iron and binds with calcium to form an insoluble salt, thus rendering the calcium unavailable as a nutrient. It also affects magnesium and zinc absorption. This might be the very food that is a contributing factor in tooth decay. However, once grains have been sprouted, the phytic acid is neutralised.
- You must only use whole grains if you are including them in your pattern of eating, for example, millet and brown rice. Refined grains such as white rice, white bread etc should not be eaten because they are practically devoid of natural fibre and moisture and this can cause constipation. They also upset normal blood sugar levels causing mental imbalances.

Observe the following rule when eating whole grains: always include a large, green, leafy vegetable salad with your meal as this furnishes the necessary alkaline minerals, especially calcium, and aids digestion.

LEGUMES – Pulses

These foods, for example, lentils, dried peas and beans have been used extensively throughout the history of human civilisation, especially in vegetarian diets. They are, however, a difficult food to digest as they contain both protein and starch in highly concentrated forms. You should add lots of green vegetables; this helps in preventing flatulence and aids digestion. As these foods are rich in nitrogen, they should be eaten sparingly.

Legumes, ideally, should be sprouted as this changes the starch-protein ratio dramatically. They then become simple sugars which the body can handle easily, and their nutritional value is increased, as well as their digestibility. Once sprouted they are still a raw food as well as a neutral food (neither a protein nor a starch food). Sprouts are an excellent addition to raw salads and sandwiches. As they are a raw food, they contain an abundance of live food enzymes and are high in vitamins B, C and E as well as minerals.

Sprouting your own seeds is very easy. I find sprouting a fine educational project for children to do themselves, because it teaches them the value and miracle of growing seeds. Initially, I suggest you choose seeds that are easy to sprout, for example, alfalfa, mung beans and lentils. Once you have developed the knack and you are growing these sprouts without difficulty, you can then try the following seeds: wheat, barley, soya beans and raw peanuts. You must only use fresh seeds that have not had their husks removed. These seeds are available at health food stores. A word of warning: do not sprout kidney, butter or haricot beans.

HOW TO SPROUT SEEDS

- Sprinkle approximately 3 – 6 tablespoons of seeds in a large-mouthed jar and pour in enough purified/distilled tepid water to cover the seeds completely. Make sure the jar is deep enough for the seeds to be able to swell to six times their original bulk. Cover the jar with some cheesecloth and hold it in place with rubber bands. The seeds should soak for about 6 – 10 hours (preferably overnight). In winter you will find you need to soak the seeds longer.

- The next morning drain all the water through the cheesecloth and rinse the seeds thoroughly in purified/distilled water. Always shake the jar gently to disperse the seeds. Never leave water in the jar, as this will cause the seeds to rot.
- After rinsing, cover with a small towel to give warmth, and make sure that the air can still enter the jar. Leave in a warmish place away from direct sunlight.
- Rinse the seeds 2 – 4 times every day in fresh purified/distilled water, making sure you remove all the water, when draining them.
- By the 2nd or 3rd day, little shoots should start appearing. Remove the towel, so that the light (not direct sunlight) can green the leaves, giving extra chlorophyll. By the 4th day the sprouts are ready to eat.
- Rinse the sprouts once more and store them in a glass jar or plastic bag in the refrigerator. They will keep fresh for 3 – 4 days. **Sprouted grains** sour easily, so eat them as soon as possible.

An alternative method of sprouting is to use "sprouting trays". These are sold at health stores. I find these the easiest to use. They are made up of 3 tiers, thus making it possible to grow a variety of sprouts in one container.

If you want to go into sprouting in a big way, I suggest you read the books mentioned in the bibliography.

HOW TO COOK LEGUMES

Legumes should be soaked in purified/distilled water before cooking. For example, soak legumes at 5pm and then again before retiring. Always throw the soaking water away and use fresh water to soak again. This increases the biochemical salts in the legumes as well as removing the troublesome sugar, hemicellulose, which is known to cause gas and flatulence.

Simmer legumes in boiling water for 15 minutes on the stove, drain and place in a casserole dish in the oven. Bake at a low temperature till tender. Remember always to serve legumes with neutral/green vegetables and not with starch vegetables.

Recent research indicates that soya beans are rich in natural oestrogens (phyto oestrogens).

"Although in small quantities, these plant-based oestrogens could help to maintain falling oestrogen levels at the time of menopause and protect us against osteoporosis in later life."
(Source: Stewart, Maryon – Beat the Menopause Without HRT)

Plant-based oestrogens can be found in the following foods: soya beans, soya flour, soya sauce, tofu (soya bean curd), miso, tamari etc.

Ultimately, to maintain a level of optimum health, we have to eat more fresh fruit and vegetables as well as other plant-based foods to ward off degenerative diseases.

Animal Products

A man of my spiritual intensity does not eat corpses

GEORGE BERNARD SHAW

These products include red meat, poultry, fish, shellfish, eggs and dairy products. I will be discussing all these foods in detail. The worst offender is animal flesh, followed by eggs, then dairy products – milk, cheese, yoghurt etc. All these foods, once metabolised, leave large residues of acid ash in the blood and tissues. Predominant waste residues are uric, phosphoric and sulphuric acid. Calcium urate residues are also deposited in the soft tissues and calcify as a result of neutralisation. In time, deposits as hard as stone form, for example:

- in the optic lens resulting in cataracts
- in the arteries resulting in arteriosclerosis
- in the kidneys resulting in kidney stones
- in the skin resulting in wrinkling
- in the joints resulting in arthritis.

FLESH FOODS – all kinds of meat

So what's wrong with meat? After all, this is what South Africans enjoy eating most. "Meat is macho". I feel that the eating of these foods is more of an emotional than a nutritional issue. Unfortunately these foods are high in cholesterol, high in protein, high in fat and low in fibre, and are therefore not very good for us. These foods also tend to cause an imbalance in the body's blood formula. Eating animal protein creates a flood of animal fat cruising through the bloodstream every 3 – 4 hours. After eating a cheeseburger and a milk shake (or other fatty meals) the blood actually becomes greasy with animal fat and stays that way for up to 4 hours. This spells trouble for the human digestive system.

People of many countries who cannot afford meat or who choose not to consume it, are by far the healthiest people in the world, for example, the Hunzas, a tribe in North India and Pakistan live to well over the century mark, in a superb state of health. Their diet consists mainly of whole grains, fresh fruits, vegetables, and goat's milk. They are also involved in a great deal of physical activity. The Tarahuma Indians in Mexico also eat an abundance of fresh fruits and vegetables. They eat no animal products and they live to a ripe old age, in the fittest of health. On the other hand, the Eskimos and Laplanders rarely live beyond the age of 40 – 45, because their diet is very high in protein and consists mainly of animal products. Avoiding flesh foods is not a new idea. It has long been part of the Hindu religion and that of the Seventh Day Adventists. Plato, Socrates, Aristotle and Buddha were vegetarians, as well as Da Vinci and Tolstoy. Meat eaters are made not born. *Dr T. Colin Campbell* claims that animal foods are implicated as the primary contributing factor in diseases such as gout, arthritis, diabetes and cancer. He suggests that the closer we approach a total plant-based diet, the greater the health benefits. *Dr McDougall* maintains that the cholesterol content of fish, meat and poultry is about equal, and each causes a similar rise in the cholesterol level, measured in the blood.

PROBLEMS REGARDING THE EATING OF MEAT

- **Meat lacks natural fibre**

  Natural fibre is found abundantly in fresh fruits and vegetables, as well as whole grains. Fibre is essential for proper digestion and for normal bowel functioning, otherwise constipation results, and haemorrhoids and other colon problems develop.

- **Meat is high in saturated fats**

  Meat fat is thicker, more saturated, solid at body temperature, and far more likely to clog human arteries than plant oils. Saturated fats in the diet tend to raise the blood cholesterol and accelerate the development of hardening of the arteries. Clogged human arteries are a major cause of heart problems, strokes and senility. No artery clogging, plaque build-up, or atherosclerosis has ever been found to be composed of rice and vegetables.

- **Animal muscle is high in protein**

  The protein of animal muscle (steak, chicken) is far more concentrated than plant protein which is found in fresh fruit, whole grains, legumes, vegetables, nuts and seeds.

  Your digestive tract cannot handle more than 120 grams of meat at a time, without some putrefaction occurring.

  Undigested protein may contribute to a host of diseases such as tumours, arthritis, cancer, osteoporosis and kidney problems. A concentrated protein load also leaches calcium from the bones.

  Meat also has a stimulating effect which is usually mistaken for a "quick pick-me-up." This stimulating effect stems from the high concentration of protein and the adrenalin which the animal secretes, as a result of the fear of being killed.

- **Animal foods are high in sodium**

  Animal foods contain far more sodium than potassium because salt is added to the meat to give it taste. The sodium/potassium content of foods is a key determinant of high blood pressure (hypertension). This disease is more prevalent among meat-eaters than among vegetarians.

- **Meat contains bacteria and parasites**

  Outbreaks of staphylococcal enteritis, shigella dysentery and salmonella have often been traced to the eating of meat, which has been improperly prepared.

  Oysters and shellfish, taken from waters contaminated with human waste, are a significant cause of infectious hepatitis. Parasitic infections can frequently be traced to a flesh diet. For example, tapeworms can be found in beef and pork. Tapeworm infestations result in chronic disability, weakness and anaemia.

- **Blood in meat can be harmful**

  Blood in the meat you eat contains considerable quantities of metabolic waste products, which are present in the animal's tissue at the time of death. The removal or metabolism of these poisonous waste products places an extra workload on your liver and kidneys.

- **Drugs used in livestock yards**

  Animal flesh is contaminated with a wide variety of drugs. These drugs include hormones, stimulants and antibiotics. They are administered to animals to speed growth and prevent disease. Animals are often slaughtered before the drugs have been cleared from their systems and we humans are exposed unnecessarily to these compounds. Many of these substances contain chemical residues which are harmful to us. Animals are definitely not raised like they used to be. Hormones and antibiotics were not given to animals years ago.

- **Meat contains chemicals**
  Some flesh foods are smoked, pickled, salted and canned using a variety of chemicals, so that they can be kept for long periods before being eaten. Sodium sulphite is often added to give meat its red colour.

- **Meat contains pesticides**
  Animal foods are high on the food chain, because they contain pesticides which have been sprayed on animal feed. These pesticides are stored in the fat molecules in the meat. You may consume in one meal, any of the poisons the animal accumulates over its entire lifetime.

Dr Michael Klaper puts it in a nutshell – "After a meal of flesh:

- *the white blood cell count increases*
- *the red blood cells become more sticky and produce sludge in the small blood vessels*
- *the levels of anti-inflammatory hormones (cortisol) and sex hormones (oestrogen and prolactin) increase".(Source: Klaper, Michael – Vegan Nutrition: Pure and Simple)*

Does all this sound beneficial to our well-being?

I am not going to insist that you give up meat initially, but I do feel that if you are going to continue to eat it regularly, you must follow these guidelines:

- Fish and fowl (white meat) are the least harmful of the meats. Choose free-range chickens (certified to be free of added drugs and hormones) as against ordinary chickens which not only have a high fat content but are injected with hormones and antibiotics. Do not eat the skin of the chicken.

- If you do enjoy red meat, eat it no more than once a week.

- Do not eat animal protein (meat, fish, chicken, eggs) more than once a day. Your portions should really not be more than 90 – 120 grams per day. You do not need protein every single day.

- You should not eat liver. The liver is the filter of the body and it contains many poisons, such as drugs and hormones, which are given to animals.

- Rather, bake, boil or grill meat. Never fry **any** foods. "Braaing" meat also has certain drawbacks, as the charcoal gives off toxins which are absorbed by the meat. We then consume these toxins when we eat the meat.

- In order to aid digestion, always add raw, red, firm tomatoes with meat of any kind and never eat meat together with a starch meal.

- If you do eat red meat regularly, and find it difficult to cut down, consume lots of carrot and celery juice the next day, to neutralise the acid of the meat in your system.

POULTRY AND FISH – are these the alternatives to red meat?

Many people are turning to chicken, turkey, duck and fish as substitutes for red meat. This is not the answer to true health. If you are consuming large amounts of animal protein in the form of either meat, chicken, fish or dairy products, you have to realise that there will be a calcium loss from the bones via the kidneys, and this causes lots of problems.

Osteoporosis is most rampant in the countries where people consume the most poultry, meat, fish and dairy products. **Osteoporosis is not so much a disease of**

calcium deficiency but rather a disease of protein excess. Vegetable protein is less prone to cause calcium loss, due to its slower absorption and less acid-forming nature.

FISH OILS

Fish oils such as salmon and cod liver oil are not as healthy as they are made out to be. They have been shown to inhibit the action of insulin – this is not good news for the diabetic. According to scientific studies, excessive consumption of fish oils could be linked to cancer and is a contributing factor in gall bladder disease. The liver of any animal is the chemical detoxifier of the body. All the pollutants consumed by the animal, as well as cholesterol, are concentrated in the liver. The potential dangers of fish oil outweigh its possible benefits to health.

If you eat fish, try to avoid the very large carnivorous species (swordfish, marlin) and species that live mostly near coastal effluents. Shellfish, for example, are very high in cholesterol as well as protein.

"Fish is not brain food – it is just the opposite. Mercury poisoning from industrial wastes is flushed into streams and rivers and washed into bays and oceans to be taken up by free swimming fish. Mercury poisons the brain and nerve cells of the fish. You will do your health (and the fish) a favor by letting them 'off the hook'."
(Source: Klaper, Michael – Vegan Nutrition: Pure and Simple)

EGGS

Eggs fall into the same category as animal protein, as they are actually animals in their embryonic state. The eggs most people consume, are from hens that lay 200 to 300 eggs a year and are fed on "rich fare" that produces diseases in them.

Eggs also contain an excess of sulphur, protein, fat, and cholesterol, and they have no fibre. The white of the egg is toxic when raw, and difficult to digest when cooked. Raw egg whites contain a protein (avidin) which combines with the vitamin biotin in the intestinal tract, causing possible damage to the kidneys and liver. Avidin also depletes the body of biotin. *"Egg protein has been found to be a leading cause of allergy, especially in children."* *(Source: Nelson, Dennis – Maximizing Your Nutrition)*

Urticaria can be exacerbated by eating eggs. If you enjoy eggs, I suggest you eat no more than two per week. Always buy free-range eggs and cook only by boiling or poaching; do not fry. Always eat raw tomatoes with eggs to facilitate digestion. You should avoid eggs if your liver and kidneys are not in perfect condition.

DAIRY PRODUCTS – do they really give us all the calcium we need?

Dairy products and meat products have so many similarities in their macronutrient content, that you can think of dairy foods as "liquid meat".

You all seem to think that milk is "nature's" most perfect food, containing all the essentials of health, including lots of calcium. Most of you will have difficulty in overcoming this conditioning, especially when emotional issues are involved, such as the dietary needs of pregnant women and young children.

WHAT ARE DAIRY PRODUCTS?

Dairy products are those foods derived from milk and include: all kinds of cheese – yellow and white, cottage cheese, yoghurt, butter-milk, ice cream, whey, and cow's milk based infant formulas, butter and cream.

COW'S MILK is designed by nature for the nutritional needs of a growing calf (to turn a 30 kg calf into a 275 kg cow in 6 months) and not for the slower growth of a smaller human being. Cow's milk is high in protein (contains 300% more casein than mother's milk), high in cholesterol, low in carbohydrates and contains no fibre. The excess of casein in cow's milk is digested and assimilated easily by the calf. No farmer in his right mind would give milk to cows as food. Cow's milk forms large, tough, dense curds which are difficult to digest.

BREAST MILK is much lower in total protein content than cow's milk, is sweeter and higher in carbohydrates and meets all the nutritional needs of a growing infant. Mother's milk forms very small, soft curds and these are easily digested by the infant. If mothers can't breast-feed their infants, then the next best choice is goat's milk, because it forms the same, easy to digest curds, as mother's milk. It is also rich in calcium, flourine, and phosphorus, and its chemical content is similar to that of breast milk.

ICE CREAM *Dr Henry Bieler says "ice cream is a highly putrefactive protein mixture, whether it be the best "homemade' or crude commercial type, rich in emulsifiers." (Source: Bieler, Henry G. – Food is Your Best Medicine)*

If you crave the occasional ice cream treat, either eat home-made using honey, or any brand that doesn't use any chemicals, petroleum products or additives. *Dr Joel Robbins* recommends that ice cream should be eaten on an empty stomach and not as dessert, and then only in small portions. Healthier ice cream substitutes are frozen bananas and fruit ices.

DISEASES ASSOCIATED WITH THE CONSUMPTION OF DAIRY PRODUCTS
- **Lactose intolerance**
  Animal milk is still not an ideal food for humans, especially after the age of three, because we do not secrete the enzyme rennin to digest the casein (protein and calcium complement), nor the enzyme lactase to digest the lactose (sugar) in milk. We humans refuse to be weaned.

  I have found during my counselling sessions, that many people are diagnosed as lactose intolerant (10% of the white population and 40% of the black population). This intolerance results in symptoms of diarrhoea, gas and stomach cramps.

- **Mucus-related diseases**
  Milk protein acts as an irritant to the immune system in many people. Dairy products clog up your system with mucus. This mucus lodges in the sinus cavities and bronchial tubes and leads to many diseases, including the various "childhood diseases", colds, flu, indigestion, stomach and bowel disorders, allergies, asthma, skin rashes, eczema, urticaria, hyperactivity, behavioural irritability and bed wetting (enuresis). Milk and dairy products are not the only factors responsible for these diseases, but their use in the diet seems to be a major contributor.

  A consultant at the *Allergy Clinic at the Children's Hospital in Rondebosch, Cape Town* observed that dairy products can cause health problems in children relating to the gastrointestinal tract, the respiratory tract and the skin.

- **Food allergies**
  Dairy products are the most frequent source of the dietary antigens that cause a great variety of food allergies. These allergic reactions may be passed on to breast-fed babies, whose mothers consume dairy products, and this could be the cause

of colic in the infant. When I look at my records of the people whom I counsel – children of all ages, adolescents and adults – all invariably show incredible improvements when cow's milk and products derived from cow's milk are removed from the diet.

- **Blood iron deficiency anaemia**
  Dairy products seem to be responsible for at least 50% of childhood iron deficiency and an unknown percentage of anaemia found in adults. This condition results from the bleeding of the small intestines caused by dairy proteins. *Dr T. Colin Campbell* found that the average Chinese adult shows no evidence of anaemia and consumes twice the iron Americans do, but the majority of it comes from plants. It is now known that as long as vitamin C is present, iron in plant food is not only easily absorbed, but is easily assimilated at cellular level. All plant food contains vitamin C.

  Professor Meyer concluded that a diet providing a variety of fresh fruit and raw vegetables will supply the necessary iron requirements.

- **Osteoporosis**
  Milk contains a lot of calcium, but how much of it is actually assimilated by the body, especially if the milk has been pasteurised? More recent research regarding milk is found in the China Study done by *Dr T. Colin Campbell*, a nutritional biochemist from Cornell University. "*Dairy calcium is definitely not needed to prevent osteoporosis. Most Chinese consume no dairy products and yet get all their calcium from vegetables, as the cow gets calcium from grass. While the Chinese consume only half the*

calcium Americans do, osteoporosis is uncommon in China. Ironically, osteoporosis tends to occur in countries where calcium intake is highest and most of it comes from protein-rich dairy products. It is the high protein diet that steals calcium from the body rather than the insufficient calcium consumed in the diet. When the fat content of milk or cheese is reduced as a low fat, skimmed milk, or low fat cheese, the relative proportion of the protein and carbohydrates (lactose) is increased. These low fat dairy products contain the same nutritional inadequacies as their whole fat counterparts".

(Source: Campbell, T. Colin – New Century Nutrition, 1996)

Fresh fruit, raw vegetables and nuts are the best source of calcium, better than milk could ever be. Green vegetables provide calcium which appears to be of greater bioavailability than that found in milk. Many legumes are also rich in calcium. These sources also provide other nutrients, as well as being free of animal protein, animal fat and lactose.

There is definite scientific evidence that dairy calcium is not needed in the diet. Research done at the Mayo Clinic, Minnesota by *Dr Lawrence Riggs*, established that people who use dairy products and/or calcium supplements on a daily basis, do not absorb more calcium than those who do not use these products. Those using the dairy products and/or supplements are the ones that develop calcium deficiencies.

Dr Neal Barnard believes that dairy advertisements give women a dangerously false sense of security, suggesting that if they drink milk their bones will be protected. He goes on to say *"excessive calcium intake does not fool hormones into*

building much more bone, any more than delivering an extra load of bricks will make a construction crew build a larger building. The problem is, calcium loss and the dairy advertisements only obscure that fact. Thus increasing milk consumption is one of the weakest possible strategies for protecting the bones and to suggest otherwise, is dangerously misleading".
(Source: Barnard, Neal D., President of Physicians Committee for Responsible Medicine)

Dietary lifestyle factors that encourage the loss of bone calcium include eating foods which are high in animal protein, sodium, phosphorus, and caffeine. Use of tobacco and a sedentary lifestyle exacerbate the problem. When these factors are eliminated, calcium lost via the urine seems to be reduced by half. Unfortunately the public have little knowledge of these factors.

Dr McDougall concludes that the most important dietary change that we can make, if we want to create a positive calcium balance that will keep our bones solid, is to decrease the amount of protein we eat each day – ie meat, fish, chicken and dairy products. Osteoporosis is rare or absent in entire populations of Asian and African women, who consume no milk products.

- **Cancer risk**
  Dr Neal Barnard also maintains that animal fats, such as meat, cheese, milk and butter are a greater cancer risk than vegetable oils. A vegetarian diet based on fresh fruit and vegetables, whole grains and legumes is the most powerful diet for health, but this power is eroded, if milk, cheese and other dairy products are added.

Lacto-ovo vegetarians might be avoiding meat, but if they still eat considerable amounts of dairy products – which contain fat and no fibre, then the cancer risk is almost as high as that of meat-eaters. These high-fat foods not only increase the levels of oestrogen in the blood, which in turn increases your risk of cancer, but are also linked to various disorders of the reproductive system, for example, ovarian cysts, tumours, vaginal discharge and vaginal infections.

- **Peptic ulcers**
  The conventional accepted treatment for this is to drink milk. Scientific studies have shown that milk can actually aggravate an ulcer, by increasing the acid production in the stomach. I have removed milk products from the diet of people suffering from peptic ulcers with favourable results.

- **Ulcerative colitis and enlarged tonsils and adenoids**
  The removal of dairy products has resulted in dramatic improvements in cases of ulcerative colitis and in the shrinkage of enlarged tonsils and adenoids.

- **Allergies to antibiotics**
  Dairy products are high on the food chain and may contain unsafe levels of environmental contaminants.
  Antibiotics are commonly used on dairy farms to treat cows for certain diseases, for example, mastitis, an infection of the cow's udder.
  Contamination of milk with these drugs can be serious, because many people are allergic to even low levels of antibiotics such as penicillin.

- **Disease-causing bacteria**
  Dairy products can also be contaminated with salmonella, staphylococci and E coli.

- **Viruses**
  Leukaemia viruses are found in more than 20% of dairy cows in the USA. There is serious concern that these viruses may be passed on to humans.

NON-DAIRY PRODUCTS

These are acceptable transitional foods. They offer people something to drink if they are allergic to milk. Enquire at health stores. You can also use nut milks.

Again, I am not going to insist that you give up dairy products initially, but I do suggest you eat limited amounts and rather choose the following:

- Unprocessed cheese – the whiter and less sharp the cheese, the better. I do however prefer goat's milk and goat's milk cheese. Ricotta or unprocessed Italian cheeses could be a second option. Cheese is very high in sodium and very difficult to digest.
- Unsalted butter – use very sparingly after foods have been cooked or as a spread on bread etc.
- Yoghurt – home-made is best. You can sweeten it with raw honey. Commercial yoghurt contains additives and artificial sweeteners.
- Milk – never mix with with any other food. If you **must** drink it, drink it alone and wait two hours before your next meal.

If you re-examine the anatomy of your digestive system and review the biochemical and nutritional requirements of the human body, you will realise that **human beings really have no nutritional requirements for the flesh or milk of animals.**

Condiments   Why we should not make a habit of using them on a regular basis

Condiments blunt the sense of taste, so that the natural flavours of foods are neither detected nor appreciated nor relished

HERBERT M. SHELTON

Condiments are used to modify the flavour or enhance the taste of food. They actually camouflage the fine, delicate flavours that nature puts into the food and possess no nutritional value. Condiments include salt, mustard, pepper, cayenne pepper, vinegar, sauces, seasonings and other cooking spices. Condiments always lead to overeating.

According to *Herbert M. Shelton "condiments irritate the lining membranes of the alimentary canal causing these to thicken, toughen and harder and this impairs their functional powers. They create a false thirst and derange digestion".* (Source: *Shelton, Herbert M. – Human Life Its Philosophy and Laws*)

Contrary to their supposed ability to make food more palatable, they actually disguise the delicate flavour of natural foods and desensitise the taste buds. Chemical analysis shows that all condiments do contain toxins. This is the reason that they are used so sparingly. You could not sit down and eat a complete meal of just a condiment and thoroughly enjoy it.

Dr Joel Robbins disapproves of condiments *"because they can lead to chronic digestive problems and are a major contributing cause of mucus build-up on the intestinal lining, which hinders the absorption of nutrients eg vinegar, actually chemically inhibits some of the digestive enzymes from doing their work".* (Source: *Robbins, Joel – Eating for Health and Wellness*)

Condiments can irritate the mucous membranes which line all the internal organs, causing inflammation, and ulceration. We receive lots of warnings that all is not right. Pain from the intestines will frequently cause headaches, lower back pain and cramps. Losing weight and using condiments do not go well together, because condiments stimulate the appetite and this leads to overeating.

Abnormal cravings often disappear when the use of condiments is discontinued.

FREQUENTLY USED CONDIMENTS

SALT. Common table salt (sodium chloride) is a powerful irritant to the body in countless ways. It is not the "spice of life". The average South African consumes 4 000 – 6 000 mg of salt daily. Heavy users consume 7 500 mg daily.

Of this daily intake 15% comes directly from the salt shaker and 85% comes from processed and packaged foods, such as chips, cold meats and biltong. Salt is thus used as a preservative (flavourant).

WHAT ARE THE BAD EFFECTS OF USING SALT?

- Salt encourages thirst by robbing the blood and lymph of the water necessary for its excretion through the kidneys, and this can lead to high blood pressure, and ultimately, to severe heart disease and strokes.
- It accumulates in the body, causing a considerable quantity of water to be retained, in order to keep the poisons in suspension, and protect the delicate tissues – 30 grams of salt hold $3^1/_2$ litres of water, ie a total weight of 2,5 kg. This accumulation of fluid is called oedema.
- Salt inhibits the absorption of vitamins from food through the intestinal membrane and retards digestion.
- Salt blunts the taste buds so that you are unable to really taste the delicate flavours of natural foods. If you have used salt for years, your taste buds become numb and the need for more salt is inevitable.
- Using excessive salt causes the delicate fluid and mineral balance of the body to change; more calcium is lost via the urine. This gives you a negative calcium balance; you need calcium for strong bones.
- The increase of water in the tissues, due to salt intake, makes the essential process of waste excretion more difficult.
- Salt not only impedes circulation, but hardens the arteries, eventually leading to premature old age.
- Regular high doses of salt lead to nephritis. Salt should be avoided by those suffering from renal disease, kidney stones, obesity and arthritis.

If you need to add salt to your food, rather use the range of herbal salts from health shops. If you prefer not to use any salt, then try the following:

- Finely chopped celery, raw or steamed, added to food gives a somewhat salty taste.
- Unsalted butter, melted on steamed vegetables, fish or chicken, after they have been cooked, adds some flavour.
- Freshly squeezed lemon juice on raw vegetables, cooked fish or chicken.
- Steamed red cabbage on steamed vegetables.
- Chopped onions browned in a pan without oil or butter. Cooked onions are better than raw onions.

All the salt we need (280 mg daily) is found in fresh fruit and raw vegetables, unprocessed and unrefined natural foods.

VINEGAR (INCLUDING APPLE CIDER)

VINEGAR stimulates the thyroid to produce more thyroxine, which causes the metabolism to work overtime. Eventually the thyroid stops working and you find it difficult to lose weight. As vinegar contains acetic acid, it retards digestion and prevents assimilation of nutrients. Vinegar can reduce the number of red blood cells, damage the kidneys and leach calcium from the bones. If you have thyroid problems, cough up phlegm regularly, and tend to be anaemic, you should avoid all types of vinegar.

I suggest you use fresh lemon juice or fresh grapefruit juice if you have the above problems. If none of these problems exists and you do enjoy the taste of vinegar, then use balsamic vinegar sparingly.

CAYENNE PEPPER contains piperidine and capsaicin which are harmful irritating alkaloids that increase the secretion of mucus. This is the body's defensive response and should be recognised as such. Continual use of cayenne pepper can eventually damage the liver and kidneys. It leaves a burning sensation in the mouth and this is the body's signal to discontinue its use.

BLACK PEPPER is also harmful to the liver. Other hot peppers eg chilies, also contain harmful substances which act as irritants to both the digestive and urinary tracts. If not in the best of health try to avoid these condiments.

GARLIC, the so called "miracle food" is generally accepted as having curative properties. We have to reconsider this belief, because of the substances garlic contains – allicin (this gives garlic its characteristic flavour and odour) and mustard oil, which are both extremely irritating to the intestinal lining of the digestive tract.

When garlic is ingested, the body tries to eliminate it immediately via the lungs and skin because it is unable to use it – hence the "notorious garlic odour" that comes from your breath even hours after you have eaten garlic. I always explain to people that if they can eat an abundance of a particular food, for example, garlic, with no other food (this I doubt), then they can regard that particular food as a real food and go ahead and enjoy it.

Garlic also destroys the balance of the resident flora in the human gut, acting like a natural antibiotic (against life).

There are also other food substances that have the same effect. For example, alcohol, coffee, meat, bread, sugar and fried foods.

The balance of the intestinal flora plays an important part in our health. If this balance is disturbed, we run the risk of problems such as candida, diarrhoea, constipation, flatulence, abdominal distention, spastic colon etc.

Healthy intestinal bacteria are essential to good health for the following reasons:
• reduce cholesterol in the blood
• produce digestive enzymes
• reduce high blood pressure
• strengthen the immune system
• produce natural antibiotics
• prevent yeast infections
• increase calcium assimilation
• produce tumour suppressing compounds
• detoxify dangerous chemicals added to foods, which act as irritants.

Correct nutrition is absolutely essential. We have to include more raw fruit and vegetables, less animal protein and less processed food. If you find this too radical initially, you could take supplementary preparations containing high numbers of probiotic bacteria (natural bowel flora).

I would like to mention something of great interest. You need 20 litres of live yoghurt to equal 1 Probiotic capsule. Consult a nutritional counsellor for guidance.

ONIONS. When you peel and chop onions, the vapours are so irritating, that they cause profuse watering of the eyes, and when you eat onions your breath smells of them. Onions, like garlic, contain mustard oil and allicin. Mustard oil is metabolised in the body to form thiocyanate, a substance which contributes to the formation of goitre, by decreasing thyroxine synthesis in the thyroid gland. This in turn slows down the metabolism of the body. The stronger the bite of onion or garlic, the more concentrated the mustard oil and allicin. By cooking garlic and onions, however, much of the mustard oil and allicin is dissipated. I prefer using leeks and spring onions. Onions also tend to lower the haemoglobin count, ie they have the ability to destroy red blood cells, thus creating an anaemic condition. People with kidney and digestive problems should avoid garlic and onions.

SUGAR. Although sugar is not a true condiment, it is found in all processed foods. *"One of the problems with regulating sugar consumption is being able to identify the foods that contain it. It's not always obvious. Many foods, however, do contain sugar. For example:*

- *The breading on many prepared foods.*
- *Luncheon meats, bacon and canned meats.*
- *Bouillon cubes and dry roasted nuts.*
- *Peanut butter and many dry cereals (even cornflakes)."*

(Source: Appleton, Nancy – Lick the Sugar Habit, 1985)

Sugar is recognised as a major allergen which can create a hyperactive condition. It also contributes to increased body acidity. Sugar also causes fermentation which results in bloatedness. Through my counselling sessions I have found that children who eat a high sugar diet suffer from a "continual irritating cough". This could apply to adults as well. There are however other contributing factors.

I am giving you this information to make you aware of the kind of condiments you are taking into your body and the long-term effects of such flavourants. By cultivating a natural taste for wholesome foods, you will in time lessen your craving for condiments.

Recreational drugs

Eat, drink and be merry – for a while

UNKNOWN

Today, there are a number of widely-used stimulants which seem to have a harmful effect upon the body's chemistry. Stimulants are substances that are taken into the body, not for their nutritive qualities, but because they exert some desired effect on the nervous system, the heart and the kidneys. The stimulants I am concerned about are: COFFEE, TEA, TOBACCO, and ALCOHOL.

COFFEE AND TEA

Coffee and tea drinking has become a habit and a way of life, to the point where it is beginning to constitute a serious health hazard.

Caffeine is a stimulant (irritant) to the central nervous system, as well as being addictive.

Caffeine affects the heart and can raise blood pressure, as well as speed up the mental processes, causing sleeplessness. It causes withdrawal symptoms when discontinued and induces both psychological and physical dependence. Decaffeinated types of drinks are actually worse than the "real thing", as they contain residues of about 90 different chemicals used to remove the caffeine. Ordinary coffee as well as decaffeinated coffee can irritate the lining of the stomach.

Coffee is devoid of any nutritional value. It is an alkaloid poison.

The main culprit in coffee and tea is caffeine. Besides being a stimulant, instant coffee contains some chemical residues from the processing of the coffee bean.

It takes 24 hours for one cup of coffee or tea to pass through the kidneys and the urinary tract.

Did you know that low bone density can be caused by only one cup of coffee a day especially during the menopause? One cup of coffee contains an average of about 100 – 150 mg of caffeine.

An average cup of tea contains about half the caffeine content of coffee, as well as tannic acid which is toxic and acts as a harmful diuretic. This increases the flow of urine, which puts harmful pressure on the delicate kidneys. Cola drinks contain 60 – 75 mg of caffeine per can.

PRODUCTS CONTAINING CAFFEINE

The following products contain caffeine: tea, coffee, cola drinks, some baked goods, chocolate (also contains oxalic acid – which prevents the absorption of calcium), ice cream, some pharmaceutical preparations such as cold remedies, codeine, diuretics, allergy pills, and anti-menstrual pain preparations.

These medicines tend to make people drowsy, so manufacturers often add caffeine to counter this effect.

82

THE BAD EFFECTS OF DRINKING COFFEE AND TEA

- People who drink 4 or more cups of tea or coffee every day may exhibit nervousness, irritability and insomnia. The effects of drinking coffee and tea are similar to those of ingesting refined sugar although its action is not so immediate. Caffeine stimulates the pancreas to produce more insulin which lowers blood sugar levels. This can result in hypoglycaemia and chronic body fatigue, which leads to more coffee and tea drinking.

- Coffee is known to destroy vitamin C in the body. Vitamin C is needed for healthy tissues and to ward off infectious diseases.

- Coffee has been linked to several diseases: increased blood pressure, increased blood cholesterol, diabetes and gastric ulcers (gastrointestinal irritation).

- Caffeine prevents the utilisation of iron.

- I have found through my counselling sessions that caffeine is a major factor in certain kinds of depressions. This could be a form of caffeine poisoning.

- Coffee and tea taken with food, force the food to leave the stomach prematurely and slow down the motility of the intestines. Undigested food in a slow functioning intestinal tract is a major cause of constipation.

- Once coffee is metabolised, the final oxidation product of caffeine is uric acid. Excess uric acid is deposited in the joints of the body as well as the muscle tissues. If you are a big coffee or tea drinker, you could be susceptible to arthritis, gout etc.

- The human foetus is potentially vulnerable to caffeine.

- There is also some evidence that high doses of caffeine may contribute to the formation of non-malignant breast lumps in women.

- The results of a recent study indicated that people drinking 5 or more cups of coffee a day were about $2 \frac{1}{2}$ times more likely to suffer from heart disease, than non coffee drinkers.

- It is not just the caffeine in coffee and tea that causes problems. Coffee and tea contain many other toxic substances, eg powerful volatile oils which can affect the bowels, thus bringing about an unnatural laxative effect in many people.

COFFEE AND TEA SUBSTITUTES

There are a number of coffee and tea substitutes on the market. Some coffee substitutes contain wheat. If you are gluten intolerant avoid these alternatives. Choose herbal teas, but do not drink in excess.

If you simply can't break the habit of drinking coffee, then try a thick wedge of lemon squeezed into black coffee. This tends to neutralise the acid effects of caffeine, as well as easing the transition to total abstinence. You must try to cut back the amount you drink, until you eventually break the habit completely. You can however drink warm water with lemon or fresh home-made fruit juices. If you enjoy any of the commercial fruit juices, make sure they contain no preservatives and always dilute them with purified water.

ALCOHOL

Alcoholic beverages, if drunk on a regular basis, can impair the body's efficiency in digesting and assimilating food, and may later damage the liver (cirrhosis of the liver) or result in diabetes, hypoglycaemia, nervous and mental disorders, heart and kidney diseases. Alcohol also interferes with and inhibits the action of vitamins found in foods. It also impairs calcium absorption, by affecting the liver's ability to activate vitamin D, which is important in the absorption of calcium. Certain drugs taken with alcohol may cause severe side effects.

TOBACCO

Smoking can shorten your lifespan by as much as 15 years. The reasons are numerous:

- cigarettes contain powerful carcinogens, eg benzopyrene which damages the cells in the lungs, nicotine which is addictive and other poisonous gases that irritate the mucous membranes causing smokers' catarrh.
- many degenerative diseases are linked to cigarette smoking eg heart disease, chronic bronchitis, emphysema, and other respiratory illnesses as well as cancer.

Secondary pollution ie smoking in a confined space with others who do not smoke, affects the non-smoker adversely. The younger the person subjected to the smoke, the more damage is done. Pets are likewise affected.

People who give up smoking suffer withdrawal symptoms. Typically they feel irritable, depressed, anxious, experience a phlegmy cough, stomach cramps and headaches. Fortunately these symptoms only last a few weeks.

My advice is, change to foods which create alkaline conditions in the body ie raw fresh fruit, and vegetables as well as steamed vegetables, potatoes, millet and almonds. You will then notice that your cravings for all stimulants will be minimised.

At this point, I feel I must make you aware of your so called "quick fixes" which really only suppress the symptoms of your problem without getting rid of the cause....

Medication

Man lives on 1/4 of what he eats. On the other 3/4 lives his doctor
INSCRIPTION FOUND IN A PYRAMID DATED 3 800 BC

The answer to being "sickness free" is not to resort to medication. Medication appeals to many because it acts as a "quick fix". You must realise that symptoms of sickness are a sign of the body's effort to eliminate toxins, which have been built up over the years. Why treat the symptom? Shouldn't we rather deal with the cause of the problem?

By taking these "quick fixes", the individual does not have to consider what he might have been doing wrong to precipitate the illness. As a result, he continues in the same incorrect lifestyle that produced the illness in the first place, and now the stage is set for more serious illnesses. Would you take medication if you were well? No! It would make you sick. Why give a sick person medication to make him/her well. How can the body be poisoned back to health. It is a known fact that many drugs and treatments have side effects.

My recommendation is to first try the conservative approach to healing if you are not feeling well, ie bed rest and total abstinence from highly stimulating and concentrated foods – rather go for raw fresh fruits and vegetables or better still, just fast and drink purified/distilled water under the supervision of a qualified doctor, trained in fasting. If your condition does not improve on this regime, then approach the medical fraternity.

Remember, nutrients and health come from gardens and orchards and not from pharmaceutical laboratories.

Now that I have explained to you all about the kinds of foods, drinks and so-called "quick fixes" that I am wary of and the dangers of making them the mainstay of your lifestyle, let me show you . . .

PART 3

How to Slowly Begin Changing Your Conventional Pattern of Eating

The Changeover

If the doctor of today does not become the dietician of tomorrow, the dietician of today will become the doctor of tomorrow

DR ALEXIS CARREL

When people come to see me regarding a health or weight problem, I realise they have come to accept to a certain extent that the old methods and procedures have failed them and they are looking for some support and guidance in improving their continual decline in health and difficulty in losing weight. You must be aware that there is no "magical road" leading to superb health and quick weight loss. You can only achieve superb health through a process of discarding bad eating and living habits, and a commitment to follow the guidelines I have to offer. I am going to provide you with reasonable suggestions and a workable plan, which can be applied immediately. When you do make these recommended changes, you will gradually begin to experience a new sense of wellbeing – something which you have not enjoyed for some years. I will make sure you are not placed in a position of strong conflict either with yourself, your family or with my recommendations. I am aware that old habits are not easily broken.

Initially you have to begin by discarding outmoded beliefs regarding health and weight loss and you have to change your attitude towards yourself. The information I am going to give you will help you to do this.

How radical do you have to be? This all depends on how bad your health is. You have to realise that some changes will have to be made. If changes are made very quickly, you will experience unpleasant symptoms immediately, but you will also gain health much more quickly. Your approach to change also depends on what degree of health you wish to achieve and how quickly.

The attainment of better health requires a planned transition. You have to start eating healthier foods, especially fresh fruit and raw vegetables.

When eating patterns change, resistance from family members or peers seems to manifest and if this is a problem, my advice is to do it gradually with the advice of a nutritional counsellor.

The general pattern of eating that I offer reduces refined carbohydrates, such as sugar and starch, is low in animal fats and animal protein and totally eliminates fried foods. Choose as many of the right foods as you can. Remember, every step forward, every replacement of a bad habit by a positive change in lifestyle, is conducive to improvement in the quality of life. I am aware that people who are accustomed to a high salt, high fat diet are not going to enjoy these so-called healthier foods at first. If you persevere, you will find that after 2 – 3 months, or possibly longer, you will actually enjoy eating these wonderful foods. In fact, when you do fast, your taste buds have a chance to rest, and after breaking the fast, you will find you actually enjoy eating these healthier foods.

A head start is to eliminate the worst cause of ill health and weight gain and that is OVEREATING. This is the most difficult of all bad habits to overcome, but if you follow my rules you will find that you eat less.

RULES TO HELP YOU CHANGE

- Do not move around and eat. You will not be aware of how much you are eating. You should thus eat at a designated place all the time.
- Always take 20 minutes or more to eat a meal. Use an egg timer.
- Now and again, put your knife and fork down. Use a serviette to wipe your mouth. All this encourages you to eat more slowly.
- Chew your food very well.
- Brush your teeth after a meal, so that you have a nice fresh taste in your mouth.
- Try to practise combining foods correctly eg never mix protein and starch. In certain cases a great improvement in health can be obtained through **just** proper food combining, without making radical changes in the diet.
- Try to replace your "usual breakfast" with a bowl of fruit salad, correctly combined.
- Where possible, buy organically grown fruit and vegetables.
- Try to eliminate snacking on high fat foods. If you have to snack, use dried fruit (sulphur dioxide free), and carob (a delicious substitute for chocolate). Both are obtainable at health stores.
- Cut down on your liquid intake. It overloads the kidneys and interferes with toxin elimination. The foods I recommend are water sufficient. Do not drink with your meals.
- If you find it difficult to give up cooked and processed foods initially, then balance them with an abundance of fresh fruits and raw vegetables.
- Read food labels, and choose foods without additives, colourants, preservatives and sugar.
- If you do eat red meat, eat it only once a week.
- Slowly change from eating red meat to poultry; use only free-range chicken – then progress to fish – then to free-range eggs – then to dairy products only, and finally, however long it takes (it does not matter), start eating only vegetarian meals.
- Initially, try to eat a vegetarian meal one day a week (no animal protein at all). Find out what vegetarian meals your family like the most, eg potato salad, pasta etc.
- Starches, for example, grains, ˙potatoes, brown rice, pasta etc, should eventually be the main energy source of your diet, and the centre of at least one meal per day.
- Add the right kind of seasoning (non-irradiated and without preservatives), ie no Monosodium Glutamate (MSG) or sugar. Enquire at health food stores.
- Try to eliminate "cheat foods" from your eating pattern as much as you can, particularly white flour and sugar. These foods contain "empty calories". Choose healthy alternatives.
- Use brown rice instead of white and if that is difficult use equal amounts of both . Use whole-wheat bread instead of white. Try to make your own.
- Use unsalted butter in place of margarine.
- Use only cold-pressed oils, for example, extra virgin olive oil in place of other oils for salad dressings, and never use oil or

butter to fry foods.
- Use raw honey or fructose instead of sugar or artificial sweeteners.

EXAMPLE OF A TRANSITIONAL EATING PLAN

This is for people who are just starting the programme. The following are only suggestions and you can choose what suits you best. I have not included flesh food, but if you feel you still want to eat it, regard it as your one protein meal of the day.

ON WAKING

Hot water with fresh lemon or herbal tea with a dairy alternative, and 1 teaspoon of raw honey. Wait $^1/_2$ hour before breakfast. Never drink with your meals.

BREAKFAST

You should always start with fruit and eat as much as you want throughout the morning till 12 pm.

Do not worry about correct combinations of fruits at this stage. Just do not mix melons with any other fruit, except from the melon family. If you cannot eat only fruit till 12 pm do not despair. Have your cereal or toast as soon as you feel hungry, but wait at least 1 hour after the fruit.

The important issue here is that if you are going to eat food other than fruit in the morning, then eat it initially 1 hour, then $1^1/_2$ hours, then 2 hours, then 3 hours later each day, till eventually you are eating fruit till 12 pm. Try and select the following:
- Subacid or sweet fruit together with $^1/_2$ a cup of macadamia nuts plus $^1/_4$ to $^1/_2$ a cup of dried fruit (sulphur dioxide free) and 2 tablespoons of wheat germ.
  OR
  Whole-wheat toast or a muffin with un-

salted butter, raw honey or raw peanut butter.

You should really not snack in between meals; try and give your digestive system a rest for about 4 hours.

Remember, if you have decided to eat fruit only in the morning, then eat as much as you want and stop 1 hour before lunch. If you want to eat your usual foods at lunch and supper time to start with, this is also fine.

This pattern of eating is very different from what you have been taught, so there is absolutely no need to be 100% perfect.

You must be happy with the choice of foods. Remember, the more correct choices you make, the better you are going to feel.

I do suggest you cut down on your coffee and tea intake during the day. You have to make changes, even if they are small changes.

LUNCH

If you really dislike eating a whole salad or even a side salad before your cooked meal, then have a whole-wheat bun or two slices of whole-wheat bread with ricotta cheese (not high in protein, so you can combine it with the bread), lettuce, tomatoes and sprouts. Vegetarians can have $^1/_2$ a cup of raw nuts (no bread).
OR
Pita bread filled with hummus or tofu spread
OR
Whole-wheat toast with raw peanut butter/avocado/tahini sauce/raw honey
OR
Salad and your choice of an animal protein dish or a starch meal.

3 HOURS AFTER LUNCH

You can snack on fresh fruit or dried fruit, or 2 – 3 pieces of carob (chocolate substitute) or any healthy confectionery.

If you want something to drink have it some time after the meal and never with it. You can have your usual drink, but cut down on the intake. Remember, at this stage you are slowly weaning yourself off the most unhealthy foods and cutting down on your liquid intake.

SUPPER

Again, have a side plate of fresh raw salad, followed by home-made vegetable soup. Try to base your main dish upon grains and potatoes ie starch, if you had animal protein for lunch. You could eat, for example, vegetable lasagna or spaghetti with preservative-free sauces. Stir fry vegetables in water and not in oil and serve them over rice or noodles, adding oil or butter after they have been cooked.

OR

Potato pancakes with green vegetables
OR
Stuffed cabbage with vegetables.

You will note that I have specifically included only vegetarian meals. I repeat, if you really want to eat your meat, chicken, fish or dairy products etc, eat them only once a day with neutral vegetables.

If you need assistance, please consult a nutritional counsellor. I have just given you some guidelines that will definitely help to improve your health. I am aware that food is important to you, but remember, food is fuel. There is more to life than food. If you want to start eating correctly right away, I suggest you do a "DETOX" (cleansing) first. Before attempting the "detox" programme, I feel you should be aware of . . .

What to expect when you improve your diet

This is a very important section which should be read very carefully and referred to regularly.

When you first begin to omit the lower grade foods such as meat, fish, chicken, tea, coffee etc and start to introduce superior foods such as fresh fruit and vegetables, whole grains and legumes, remarkable things begin to happen to your body and mind. You must be aware that when the food coming into the body is of a higher quality than the elements present in the tissues, the body begins to discard the lower grade materials, to make room for the superior materials which it uses to make new and healthier tissues. The body starts to eliminate previously retained proteinaceous waste. Fat cells are broken down and the toxins stored in the fat cells are released into the bloodstream. During this process the body is able to "clean house" more efficiently and as a result you are going to experience uncomfortable symptoms. These unpleasant symptoms are the temporary result of going on a Detoxification (cleansing) Programme. Do not let any temporary discomfort persuade you to abandon your new eating habits. Whenever people hear the word detox it conjures up visions of unpleasant symptoms, discomfort and inconvenience that will prevent them from getting on with their daily activities. They are not wrong in their thinking. If, however, the body is very toxic, they will experience more severe symptoms than those individuals whose eating patterns do not include a tremendous amount of junk food and high animal protein.

You will also have to look at your genetic disposition. How good are the genes you have inherited? You can't change your genes, but you can change your existing bad eating patterns for a more healthy diet. This will help break weak genetic links.

When you begin this Detox Programme, which is low in protein and low in fat, you will find that after 3 days you feel like quitting, because you think you actually felt better and stronger on your old pattern of eating. This initial feeling of reduced energy is due to the redeployment of your forces and energy for the rebuilding of vital organs.

The feeling of weakness and lack of energy is the result of the exclusion of animal food (meat, dairy products) and recreational drugs. This results in slower heart action and a decrease in energy, which can last about 10 days. You have to give the body a chance to adjust and complete its recuperation. You must be patient, because you are definitely going to feel better. Never judge results prematurely. Although it takes 7 years to **completely replace** every cell in the body, you are still going to feel better in the long term.

During the Detox Programme it is also important to get more rest and sleep. You should not be tempted to fall back on stimulants of any kind. Remember that it took time to put the body in its present state and patience will be required to correct unhealthy conditions. You cannot accomplish healing overnight. The long-term rewards of improving your diet are: increased vitality, improved sleep, more energy, regular and soft bowel movements, lower cholesterol, a healthy heart, lower cancer risk, stronger bones and much more. I feel all this is well worth any temporary discomfort. You might just have to live through a few uncomfortable symptoms for a few days. Don't give up!

WHAT HAPPENS TO THE BODY WHEN YOU EXPERIENCE UNPLEASANT WITHDRAWAL SYMPTOMS

When the use of toxic stimulants, such as coffee, tea, chocolate or cocoa, alcohol and cigarettes is stopped, headaches are common and a feeling of dejection is experienced. Headaches are due to the discarding by the body of the toxins eg caffeine and theobromine which are removed from the tissues and transported through the bloodstream to the elimination organs. When the blood circulates through the brain during its many bodily rounds before the noxious agents reach their final destination, these irritants register in our consciousness as pain – in other words – a headache. Another sign of body detoxification is lower back pain, due to the concentration of toxic materials there. The symptoms usually vanish within 3 days and we feel stronger, due to the recuperation which follows. Have you noticed that when you skip a meal you often get a headache? Missing the meal doesn't cause the headache, but missing the meal will cause an increase in toxic blood levels, as the body moves accumulated waste out of the cells into the bloodstream for elimination.

People who have had tendencies in the past to recurring skin rashes or eruptions, will frequently tend to eliminate poisons and harmful drugs through the skin, precipitating new rashes or eruptions. Doctors not familiar with this pattern of eating may diagnose the individual's problem as an allergy. Many ask "although I am eating better than I ever did before, why am I feeling worse?" They don't understand that the body is "retracing" illnesses they had previously. The skin is becoming more alive and more active and is thus able to rid the body of toxins. The body is throwing out more poisons more rapidly, because it has more energy now that it no longer has to digest heavy concentrated meals.

By discarding the toxins, your body is saving you from more serious diseases, such as hepatitis, kidney disorders, blood disease, heart disease, arthritis, nerve degeneration and even cancer, depending on your structural weaknesses. These illnesses can come about if you keep poisons in your body too long. Some people may develop colds, which they haven't had for a long time, or even fevers. This is nature's way of house cleaning. You should not stop the symptoms with medication or massive doses of vitamins. These symptoms are evidence of a remedial process (house cleaning). They are not a manifestion of allergic or deficiency conditions. You might be **eating perfectly** and observing all the correct rules and still symptoms occur – why? Those who have eaten more natural foods and have abused their bodies less with overeating, will have reactions ranging from almost none at all or very mild, to symptoms which may be uncomfortable or acute. Those who have abused their bodies more, will experience more severe symptoms especially if their liver, kidneys and other important organs have been damaged.

The following are some of the symptoms you might experience:

- headaches may manifest at the beginning of the Detox Programme
- fever, colds, skin rashes
- a short interval of bowel sluggishness, occasional diarrhoea, and frequent urination
- feelings of tiredness or weakness
- disinclination to exercise
- nervousness, irritability, negativity, or depression may occur later on.

Let me explain the symptoms of diarrhoea and constipation. The average person generally consumes a low-fibre diet. When you increase the consumption of high-fibre food, the digestive tract is not accustomed to this new food. As a result, the stools now contain more weight, allowing them to pass through the digestive tract at a faster rate. The peristaltic waves that propel the food now have to adjust to the new type of stool. This adjustment can take weeks or longer. You have to be patient. You will either experience constipation or diarrhoea. This does not indicate that you must change your new eating pattern. Just carry on with the Detox Programme.

My suggestion to those who are experiencing indigestion and cramping on this Detox Programme, is not to eat asparagus, cabbage, cauliflower, broccoli or Brussels sprouts for the first two weeks. Fruit juices can also increase gas, so these must be avoided temporarily, if you are experiencing these problems.

The majority of people find detoxification symptoms tolerable and feel encouraged to bear with them, because of the many improvements which have already occurred and which are becoming more evident each day. All this acts as an inspirational force. Remember, the more you rest and sleep when these symptoms are present, the milder they become and the quicker they subside. Be happy you are having these symptoms. Your body still has vitality. It is rejuvenating by reacting to toxins every day, throwing off more and more waste, which eventually would have brought pain, disease and much suffering. I would like to emphasise that those who experience the worst symptoms and who still persevere with the Detox Programme, are avoiding some diseases, which would have eventually developed, had they continued their old pattern of eating.

Remember – you are not going to stop experiencing uncomfortable symptoms in the future even though you really feel better each day. The body is cyclical in nature and health returns in a series of gradual, diminishing cycles; you progress from one healing crisis to the next, but they become less frequent and less severe, until the body, mind and soul reach perfect harmony.

HOW HEALING OCCURS
You start a better diet, and for a while you feel much better. After some time a symptom occurs. You may feel nauseous for a day and have diarrhoea with foul smelling stools. After a few days you start feeling even better than before, and all goes fine for a while. Then you suddenly develop a cold, feel uncomfortable and lose your appetite. It really is unnecessary to resort to medication. That is your choice but just bear in mind what is happening to the body. Again, after about 2 – 3 days you suddenly recover from the cold and feel better. This continues usually for about another 2 months, at which time you suddenly develop an itch or a rash. Again, don't halt this elimination process by taking medication (this is, of course, your choice). Medication suppresses symptoms. The rash flares up, continues for 10 days and suddenly

subsides. At this point in time you may find your energy has increased more than ever before. This rash is usually an outlet for the poisons in the liver.

Recovery occurs in cycles; you feel better, a reaction occurs and you don't feel well for a short while. You recover and feel even better and so it continues, each reaction milder than the last. Eventually the body becomes purer, and reactions become shorter in duration. You begin feeling better than ever before and this lasts longer, until eventually you reach a plateau of vibrant health.

I am often asked "how can we avoid these uncomfortable detox symptoms?" Please remember that uncomfortable symptoms are a result of toxins in the bloodstream. In order to help you handle these symptoms, I suggest you see a nutritional counsellor, who will adjust the Detox Programme.

If you want to change your eating pattern on your own, then I suggest you introduce raw foods **slowly** into your diet. Start by replacing one of your normal meals each day with a raw one. Gradually eliminate meat and processed foods from your diet until you reach a balance of about 75% raw and 25% cooked.

You must learn to understand and interpret the symptoms and changes which follow the beginning of a better nutritional programme, as being of tremendous benefit to you. The body will never harm itself if given the right conditions. Now that you are aware of how the body reacts to an elimination diet you are ready to follow . . .

The Detox – Cleansing Programme

If you are on any medication, have severe health problems, are pregnant, or breast-feeding, I insist you consult a nutritional counsellor before embarking on this programme.

If you find the Detox Programme too restrictive, you can start with the Maintenance Programme which will also improve your health, but will take a little longer. In order to gain the maximum benefit from the Detox Programme, I suggest you follow it exactly. You can however interchange lunch and supper. If you are taking laxatives, please stop them and don't ever use them again. You **can** cut down on the quantity of food given, if you feel rather full after eating the amounts I suggest. You will however not feel hungry on this programme.

Not only will you lose weight, but you will find, for example, that your constipation problem will correct itself without the use of laxatives. A Detox Programme is absolutely essential at least twice a year, to rid the suffering body of built-up toxins. It is not always easy to tell how well your body is coping with toxins and stress. A toxic body doesn't have sufficient vitality to react to every negative input. It just gets heavier in weight and works less efficiently over a period of time. This is a result of your eating pattern and lifestyle over the years as well as your inherited genes. The food that I suggest on the Detox Programme requires minimal digestion and subsequent elimination. If you do experience headaches etc, try not to resort to medication. My suggestion is, don't eat anything, just drink purified water and go to sleep. Consult a nutritional counsellor if you can't handle the symptoms.

This detoxifying diet is guaranteed to shed kilos, speed up circulation and metabolism, eliminate bodily poisons and generally make you feel much better in the long run.

RESOLVE TO GIVE UP FOR 4 WEEKS
- Coffee, tea, cold drinks and all kinds of fruit juices, even home-made
- Sugar and sugar substitutes
- Animal protein ie red meat, chicken, fish etc, and dairy products (milk included)
- Seasoning ie salt, pepper and spices, except where permitted
- Snacks between meals
- Oil (except cold-pressed oil)
- Nuts (except unsalted, unroasted almonds or pecans)
- Fried foods.

WEEK 1
On waking:
Have a glass of purified water with a slice of lemon or herbal tea. Wait at least $1/2$ hour before breakfast.

Breakfast:
2 kinds of fruit in season – eat as much as you want, eg 3 pears and 3 mangoes mixed with a $1/2$ cup of ground almonds or pecans, plus 1 teaspoon of raw honey (honey that has not been heated). Correct combinations of fruits during week 1 is not important but do not mix the melon family with any other fruit, nor with nuts. You can however mix the various types of melons together or you can just eat one kind only. Stop eating 4 hours before lunch. Do not drink with your meal. If you are thirsty you can drink herbal tea or

purified water. Only drink 2 hours after a meal or $1/2$ hour before the next meal.

Lunch:
- A large raw vegetable salad with any raw vegetables plus $1/2$ a cup of ground almonds or pecans and 1 teaspoon of raw honey.

OR

- A large raw vegetable salad with 1 small avocado pear.

  You can add a dressing to both the above, made up of 2 tablespoons of cold-pressed oil (sunflower, sesame, almond, olive or flaxseed), 1 tablespoon of fresh lemon juice (not vinegar), plus 1 teaspoon of raw honey. If you need more dressing, just double up on the ingredients but not the honey.

OR

- 1 small avocado pear, plus 1 kind of subacid or acid fruit (as much as you want). Do not add any dressing. You can add lettuce and/or celery only, if you wish. If you are thirsty, drink only herbal tea or water $1/2$ hour before the meal or 2 hours after the meal. Wait 4 hours before supper.

Supper:
Lots and lots of steamed neutral vegetables and/or a raw vegetable salad (no tomatoes) with the same dressing as for lunch, but without the honey. (If you suffer from heartburn don't add the lemon juice to your salad dressing at supper.) You can add 2 – 3 baked potatoes or 3 mealies or 2 – 3 sweet potatoes (with either the raw salad or steamed vegetables).

You can add a dab of unsalted butter to your starch vegetables, and oil and lemon dressing (without the honey) to the neutral vegetables. 1 hour later have $1/2$ a cup of dried fruit (sulphur dioxide free).

WEEK 2
On waking:
The same as for Week 1. Remember, wait $1/2$ hour before breakfast.

Breakfast:
Have as much fruit for breakfast as you like, **correctly combined**. Try not to have more than two types of fruit at the same meal. Do not add nuts and honey this time. Wait 4 hours before the next meal.

Lunch:
The same as for Week 1. Wait 4 hours before supper.

Supper:
The same as for Week 1.

NOTE: Drink only herbal tea or purified water $1/2$ hour before the meal or 2 hours after the meal.

WEEK 3
On waking:
No herbal tea. Drink only water with fresh lemon or home-made fresh fruit juice. Wait **1 hour** before breakfast.

Breakfast:
The same as for Week 2.

Lunch:
A side salad (you could have more) with oil and lemon juice (no honey). Straight after the salad, a piece of grilled chicken (free-range) or fish and steamed neutral vegetables. You can season the salad, chicken or fish with vegetable salt. If you're a vegetarian, choose $1/2$ a cup of any nuts or seeds except peanuts, or an avocado pear. Wait 4 hours before supper.

Supper:

A large raw vegetable salad with oil and lemon dressing and 2 – 3 mealies steamed, **or** 2 – 3 slices of whole-wheat bread **or** a big bowl of brown rice, millet or polenta **or** 2 – 3 baked sweet potatoes. You can add a blob of unsalted butter to your starch dishes as well as your whole-wheat bread. You can add steamed neutral vegetables to the meal if you are still hungry. Remember, if you do suffer from heartburn, don't add lemon juice to the salad dressing or tomatoes to the salad.

NOTE: Drink only herbal tea or purified water $^1/_2$ hour before the meal or 2 hours after the meal.

WEEK 4

Eat raw fruit correctly combined throughout the day until 1 hour before supper. After 12 pm you can add lettuce and celery to any fruit, except those of the melon family. If you change your combinations, wait at least 1 hour.

Supper:

Salad first (you need only eat a side plate) and immediately after, choose either a protein or a starch meal with steamed neutral vegetables.

Do not have a protein meal every single night. My suggestion is to alternate with a starch meal one night and a protein meal the next night.

During Week 4 try to eat raw food **only** for one whole day, ie fruit correctly combined till you go to sleep.

OR

Fruit till 1 hour before supper, then have a raw vegetable salad and $^1/_2$ an avocado. Do not add the oil and lemon dressing.

OR

Raw vegetable salad and $^1/_2$ a cup of nuts only. You can add an oil and lemon dressing, but no honey. Do not be scared to eat an enormous salad – the only restrictions are the nuts and avocado. You can add vegetable salt to your salad.

Remember your drinking rules.

IMPORTANT:

If you find your symptoms too difficult to handle, please consult a nutritional counsellor who will adjust the Detox Programme accordingly. **The more severe the symptoms, the more toxic the body.** Now that you have completed the Detox Programme, I am going to show you...

How to eat correctly

Healthy eating is a gold mine

NEAL D. BARNARD

After the initial detox programme you should follow a correct eating and lifestyle management plan, which should help keep degenerative diseases at bay, as well as maintaining weight loss. This eating pattern can be followed in your normal day-to-day living. If you find you need to indulge in a binge now and again, "be my guest" but remember, the **day before**, the **day of** the indulgence, and

the **day after** are very important.

I do not suggest you indulge in binges on a regular basis. It's not what you do now and again that will harm you, it's what you do on a daily basis that will eventually bring on degenerative diseases.

The Maintenance Programme I recommend is in harmony with human physiology. The body works in physiological (metabolic) cycles. When you eat in accordance with these metabolic cycles you will bring about more efficient digestion, efficient assimilation of food, cleansing of toxic cells and overall health benefits, as well as weight loss.

METABOLIC CYCLES

From 8 pm till 3 – 4 am, the body is engaged in digesting and assimilating food eaten that day, by mobilising nutrients to the cells. Sugars are converted to glycogen and stored in the liver and muscles. This glycogen is made available for use by the body through-out the rest of the early morning and the following day, until the supply is exhausted.

From 3 – 4 am till 12 pm, the body is involved in a cleansing, repairing and rebuilding phase. The cells are dumping waste products (toxins) into the bloodstream and are manufacturing and/or repairing cells. During this phase it is very important not to eat the wrong foods so early in the morning, because this will interfere with the elimination cycle.

We have plenty of stored sugar in the form of glycogen to use for energy. This elimination phase ends late in the morning, after you've been up and active for several hours. The kind of food you should eat is fruit – it is the most easily digested. If it makes you feel weak or you happen to experience headaches or other unpleasant symptoms, this is not because you need heavy foods eg cereals, it is because your body is cleansing and repairing itself (making itself healthy).

From 12 pm till 8 pm, the body's metabolism is geared to digesting foods.

You should also eat in accordance with energy demands on the body. During the early part of the day we need more energy for physical/mental activities than at other times. The digestion of food demands a tremendous amount of energy, therefore it would be more sensible to eat the more difficult to digest foods when our physical activities ie our energy needs are lowest and that is in the evening. On the Maintenance Programme, I am including foods you are accustomed to eating, but I am going to show you what to eat, how to eat and when to eat these foods. Remember, this is all based on your 24 hour metabolic cycles.

GENERAL RULES

- Use dressings, condiments and seasonings without chemical additives and preservatives, sugar or Monosodium Glutamate (MSG). These only add toxins to your body.
- Avoid vinegar in salad dressings. Substitute fresh lemon juice.
- Avoid the excessive use of raw onions and garlic. They disturb the taste buds and encourage the craving for heavy foods.
- Use only cold-pressed oils (sunflower, sesame, olive, almond and flaxseed) when adding a dressing to the salad. Use 2 tablespoons of cold-pressed oil and 1 tablespoon of fresh lemon juice. Adjust the amount, using this ratio, according to the size of the salad.
- If you are hungry you may snack on 1 fruit or 2 – 3 pieces of carob (chocolate substitute) or dried fruit 3 hours after lunch.
- Do not have more than a $1/2$ a cup of dried fruit (sulphur dioxide free) per day and soak the dried fruit to reconstitute the water content.
- Choose unprocessed cheeses, cultured yoghurt, raw unsalted butter (never use margarine) and goat's milk, if you are not a vegetarian.
- Do not eat red meat more than once a week. Eat animal protein no more than 3 times a

week. Any salted, smoked meats or fish are not recommended eg frankfurters and sausages. Choose free-range chickens and eggs (from fowls that have not been injected with antibiotics or hormones). If you are a vegetarian choose raw, unsalted, unroasted nuts or seeds (no peanuts). Do not have more than $1/2$ a cup per day.

- Never drink with your meals. You should drink only 4 cups/glasses of liquid per day unless you are involved in strenuous activities. I recommend drinking purified water or herbal tea, but initially if you must, you can have your usual tea and coffee. Remember, however, that the quantity is restricted. Try to substitute them for herbal teas and health coffees.

- Before eating any processed, cooked, tinned and bottled food eg bread, cheese etc, eat a side plate of raw vegetable salad first.
- Don't use sweeteners or sugar in your tea or coffee. Use raw honey. Commercial honey is heated, and this changes its molecular structure.
- Never use oil in salad together with avocado pear if you want to lose weight.
- Never have nuts and avocado at the same meal or on the same day.
- Do not eat later than 9 pm as this will affect your body cycles.
- Make a habit of eating 75% raw food and only 25% cooked food.
- **Do not overeat.**

Your daily eating plan – Maintenance Programme

On waking:
Purified water with a slice of fresh lemon or freshly made fruit juice (not commercial fruit juices). Wait at least 1 hour before eating breakfast. If you don't want to drink anything in the morning, you need not. You should not have tea or coffee on waking.

Breakfast:
Eat as much fresh fruit as you want, correctly combined till 12 pm or 1 hour before your lunch. You can include dried fruit (sulphur dioxide free) especially in the winter time. Don't eat more than $1/4 - 1/2$ a cup per day. Dried fruit helps eliminate cravings for sweets and chocolates.

Wait 1 hour after fruit or 2 hours after other foods before drinking.

Lunch:
Always eat a raw vegetable salad first and then choose either a starch meal with a small avocado (if desired) or a protein meal (no avocado) together with as many steamed neutral vegetables as you desire. You can also have a legume dish but regard it as a protein meal even though it is both high in protein and starch. Do not eat together with any starch food. If you find these meals too much to consume, then choose one of the following: Salad and avocado pear only (steamed neutral/green vegetables optional).
OR
Salad and $1/2$ a cup of nuts/seeds only (steamed neutral/green vegetables optional).
OR
Acid fruits and $1/2$ a cup of nuts/seeds only

(lettuce and/or celery optional).

OR

Avocado pear and subacid or acid fruit only (lettuce and/or celery optional).

OR

Fruit only, correctly combined. I suggest you add lettuce and/or celery to any fruit except the melon family.

You can **snack** 3 hours after eating a concentrated meal (fruit only is not a concentrated meal). You can snack on 1 fruit, carob or dried fruit etc, provided you haven't had your quota of dried fruit for the day. Wait at least 1 hour before eating supper.

Supper:

Always eat a raw vegetable salad first and then choose what you didn't have at lunch. If you had a protein meal at lunch you should have a starch meal at supper or just a fruit meal.

THE RULE OF THUMB

- Only 1 protein meal per day, if you wish. You do not need protein every day.
- If you want to, you can have 2 starch meals per day, eg starch at lunch and supper.
- You could even have 3 fruit meals per day.

The more raw meals you eat in a day, the stronger the detox symptoms initially.

You must decide which meals are the most suitable for you. Whichever meal you choose, on the Maintenance Programme, your health is going to improve.

WHAT TO DO IF YOU REALLY FEEL LIKE A BINGE (PIG-OUT)

Eat and enjoy. Don't feel guilty, because I am going to give you the rules on how to handle the binge.

The day before the binge

Eat only fruit correctly combined till you go to sleep.

The day of the binge

Eat as much as you want of one type of fruit throughout the day till 1 hour before the binge, then eat whatever your heart desires.

The day after the binge

Eat only one type of fruit, starting 12 – 18 hours after you have finished the binge till 1 hour before supper.

Supper:

Preferably a raw meal such as salad and avocado pear or avocado pear together with subacid or acid fruit or just fruit. Do not have any protein.

If you feel really awful the day after the binge, just drink purified water throughout the day or eat only fruit for all your meals.

I hope these rules will ease the feeling of guilt you might experience. I would also like you to take good note of the following.

When you decide to change your diet in a radical way by first following the Detox and then rigidly sticking to the Maintenance Programme, without indulging in binges for some time, when you **do binge** you are not going to feel good at all.

The body has reached a stage where it will not tolerate the wrong foods so readily. Remember – there is a price to pay for going off track. You will find, however, that in time you won't be going on binges on a regular basis, because the feeling you have after the binge is not pleasant.

A RULE TO REMEMBER

If you are not feeling well, for example, if you

have a cold, upset tummy etc, follow the advice given for **the day after the binge** or better still, eat only fruit or fast till you feel better. It might take a little longer to resolve your problem, but it's absolutely worth it. Only use medication as a last resort.

This new lifestyle of high water content food, correct combinations etc. will help you deal with the causes of overeating, by cleansing the intestines and unclogging the villi, so the body can absorb the nutrients and stop you from eating more. In short, your body will no longer need to sound the alarm for more food, since it will regularly be receiving food that will cleanse and nourish it.

Remember to include the **other essentials of life** (see section on Correct Lifestyle)

If you can follow this kind of lifestyle most of the time and I suggest you at least try, then you are assured of better health and a more contented attitude towards life.

Do it, not because it's easy, and it's not, but because it's right.

The toughest part of my life isn't watching what I eat, it's watching what other people eat. I have realised that education is an essential part of healing, so I have put together a whole set of recipes on . . .

102

PART 4

How to Get Started with Your New Programme

Mouth-watering Menus

Rather than subsist on the dull foods that may be all that is left when everything unhealthy is subtracted from one's diet, we can branch out into new and delicious foods
NEAL D. BARNARD

These recipes are for all those people who now realise they must begin a new healthy eating pattern, so that they can enjoy vibrant health. I have realised that it is not enough to tell people what not to eat, they must rather taste foods free of animal flesh and judge for themselves. Here are some practical step by step tips to help you improve your life by adjusting your existing eating habits. It is easy and you can do it!

It all starts in the kitchen, the one place where you have total control of what you eat. Begin with your refrigerator and then move on to the grocery cupboard.

Start removing commercial salad dressings, sauces made with preservatives (read your labels), replace margarine with unsalted butter and choose free-range chickens and eggs. Use unprocessed cheeses and preservative-free yoghurts if you still want dairy products, otherwise use tofu in place of dairy. Replace salty crackers and sugary cereals with healthier alternatives like rolled oats, unsalted rice cakes, brown rice, millet and polenta. Use whole-wheat flour, raw peanut butter and raw honey instead of sugar or sweetener. Replace tea and coffee with herbal teas and coffee substitutes. Use a water filter. By boiling the water you might be getting rid of germs, but you are still not getting rid of the chemicals.

With regard to meal preparations, start by cutting back on your animal food intake. If you eat meat 6 times a week then cut back to 5, then 4. If you eat eggs for breakfast quite often, then substitute 1 or 2 egg meals per week with cereal or fruit. Use cold-pressed oils (see list under criterion 4) rather than ordinary oils. Use herbal salts as against ordinary salt, which is sodium chloride. Use pastas made without egg. Try to use whole-wheat pastas or gluten-free pastas. Use carob products as an alternative to chocolate. Choose healthy sweets without tartrazine. Choose juices without preservatives. Use dairy alternatives. Enquire about all these products at your nearest health store.

EQUIPMENT

You need fruit and food combination charts, a large cutting board, a seed sprouter, a melon ball scoop, a salad spinner, a vegetable steamer and a set of chopping knives. You should purchase a juice extractor and a blender. I have a **Vita-Mix**® and a **Magimix**® blender and I find these the best on the market. There are however other makes. You must choose what is best for you. With this equipment you can make the most appetising meals.

Make these positive changes at your own pace. Give yourself credit for each step you take. Don't make comparisons, especially with someone who might be farther along the path to good health. This is very important as you **are** going to continue to make better, healthier changes in your eating habits. The most important thing is to take things slowly. Don't try to change your family's eating habits overnight and don't impose strict rules on your family's eating pattern. This is not a realistic way to go about making healthy changes, especially if you don't have the day-to-day support of family and friends.

I'm going to give you mouth-watering menus which are quick and easy to prepare, and which will please the taste buds of even the most difficult eater. The recipes in this book include hearty breakfast foods, such as luscious fruit salads with fantastic fruit sauces as well as nutritious nut butters. There are satisfying main course salads with sensational dressings and dips, followed by superb soups and mouth-watering main dishes. I have also included divine drinks, delectable puddings and super-delicious natural ice creams. There are captivating cakes, tempting sandwiches and a variety of breads to choose from. I have of course included some transitional recipes, to help you make the change from traditional fare to more wholesome foods gradually, instead of suddenly. Bon Appétit! But don't let your life revolve around what and when you are going to eat.

IMPORTANT INSTRUCTIONS
I use very little seasoning in my recipes. I sometimes don't even mention "add seasoning to taste". If you feel the need to season, go ahead, but use those seasonings without preservatives. Many seasonings contain harmful ingredients such as sodium chloride, yeast, textured proteins, artificial sweeteners, harsh spices and herbs, MSG and fermented residues. Avoid aluminium cookware especially if the cooking surface itself is made from this metal. Acid-forming foods cooked in aluminium interact with the metal to form aluminium salts, which are toxic. Use stainless steel or glassware. Pots and pans with non-stick finishes scratch easily and can contaminate foods with bits of plastic while cooking is taking place. Use dried fruit (sulphur dioxide free) and unsalted, unroasted nuts. **Wherever I have put an * please refer to the recipe index.**

OVEN TEMPERATURES
Cool	150 °C	(300 °F)
Warm	160 °C – 180 °C	(325 °F – 350 °F)
Hot	200 °C	(400 °F)
Very Hot	230 °C	(450 °F)

1 cup (8 oz)	=	240 g
1 oz	=	30 g
tsp	=	teaspoon
tbsp	=	tablespoon

Breakfast Dishes

Fresh fruit makes a great breakfast. What a wonderful way to start your day! There are so many different fruits and so many varieties of each fruit. Each season brings with it a kaleidoscopic array of new choices. Quantities given may only be sufficient for 1 – 2 persons.

Swiss Breakfast

1 grated apple (not peeled)
½ cup rolled oats
2 tbsp macadamia nuts, chopped
2 tbsp raisins
¾ cup fresh apple juice

Mix all 4 ingredients and then add apple juice. Let stand for 10 minutes.

Crunchy Fruit Munch

1 cup ground macadamia nuts
1 banana, diced
1 small pear, diced
½ cup currants/raisins
4 dried figs, chopped
2 tbsp wheat germ

Mix above ingredients together in a bowl.
Add any flavour soya milk or other dairy alternatives.

Do-it-yourself Granola

3 cups rolled oats
2 cups wheat germ
½ cup dates or dried apricots
1 cup chopped macadamia nuts
½ cup raisins

Mix all ingredients together and store in a cool place or refrigerator. This mixture can be browned in the oven until crunchy.
Add any flavour soya milk or dairy alternative or fresh apple juice.

Muesli

2 cups raw oats
4 apples (red or yellow – not peeled)
½ cup macadamia nuts
¼ cup raisins

Grate apples. Grate or chop nuts. Mix all ingredients together. Add dairy alternatives or fresh apple juice or 2 ripe mashed bananas, moistened with purified water to make a milk. Eat immediately.

Rice Pudding (transitional)

(children really enjoy this)
1 cup brown rice
3 cups purified water
½ tsp vegetable salt
2 – 3 ripe bananas, mashed
1 cup fresh cream or 1 cup soya milk
½ tsp cinnamon
1 cup raisins and/or sultanas
1 – 2 tbsp raw honey (optional)

Bring rice, water and salt to the boil.
Simmer for about 30 – 45 minutes or until water is absorbed.
Add remaining ingredients to the cooked rice.
Pour into an oven-proof dish. Bake at 180 ˚C for about 35 minutes.

Cocobanana Cereal

4 crisp red apples or pears
4 medium ripe bananas
½ cup chopped dates or raisins
1 – 2 tsp ground cinnamon
½ cup desiccated coconut
½ cup soya milk (flavour of your choice)

Core and slice apples/pears Slice bananas. Combine apples and bananas in a bowl. Add remaining ingredients and mix well.

Oats with a Difference

1 cup raw rolled oats
½ cup purified water

Bring water and oats to the boil. Simmer on low heat for a short time until desired consistency is reached. Serve with diced or mashed bananas. Sweeten with "date fudge" (macerated dates or ordinary dates blended) or raw honey.

Variations:
Use coarse yellow mealie meal or polenta if there is a gluten intolerance. This takes longer to cook.

Slimmer's Porridge

1 cup rolled oats soaked overnight in purified water
$\frac{1}{2}$ cup raisins
1 banana, finely chopped
juice of 1 apple
dash of cinnamon

Combine the soaked oats with the fruit juice. Add remainder of ingredients. Eat and enjoy!

Basic Granola (transitional)

7 cups rolled oats
1$\frac{1}{2}$ cups macadamia nuts, roughly chopped
1 cup desiccated coconut
1 cup chopped dates/raisins

Mix all ingredients together. Bake at 160 °C stirring occasionally until slightly brown. Cool. Store in a glass jar. Before serving, you can add either wheat germ, sesame or sunflower seeds, or all 3.

Home-made Dairy Alternatives

At breakfast time, when contemplating what to pour over your children's porridge or even your own, non-dairy milks are a quick and easy alternative. The secret is to own a good blender and use very cold purified water.

You could also use fresh apple or pear juice to pour over cereals.

A word of warning: Do not use any of the following beverages as "formula" for feeding infants.

Nut Milks

Use $\frac{1}{2}$ cup nuts (no peanuts) or seeds with 1 cup ice cold purified water. If using almonds, always blanch first. Blend for 30 – 90 seconds until smooth. You may want to add more water. You can add raw honey as a sweetener.

Banana Milk

Fill $\frac{1}{2}$ the blender with ice cold purified water. Slice 2 – 3 ripe bananas and add to blender. Add 1 tbsp raw honey or barley malt and $\frac{1}{2}$ tsp vanilla essence (tartrazine free – this is very concentrated), Blend well for about 30 – 90 seconds. Serve immediately.

Soya Milk (home-made)

2 cups purified water
8 tbsp soya milk powder

Blend ingredients with vanilla essence and sweetener to taste, eg raw honey. You could also use commercial soya milk preparations. Enquire at health food stores.

Fruit Meals – Fruit Sauces – Fruit and Nut Drinks

For those who just want to eat only fruit throughout the morning I have given you a choice of divine fresh fruit juice drinks, delicious fruit combinations with fantastic sauces, as well as nuts which you can add to your fruit. Take your pick. Remember to wait 1 hour after having a fruit juice, before your fruit meal. The natural sugars in fresh fruits are not harmful and a variety of fresh fruits will give you lots of energy.

Do not eat more than $\frac{1}{4}$ – $\frac{1}{2}$ cup of dried fruit per day. For weight loss eat a $\frac{1}{4}$ cup only three times per week.

The best form of protein is nuts and seeds. If you are a vegetarian, eat no more than a $\frac{1}{4}$ – $\frac{1}{2}$ cup of nuts or seeds per day and eat them no less than three times per week.

For those who still want their flesh foods during the rest of the day, remember you are only allowed one protein meal per day. So if you have nuts with any of your meals, that is your protein quota for the day.

The "converted" can eat a fruit meal for breakfast lunch and supper; don't eat fruit only for all meals for longer than a month at a time.

These recipes are sufficient for 1 person.

Fruit Meals

Papino Surprise

Slice papino (pawpaw) lengthwise and scoop out pips.
Fill papino with sliced ripe bananas.
Roughly chop dates and sprinkle over bananas.

For small children:
Dice the papino into small cubes and serve with puréed banana as a custard. Raisins or sultanas can be used in place of dates.

Sweet Fruit Salad

Dice and combine red and yellow apples, papinos, bananas and pears. Use as much as you want of each fruit.
Add fresh apple juice to moisten. Sweeten with dates, raisins or sultanas.
You can soak the dried fruit overnight and add it to the fresh fruit. Use the juice of the soaked fruit to moisten the fruit salad, instead of the apple juice.

Fabulous Fruit Salad

1 Golden Delicious apple
2 apricots
1 cup green seedless grapes
1 cup red seedless grapes
2 pears

Dice apple and pears, and slice apricots into small pieces. Mix together with grapes. Serve with Peach-Grape Sauce.*

Summer Fruit Medley

1 cup green seedless grapes
1 cup red seedless grapes
1 cup sliced peaches
1 cup sliced nectarines
1 cup blueberries

Combine all ingredients in a clear glass bowl. Add Mango-Plum Sauce* and stir gently into fruit medley.

Stuffed Pears

Pare and core large pears.
Stuff with raisins, dates, and finely chopped macadamia nuts.
Sprinkle with desiccated coconut. Serve on lettuce leaves.

Pineapple, Mango and Berry Salad

3 butter lettuce leaves
1 sliced mango
1 cup finely diced pineapple or puréed pineapple
1 cup blueberries
1 cup strawberries

Arrange lettuce leaves on a plate.
In the centre make a mound of cubed or puréed pineapple.
Arrange blueberries, mango slices and strawberries around the pineapple.

Pineapple Deluxe

1 pineapple cut into chunks
1 cup sliced strawberries or nectarines
2 kiwi fruit, peeled and sliced
almonds, pecans or sunflower seeds (optional)

Liquidise pineapple chunks in a blender. Place in a bowl. Garnish with sliced strawberries or nectarines and peeled, sliced kiwi fruit. Sprinkle with $1/4 - 1/2$ cup of nuts of your choice.

Sweet Waldorf Salad

(also delicious as a light lunch)
4 Golden Delicious apples, diced
2 cups celery, chopped
1/4 cup macadamia nuts, chopped
1/4 cup raisins
2 tbsp fresh apple juice

Combine apples, celery, raisins and nuts. Add apple juice to moisten. Toss ingredients well. Serve immediately.

Apple Delight

Juice of 1 orange
2 coarsely grated Granny Smith apples
¼ cup ground almonds

Pour orange juice over apples and sprinkle ¼ cup of ground almonds over fruit mixture.

Banana Frulatta

4 bananas
1 medium papino
¼ to 1 cup Date-Apricot Topping*
½ cup soaked raisins

Purée bananas and papino together. Add Date-Apricot Topping. Mix well. If too thick add juice of soaked fruit. Pour into a tall glass and sprinkle with chopped, soaked raisins.

Fruit Salad with Pear Custard

¼ cup dried pears
4 bananas
1 large sliced mango
3 sliced peaches

Soak dried pears overnight in purified water. Blend pears with water and bananas to make a custard consistency. Pour pear-banana custard over sliced mangoes and peaches. Garnish with a mint leaf.

Citrus Fruit Delight

1 pink grapefruit (remove pips)
1 large orange (remove pips)
1 kiwi fruit
½ cup diced celery
½ cup strawberries

Peel both grapefruit and orange and cut into small pieces. Peel kiwi fruit and slice. Combine all fruit in a bowl. Sprinkle with diced celery. Top with strawberries. Chill and serve immediately.

Rainbow Fruit Salad

1 pineapple
1 punnet strawberries
4 ripe kiwi fruit
1 mango
1 punnet blueberries

Wash fruits well. Peel, core and dice pineapple. De-stem strawberries and cut into slices. Peel and slice kiwi fruit and mango. Combine all fruits and enjoy the different flavours, colours and textures.

Fruit Medley

oranges and berries
(strawberries, blueberries or raspberries, etc)
30 – 60 g almonds, chopped coarsely or sunflower seeds (optional)

Wash fruit. Arrange attractively on a bed of lettuce. Sprinkle nuts or seeds over fruit.

Deluxe Fruit Salad

1 cup peeled, sliced peaches
1 cup blueberries, raspberries or mulberries
1 cup sliced apricots

Wash peaches, berries and apricots. Cut into bite-sized pieces. Mix together and serve.

Melon Delight

Choose from watermelon as well as other melons in season. Scoop melons into balls or cut into cubes. Arrange attractively. Enjoy!

Strawberry Kiwi Delight

½ – 1 punnet strawberries
1 orange
1 kiwi fruit
red lettuce leaves
Raw, unsalted almonds or cashews, coarsely chopped (optional)

Wash lettuce leaves and place in a dish. Wash strawberries, de-stem and place around the outside of the dish. Peel orange, separate segments and arrange next to strawberries. Slice kiwi fruit. Place kiwi fruit in the middle of the dish. Add a small amount of almonds or cashews for a wholesome, delicious meal!

Pineapple Orange Dish

1 pineapple
1 orange
1 cup strawberries
mint leaves

Dice pineapple into small pieces. Peel orange, remove pips, and cut into chunks. De-stem strawberries and slice into small pieces. Mix all ingredients together. Garnish with mint leaves.

Winter Fruit Salad

1 banana, sliced
60 g chopped macadamia nuts
1 apple, sliced thinly (Golden Delicious or red)
30 g figs or dates, chopped

Mix banana and apple in a bowl. Add dates or figs, and nuts to the fruit.

Pear Persimmon Delight

1 pear
1 persimmon
1 Golden Delicious/Starking apple
6 – 8 dates or $^1/_3$ cup raisins
romaine or butter lettuce leaves

Arrange lettuce on a plate. Core pear and apple and cut into cubes. Cut persimmon into slices. If it is very soft, you can just break the skin and 'spoon' the fruit onto the lettuce leaves with the cubed apple and pear. Add dates or raisins. This fruit arrangement is very sweet-tasting, colourful and beautiful to look at. It's like eating dessert for the main course.

Fruit Sauces

Fruit can be made into the most delicious sauces which can be used in a variety of ways. It can be used as a sauce with fresh and/or dried fruits correctly combined, or eaten as a thick fruit soup with one or more kinds of bite-sized fresh and/or dried fruits added. Sauces can be used as dips for fruit, such as bananas and strawberries or as spreads for fruit sandwiches or as excellent toppings for "banana ice cream".

You can substitute a particular dried fruit mentioned in recipes for any dried fruit of your choice (sulphur dioxide free). Always use 3 parts purified water to 1 part dried fruit, to reinstate the moisture content of the fruit.

Apricot Sauce

3 apples (Golden Delicious/Starking)
$^1/_2$ cup dried apricots
dates

Soak dried apricots overnight in purified water. Wash, quarter, core and dice apples. Chop some dates, add to blender with a few soaked apricots and blend at high speed. Add remainder of the soaked apricots, blending until desired consistency is obtained. If you need more liquid, add some apple juice or use purified water from the dried fruit. Pour this over sweet or subacid fruit.

Apple Sauce Supreme

3 apples (Golden Delicious/Starking)
$^1/_2$ cup dates or raisins soaked
in purified water (optional)

Wash apples. Cut into quarters, removing seeds. Put into blender with enough purified water to get the blender going. Blend until smooth. If you want to make your apple sauce sweeter, add dates or raisins that have been soaked overnight and blend till smooth. Garnish with a sprig of mint.

Pear Sauce (a delicious winter sauce)

2 fresh pears + $^1/_4$ – $^1/_2$ cup dried pears
purified water
dates (optional)

Soak dried pears overnight in purified water. Cube pears and put in blender. Add soaking water and dried pears to blender and blend till mixture becomes creamy in texture. Dried pears provide enough sweetness, but if you desire more sweetness, or if you use fresh pears only, you may want to add a few dates and blend them with your mixture. Pear Sauce is delicious on top of sliced ripe bananas or mixed in with cubed bananas.

111

Fig-Apple Sauce

6 red/Golden Delicious apples
6 dried figs soaked overnight in purified water

Drain figs and cut into slices. Slice and core apples. Blend apples and figs, adding a small amount of soaking water to make the consistency of a sauce. Can be poured over sweet or subacid fruit. Absolutely delicious over mangoes!

Fruit Sauce

1 ripe mango, peeled
1 papaya (pawpaw or papino), halved and seeded
2 peaches, peeled and pitted

Place peeled mango in blender or food processor. Scoop out pulp of papaya. Add papaya and peaches to blender with mango. Blend until smooth. Use immediately. Serve as a thick drink by itself, or as a sauce over subacid or sweet fruit.

Mango-Plum Sauce

1 mango, peeled
4 plums, peeled

Put mango and plums into blender. Blend until smooth. Pour over Summer Fruit Medley.*

Peach-Grape Sauce

2 peaches
1 cup seedless grapes

Peel peaches and remove stones. Cut into pieces and put into blender with grapes. Blend until smooth. Pour over Fabulous Fruit Salad.*

Date-Apricot Topping

1 cup dried apricots
1 cup dried dates
3 cups purified water

In a medium bowl, combine apricots, dates and water. Cover and soak for 12 – 24 hours. Blend entire mixture in a blender. Topping can be served over subacid or sweet fruit.

Raisin Sauce

Soak ½ cup raisins overnight in purified water. Blend bananas with raisins, dates or any other dried fruits. Pour over any sweet or subacid fruits, or stuff lettuce leaves with the sauce.

Sweet Fruit Sauce

¼ cup dried prunes/currants
2 bananas
1 papino

Soak prunes overnight in purified water. Stone and blend with bananas and papino. Also delicious with currants instead of prunes. Pour over sliced peaches, mangoes or subacid fruits in season.

Cashew-Apple Cream

2 Golden Delicious apples, peeled, cored and diced
1 cup cashew nuts
½ cup purified water

Blend apples with a little water. Add cashews and more water if needed. Blend well to make a smooth cream. Serve over subacid or acid fruit or Pineapple Pom Pom.*

Dried Fruit Sauce

500 g pitted dates
500 g dried figs
500 g raisins
3 bananas
1 tsp ginger

Soak dried fruit overnight. Strain and save juice for drinking. Blend dried fruit together with bananas and ginger. Serve as a thick fruit sauce over sweet or subacid fruit.

112

Fruit and Nut Drinks

These drinks are as healthful as they are delicious. They can be used as meals or served ¹/₂ hour to 1 hour before a meal. In this manner, they do not interfere with digestion.

You can just use fresh fruit and make delicious combinations of juices or you can blend fruits and drink thick "smoothies".

Why not add nuts or seeds and make delicious shakes! Nuts and seeds provide readily usable high quality protein. They are superior sources of essential fatty acids, calcium, magnesium and other valuable minerals as well as B complex vitamins. Vegetable juices can be used as your raw choice before a cooked meal (but you have to wait ¹/₂ hour before eating the meal) or you could drink them as a snack in the late afternoon. Vegetable juices are very high in organic minerals.

Cashew-Pine Shake

1 cup grated pineapple
¹/₂ cup chopped celery
¹/₄ cup cashews

Blend all ingredients together. Delicious as a shake or "custard" over sliced acid fruits, served on a bed of lettuce.

Date-Macadamia Shake

1 cup macadamia nuts blended with purified water to make a milk. If you want it thicker use less water. Add water slowly to get desired thickness.
2 frozen bananas (take overripe bananas, peel them, cut into thirds, put into a plastic bag and freeze till required)
Add 6 chopped dates to the mixture.
Blend frozen bananas first. Then add other ingredients to blender and blend until thick and creamy. This is absolutely delicious!

Fruity Almond Milk Shake

Blend together any mix of acid fruits (strawberries, pineapples, kiwi fruits etc). Add ¹/₂ cup almonds to mixture and blend again. Pour into tall glasses and serve.

Almond, Pineapple and Orange Juice Milk Shake

1 pineapple, liquidised
3 oranges, juiced
¹/₂ to 1 cup almonds

Blend almonds to make a fine powder. Add orange juice and liquidised pineapple to nut mixture. Mix well. Pour into tall glasses and serve.

Almond Milk

Place ¹/₄ cup almonds in enough boiling water to cover for about 10 minutes, to remove skins. Skins will peel off easily. Blend almonds into a fine paste. Add one cup purified water and blend again. You can also add raw honey to sweeten. This milk is very high in calcium. If used for infants, don't use honey and put mixture through a muslin cloth.

Strawberry Smoothie

(not the ideal combination, but mouth-watering)
3 bananas
¹/₂ punnet strawberries

One of the fruits must be frozen. Blend together and serve immediately.

Apple-Date Smoothie

2 frozen bananas (fresh can also be used if desired)
2 apples, cored
2 – 4 mejool dates, seeded
1 cup fresh apple, grape or pear juice

Purée all ingredients together in a blender until smooth. Serve in a tall glass.

Strawberry Punch (without the alcohol)

¹/₂ jug freshly squeezed orange juice
¹/₂ jug blended pineapple
1 punnet strawberries, sliced
2 kiwi fruits, diced
¹/₂ cup fresh granadilla pulp

Mix orange juice together with above fruits. Chill. Serve in a tall glass, garnished with a sprig of mint.

Lip-smacking Date Smoothie

¹/₂ cup fresh fruit juice (apple, pear or grape)
dates (2 – 4 per serving)
2 frozen bananas

Use freshly made juice as a base. Place juice in a blender. Add seeded dates to juice and blend at high speed. (Dried apples instead of dates may be used.) Add frozen bananas one at a time, through opening in blender. This must be done while blender is running at high speed. (Fresh or ripe bananas can also be used if you have no frozen bananas.) Blend well. Serve in a tall glass.

Pineapple Pom Pom

1 pineapple, peeled and cored
4 Golden Delicious apples, peeled and cored
strawberries/nectarines (optional)

Cut pineapple and apples into cubes and place in blender. Blend till chunky – not smooth. Put mixture into glasses, filling each about two thirds full. Cover with Cashew Cream.* Fill the rest of each glass with diced strawberries or nectarines. This is really delicious.

Smile-inducing Pink Juice

¹/₄ ripe pineapple
1 punnet strawberries
2 Starking apples

Peel and cut pineapple into 6 – 8 large chunks. Place pineapple chunks in blender. De-stem and wash strawberries. Wash apples and cut into slices, to fit juicer. (The core and seeds can be handled by the juicer.) Put apples through juicer. Then add juice to blender and liquidise with blended pineapple for a couple of minutes on high speed. With the blender still running add strawberries, a few at a time. Continue blending for a minute or two. Pour into 2 tall glasses and enjoy.

Coconut Milk Shake

1 cup coconut milk (¹/₂ cup desiccated coconut mixed with 1 cup purified water). Blend with 1 small banana, ¹/₂ tbsp carob powder and several dates without seeds. 60 ml grape, apple or pear juice can be added.

Banana Tahini

(not a perfect combination, but yummy)
2 cups purified water
2 frozen bananas
1¹/₄ tbsp tahini
¹/₂ tsp vanilla essence
(tartrazine free – this is very concentrated)

Combine all ingredients in blender. Blend at high speed for a minute until creamy and smooth. If mixture is too thick, add more water. If too thin, add more frozen bananas. This really tastes like a thick vanilla milk shake.

Fresh Vegetable Juices – Afternoon Drinks

Use a juice extractor and not a blender to make these juices. Always drink juices as soon as they are made. Use carrots as a base for most juices. You do not have to scrape carrots, just simply wash well. You can add apple juice to sweeten some vegetable juices.

Celery is a source of natural sodium and will help to neutralise the acid build-up in the body. These juices are very high in organic mineral content (calcium and iron).

Carrot and Celery Juice

2 stalks of celery (no leaves)
7 carrots

Put through juice extractor.

Apple and Cabbage Juice

300 ml apple juice mixed with 180 ml cabbage juice

Carrot, Celery, Spinach and Lettuce Juice

7 carrots
2 stalks celery (no leaves)
2 spinach and 2 lettuce leaves (green ones)

Put all ingredients through a juice extractor. This combination has a strong, laxative, cleansing effect.

Apple and Celery Juice

300 ml apple juice mixed with 180 ml celery juice

Broccoli-Carrot Blend	Carrot, Celery and Cucumber Juice
300 ml broccoli juice mixed with 180 ml carrot juice	Mix 240 ml carrot juice with 120 ml celery juice and 120 ml cucumber juice (peel cucumber first).

Lunches and Dinners

There are so many options. You can interchange lunch meals for evening meals and vice versa. Just remember, you cannot combine a protein meal with a starch meal. You can choose from a variety of raw dips, cold soups, hot soups, satisfying main course salads, mouth-watering hot vegetables, with delicious dressings and sensational and tempting breads. You will never go hungry eating vegetarian meals. There are wonderful choices for children and the foods I recommend are as wholesome as they are appetising. Fruits, vegetables, sprouts, nuts, seeds and avocados are extremely rich in vitamins, minerals and essential fatty acids and supply plenty of high quality usable protein. Remember, you can have 1 protein meal per day, or 2 starch meals per day, or if you are into Natural Hygiene, 3 fruit meals per day. The main dishes that are presented here are more healthful versions of some of the foods you may be accustomed to eating.

Always start a cooked or processed meal with a side plate of raw salad.

You have a wonderful choice of salads which are easy to prepare. You can always serve them with any healthy oil dressing or just squeeze fresh lemon juice over the salad. In order to tempt children to eat raw vegetables, I have given you the most delicious dips. I have found that children absolutely love to eat these delicious dips and vegetables in front of the TV, just before supper. I have also included some lightly steamed vegetables and pasta dishes, with lots of raw vegetables to make the transition from eating a great deal of cooked foods to eating more raw foods much easier.

The recipes are sufficient for 2 people only.

Raw Salads

There are a variety of raw salads that you can choose from before eating anything that is cooked. I can assure you that after eating these salads you will not actually feel like eating more. If you are going to eat flesh foods after these delicious salads, make sure you don't eat salads with starchy vegetable ingredients or with avocado in them.

Corn Salad (starch meal)

2 cups butter lettuce
½ cup shredded carrots
1 cup fresh mealies, cut off the cob
½ cup alfalfa sprouts
½ cup chopped red peppers

In a medium bowl, combine the lettuce, carrots, mealies, sprouts, and red peppers. Toss with your favourite healthy dressing.

Tossed Salad

2 cups butter lettuce
1 sweet red pepper
2 stalks celery
2 tomatoes
½ cup alfalfa sprouts

Wash vegetables. Tear lettuce into small pieces. Slice sweet red pepper, tomatoes, and celery into bite-sized pieces. Toss all ingredients together and add any dressing of your choice.

Avocado-Orange Salad

4 navel oranges, peeled and sectioned
2 grapefruits, peeled and sectioned
2 avocados, peeled, cubed or sliced
4 large leaves butter lettuce
1 cup Avocado-Orange Dressing*

Arrange avocados and orange and grapefruit sections on a bed of lettuce leaves. Top with Avocado-Orange Dressing.* This is a meal on its own.

Cabbage Salad Extraordinaire

(not the ideal combination, but very tasty)
1 cup grated cabbage
1 cup grated carrots
1 cup grated zucchini (baby marrows)
½ cup raisins
½ cup sprouted mung beans
½ cup diced apples

Mix above ingredients together in large bowl. Serve with Avocado-Orange Dressing.*

Carrot Salad (starch meal)

2 cups grated carrots
1 cup grated sweet potato
2 yellow mealies (cut off cob)
4 Brussels sprouts, thinly sliced
1 cup alfalfa sprouts
Cucumber-Celery Dressing*
lettuce leaves for two
½ cup chopped olives (optional)

Prepare a bed of lettuce. Combine the first 5 ingredients. Scoop onto lettuce leaves. Pour over Cucumber-Celery Dressing. Garnish with olives.

Stuffed Red Peppers

½ cup celery, finely diced
2 tomatoes, cut up
½ red pepper, sliced
1 cup mixed sprouts
1 avocado, mashed well
1 medium red pepper per person

Mix first 4 ingredients well with mashed avocado. Cut tops off peppers and stuff with avocado mixture.

Green Crêpes

1 cucumber
1 large or 2 small tomatoes
½ cup fresh peas
1 sweet red pepper
1 tbsp fresh basil
butter lettuce or red lettuce leaves

Dice cucumber, tomatoes and pepper into small cubes. Mix with fresh peas. Chop basil finely and add to salad. Add oil and lemon dressing. Spread mixture onto lettuce leaf and roll up the leaf. Secure with toothpicks. Be sure to remove the toothpicks when you serve the crêpes.

Pea Salad (starch meal)

2 cups sugar snap peas
1 cup raw corn (mealies taken off cob)
1 cup chopped cucumber
1 cup grated red cabbage
¼ cup chopped celery
½ cup chopped red pepper
alfalfa sprouts for garnish

Slice the sugar snap peas diagonally. Toss all ingredients together in large bowl and garnish with alfalfa sprouts. Add any dressing of your choice.

Kohlrabi-Red Pepper Salad

½ large red pepper
½ tsp fresh dill, minced or chopped very finely
1 avocado
1 medium kohlrabi
juice from 1 lime or ½ lemon
romaine lettuce

Dice red pepper. Peel kohlrabi and cut into julienne strips. Combine with red pepper, and chopped dill. Cut avocado in half, remove seed and peel. Put several slices of avocado aside. Mash rest of flesh with a fork. Combine mashed avocado with lemon/lime juice to taste. Toss mashed avocado with kohlrabi, red pepper and dill. Serve on a bed of romaine lettuce. Add avocado slices in spokes around salad.

Pine-Carrot Salad

(not the perfect combination)
2 large grated carrots
1 pineapple, finely cubed
½ cup desiccated coconut
½ cup roughly chopped pecans
½ cup finely chopped celery
fresh orange juice

Toss together first 5 ingredients. Add orange juice as your dressing. Children really enjoy this salad.

Carrot Salad with Tahini Dressing (protein meal)

5 carrots, grated
2 tbsp sunflower seeds
juice of 1 lemon
5 tbsp cold-pressed olive oil
5 tbsp tahini
5 tbsp purified water
1½ tsp soya sauce (without MSG)
fresh parsley, chopped to garnish

Place first 2 ingredients in bowl. Blend remaining ingredients together. Pour over salad and sprinkle with parsley.

Baby Spinach and Avo Salad (starch meal)

1 packet baby spinach
½ cup diced olives
1 red pepper, sliced
2 ripe avocados, cubed
2 yellow mealies (cut off cob)
4 tomatoes, diced

Combine ingredients together in glass bowl. Add your favourite dressing.

Beetroot Coleslaw

½ cabbage, shredded
6 medium carrots, grated
2 – 3 beetroots, grated
1 small onion, grated and blanched in boiling water

Combine ingredients in bowl. Add the following dressing:

Dressing

juice of 1 lemon
4 – 6 tbsp cold-pressed sunflower oil
2 tsp health salt

Blend all ingredients well. Pour over salad mixture.

Sweet Potato and Beet Salad (starch meal)

2 cups butter lettuce
½ cup shredded zucchini (baby marrows)
¼ cup peeled, grated sweet potato
½ cup peeled, grated beetroot
1 avocado, peeled and cubed
1 tomato, sliced

Blend all ingredients in medium-sized bowl. Toss with any dressing of your choice.

Zucchini Salad

1 packet zucchini (baby marrows) finely chopped
4 stalks celery, finely chopped
2 small cabbages, finely sliced
1 stalk broccoli, broken into small florets
celery and carrots for juicing
2 avocados

Place chopped zucchini, celery, cabbage and broccoli in a bowl. Juice enough carrots and celery to make a dressing. Blend juice with avocados. Lightly toss vegetables with blended ingredients. Season to taste.

Veggie Salad

1 butter or romaine lettuce
½ small purple cabbage
2 stalks celery
1 – 2 turnips
3 avocados
alfalfa sprouts

Wash, dry and break up lettuce into small chunks. Grate purple cabbage. Wash celery, and peel turnips and avocados. Dice celery, turnips and avocados. Toss all ingredients together. Add Avid Avocado Dip* as a dressing. Garnish with alfalfa sprouts.

Avocado Burgers

2 cups celery
½ cup carrots
½ cup cabbage
2 ripe avocados
2 tsp lemon pepper
pinch vegetable salt
juice of 1 lemon

Blend celery, carrots and cabbage in a food processor. Add avocados, seasoning and lemon juice. Blend well. Shape into flat burgers. Serve on salad greens or on a whole-wheat roll.

Tropical Avo Salad

1 firm, ripe avocado cut in half, sprinkled with lemon juice
1 pineapple, peeled and cubed
1 – 2 guavas or kiwi fruit, cubed
1 – 2 stalks celery, cubed

Mix pineapple and guavas or kiwi fruit together. Add cubed celery to fruit. Mix well. Fill avocado halves with fruit and celery mixture.

Italian Mixed Salad

1 lettuce
1 fennel bulb, cut into strips
$^1/_2$ small cucumber, sliced
6 radishes, sliced
1 stalk celery, finely sliced
1 small red pepper, sliced
4 spring onions, finely sliced
2 ripe, firm tomatoes cut into eighths
vegetable salt
4 tbsp cold-pressed olive oil
2 tbsp fresh lemon juice

Tear lettuce into bite-sized pieces and place in salad bowl. Add fennel, cucumber, radishes, celery, pepper and spring onions. Lastly add in tomatoes. When ready to serve, sprinkle with a little health salt. Add oil and lemon juice and toss lightly. Serve immediately.

Avocado Boat Salad

1 avocado, peeled and cut in half
4 – 6 spinach leaves
3 tbsp carrots, shredded
3 tbsp spring onions, finely chopped
3 tbsp celery, finely chopped
2 tbsp cold-pressed olive oil
1 tbsp freshly squeezed lemon juice

Place peeled avocado halves on a bed of spinach leaves. Mix chopped vegetables with oil and lemon. Pile this mixture in the centre of each avocado.

Quick Cabbage Salad

1 medium cabbage, finely sliced
1 – 2 stalks celery, chopped
2 tomatoes, chopped

Mix all ingredients together and serve with your favourite dressing.

Nut and Pepper Salad (protein meal)

1 medium red lettuce
4 broccoli florets
1 ripe tomato, sliced
$^1/_2$ sweet yellow pepper
$^1/_2$ sweet red pepper
1 stalk celery
raw cashews or almonds

Break lettuce into bite-sized pieces and place in bowl.

Add sliced tomato and sliced vegetables. Toss lightly with your favourite dressing. Garnish with raw cashew nuts or almonds.

Cashew Slaw (protein meal)

$^1/_2$ head green cabbage
$^1/_4$ head red cabbage
6 stalks celery
1 large red bell pepper
caraway seeds for garnish

Grate above ingredients and mix well together. Top with Cashew Cream*. Sprinkle lightly with caraway seeds.

Ethiopian Tomato Salad

$^1/_2$ red pepper, seeded and finely chopped
$^1/_2$ fresh chili, very finely chopped
$^1/_4$ cup red onions, chopped
$1^1/_2$ tbsp fresh lemon juice
$^1/_4$ tsp vegetable salt
3 ripe tomatoes, chopped

Combine in a bowl pepper, chili, onions, lemon juice and vegetable salt. Stir in tomatoes. Add more vegetable salt if necessary. Chill and serve cold.

Raw Pea Salad

1 cup raw peas
2 cups grated carrots
1 cup sunflower seeds
1 spring onion, chopped

Mix all ingredients together. Add Honey Dressing.*

Broccoli and Cabbage Toss

$^1/_2$ head small cabbage
$^1/_2$ head butter lettuce
$^1/_2$ head broccoli, broken into florets
2 tomatoes, thinly sliced

Mix all raw vegetables together. Serve with your favourite dressing.

Savoury Nut Balls (protein meal)

4 tbsp carrots, finely grated
1 cup ground almonds or cashews
2 tbsp cold-pressed olive oil
2 tbsp spring onions, finely chopped
$^1/_4$ tsp kelp or vegetable stock powder
$^1/_4$ tsp curry powder (no preservatives)

Mix all ingredients together. Add more oil if too dry. Roll into balls. Serve together with a French salad.

Tabouleh Salad (starch meal)

³/₄ cup bulgur wheat (cracked wheat)
2 tomatoes, finely chopped
1 cup red pepper, finely chopped
¹/₂ cup spring onions, chopped
¹/₂ cup parsley, finely chopped
1 avocado, finely chopped
vegetable salt to taste
freshly squeezed lemon juice to taste

Soak bulgur wheat in 1¹/₂ cups purified water for 2 hours. Drain off water, squeezing excess moisture out with a cloth. Combine bulgur wheat with remaining ingredients. Chill for approximately 2 hours before serving. Garnish with extra chopped parsley, red pepper and spring onion.

Italian Style Tomatoes

Tomatoes, cut into wedges
cold-pressed olive oil to cover tomatoes
origanum to taste
garlic seasoning (optional)
vegetable salt to taste

Mix tomatoes, oil and seasoning in bowl. Eat this with freshly baked health bread.

Avocado Shells

Cut avocado in half and remove seed. Scoop out centre and mash well. Gently mix with minneolas or naartjies or any subacid or acid fruits. Refill shells with this mixture. Delicious!

Sour Cream Coleslaw

¹/₂ head green cabbage
2 medium carrots
1 medium red pepper
¹/₂ – 1 cup cream, soured with lemon juice
1 tsp vegetable salt
¹/₄ tsp lemon pepper

Mix all raw vegetables in bowl. Lightly fold in soured cream. Season to taste. Serve immediately.

Citrus Delight

3 oranges, cut into cubes
2 granadillas
1 cup fresh grapefruit juice
1 avocado, mashed

Mix grapefruit juice with mashed avocado. Carefully blend in oranges and granadillas.

Pickled Mushroom Salad

3 cups button mushrooms, sliced
3 stalks celery, finely sliced
¹/₂ tsp chopped spring onions
2 tbsp fresh parsley, chopped
1 cup sprouts of your choice

Mix all ingredients together and prepare the following dressing:

Dressing

juice of 1 lemon
¹/₃ cup cold-pressed olive oil
¹/₂ medium carrot, coarsely grated
1 tsp health salt

Blend all above ingredients well and pour mixture over salad. Serve salad the following day.

Creamy Chickpea Casserole (protein meal)

chickpeas (garbanzo beans), sprouted
¹/₂ lemon
1 medium tomato
2 stalks celery (without leaves)
1 medium avocado pear

Pour sprouted chickpeas into salad bowl. Juice lemon and place in blender along with washed and quartered tomato and liquidise on high speed. Wash celery, and gradually add to blender. Add peeled, sliced avocado and liquidise until smooth and creamy. Pour avo-tomato sauce over sprouted chickpeas. Mix well and serve.

Avo-filled Red Pepper (protein meal)

1 red pepper
1 avocado pear
¹/₄ cup olives (in brine)
¹/₄ cup feta cheese
¹/₂ English cucumber

Scoop out and chop flesh of red pepper. Dice peeled cucumber, mash avocado and chop olives and feta cheese. Mix all ingredients together and fill red pepper.

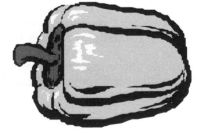

Salads with Cooked Ingredients

The following salads have some cooked ingredients. Don't forget to eat something raw beforehand, eg a small raw vegetable salad, and then make a meal of any of the following salads if you wish.

Cauliflower-Broccoli Salad

2 cups cauliflower
2 cups broccoli florets
2 cups torn romaine lettuce
2 cups torn butter lettuce
1 cup chopped tomato
1/2 cup chopped celery
1/2 cup chopped yellow pepper
1/4 cup chopped red pepper
1/4 cup shredded zucchini (baby marrows)
chopped parsley and spring onion to garnish

Steam cauliflower and broccoli until tender. Slice cauliflower and broccoli into small pieces. Combine all ingredients in large bowl. Toss with Nut Butter* or another dressing of your choice. Garnish with chopped parsley and spring onion.

Eggplant Salad

1 eggplant, peeled and diced
1/4 head broccoli, broken into florets
3 – 4 tomatoes, diced
1 stalk celery, diced
1 red pepper, sliced
1 avocado, diced
butter lettuce

Steam eggplant and broccoli. Allow to cool and mix with remaining diced ingredients. Serve on a bed of lettuce and drizzle with dressing of your choice.

Millet Salad (starch meal)

1 cup cooked millet
1/2 cup chopped red pepper
1/2 cup chopped celery
1/2 cup chopped carrots
1/4 cup chopped parsley
1/2 cup frozen peas, defrosted
1/2 cup lightly steamed broccoli florets

Combine above ingredients in large bowl. Mix well. Toss with your favourite dressing. Cover and chill for at least 2 hours.

Stuffed Tomatoes (starch meal)

6 butter lettuce leaves
6 large tomatoes
4 cups Millet Salad (see previous recipe)
parsley for garnish

Place lettuce leaves on dinner plate. Cut tomatoes into 6 sections, nearly to the base, and fill centre of each with Millet Salad. Garnish with parsley.

Asparagus Salad (protein meal)

1 punnet fresh asparagus
120 g raw pumpkin seeds
(or chopped almonds)
4 butter lettuce leaves
2 large or 4 small tomatoes
1 grapefruit (optional)
2 stalks celery, chopped

Cut off the very tough and discoloured bottom ends of asparagus stalks and steam the remainder for 2 – 3 minutes, taking care not to overcook. Cut up asparagus and place in large mixing bowl, along with pumpkin seeds (or chopped almonds). Wash, dry and break up butter lettuce into large bowl. Add cut up tomatoes and chopped celery. Juice 1/2 grapefruit and add to salad. Cut remaining 1/2 grapefruit into small chunks and add to salad.

Lentil and Tomato Salad (protein meal)

250 g lentils (soak for 1 hour and then throw soaking water away)
vegetable salt to taste
6 – 8 tbsp Tomato Dressing*
3 spring onions, finely sliced
1/2 red pepper, finely sliced
4 tomatoes, skinned and chopped
2 celery stalks, sliced
1 tbsp parsley, chopped

Place lentils in a pan and cover with purified water. Add a little salt and simmer gently for 30 – 40 minutes until softened. Drain well and mix with Tomato Dressing* while still warm. Leave to cool. Add remaining ingredients with seasoning to taste. Mix together thoroughly. Garnish with parsley.

Spinach and Mushroom Salad

(not an ideal combination)
½ bunch spinach
½ punnet mushrooms
alfalfa sprouts
½ red pepper
2 slices health bread
olive oil
¼ cup Parmesan cheese

Shred spinach, add sliced mushrooms, sliced red pepper and sprouts to salad bowl. Sprinkle Parmesan cheese over cubed bread, and brush with oil. Grill in oven till brown. Add to salad. Choose a dressing of your choice.

Simple Macaroni Salad (starch meal)

4 – 5 cups cooked whole-wheat pasta
1 cup fresh peas
1 red pepper, sliced
1 cup celery, chopped
1 English cucumber, peeled and diced
4 spring onions, chopped
1 cup carrots, grated
1 avocado pear, peeled and diced
½ cup fresh carrot juice

Add raw vegetable ingredients to cooked pasta except for last 2 ingredients. Purée avocado pear together with ½ cup fresh carrot juice. Use this as a dressing over vegetable pasta.

Dill-Pasta Salad (starch meal)

500 g pasta
2 tbsp fresh parsley, chopped
¼ cup finely diced celery
1½ cups chopped tomatoes
¼ – ⅓ cup cold-pressed oil
2 tbsp fresh dill, chopped
2 tbsp fresh basil
vegetable salt to taste

Cook pasta according to instructions on packet. Pour into colander. Run under cold water and drain thoroughly. Combine parsley, celery and tomatoes. Gently stir into pasta. Blend oil, fresh basil and dill in processor. Pour dressing over pasta salad. Season to taste. Mix well to combine all ingredients. Serves 3 – 4 . The more raw vegetables added to your pasta, the easier it will be to digest.

Avo-Brinjal Salad

1 brinjal (eggplant)
3 – 4 tomatoes
1 stalk celery
1 avocado
butter lettuce
sprouts

Peel and dice brinjal into bite-sized chunks. Steam till tender. Allow to cool. Dice tomatoes, and slice celery into very thin pieces. Peel avocado, remove seed, and chop coarsely. Mix above ingredients with brinjal. Put mixture on a bed of lettuce and garnish with sprouts.

Dips and Spreads

You can use a variety of sliced or whole raw vegetables, rice cakes or wedges of health bread with dips, or use the recipes as dressings (add more liquid) or as spreads on sandwiches.

Avid Avocado Dip

¼ cup juice of either carrots, or celery and/or red pepper or all 3)
2 avocados

Cut avocados in half and remove seed. Scoop out pulp and mash with a fork. Add vegetable juice and mix by hand until smooth. Pour mixture into small bowl and serve with fresh vegetables, rice cakes etc.

Raw Sweetcorn Dip (starch meal)

1 spring onion
2 yellow mealies
¼ head raw cauliflower
1 avocado
health salt to taste
¼ – ½ cup freshly squeezed lemon

Remove mealies from cob. Purée mealies, avocado, spring onion and cauliflower. Add 1/4 – 1/2 cup of freshly squeezed lemon juice. Season with health salt.

Cashew and Tomato Blend (protein meal)

1 cup cashews
4 fresh tomatoes
approximately 250 g tomato purée or purified water
2 tbsp fresh basil
2 stalks celery, finely chopped
1 spring onion, finely chopped
juice of 1 lemon
$^{1}/_{2}$ tsp marjoram
$^{1}/_{2}$ tsp vegetable salt
English cucumber and parsley to garnish

Blend cashews until a fine powder is formed. Add tomatoes, basil, lemon juice and seasoning to blender. Add tomato purée or purified water according to desired thickness. Blend well, add in celery and spring onion and mix by hand. Garnish with finely chopped English cucumber and chopped parsley. Serve with sliced raw vegetables of your choice.

Garlic-free Hummus

(not an ideal combination)
$1^{1}/_{2}$ cups chickpeas
2 lemons, juiced
$^{1}/_{4}$ cup finely minced parsley
$^{3}/_{4}$ cup tahini
purified water

Soak chickpeas for $1^{1}/_{2}$ hours in 5 cups of purified water. Throw soaking water away. Add fresh water and bring to boil. Reduce heat. Cover and simmer for 2 hours until tender. Drain and blend with remaining ingredients. Serve with raw vegetables. If you are just starting on this programme, you can use this recipe with rice cakes, or as a filling for pita bread.

Guacamole Dip

1 avocado
1 peeled cucumber, diced
1 stalk celery, diced
1 tomato, diced
1 tsp fresh lemon juice
seasoning to taste

Peel avocado and remove seed. Mash pulp with a fork. 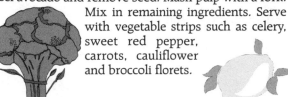 Mix in remaining ingredients. Serve with vegetable strips such as celery, sweet red pepper, carrots, cauliflower and broccoli florets.

Carrot and Sweet Potato Dip (starch meal)

$^{1}/_{2}$ medium cucumber, peeled and chopped
2 tbsp lemon juice
1 cup finely shredded carrots
1 cup finely grated sweet potato
$^{1}/_{2}$ cup coarsely ground macadamia nuts (low in protein)
$^{1}/_{2}$ tsp finely chopped fresh dill

Purée cucumber and lemon juice in blender. Add remainder of ingredients and blend well. Serve with raw vegetable crudités or bread sticks.

Cashew-Orange Dip (protein meal)

$^{1}/_{2}$ cup orange juice
$^{1}/_{2}$ cup cashews

Blend cashews first. Add orange juice until desired consistency is obtained. Serve with acid fruit or vegetable crudités. Delicious as a dressing.

Avocado and Tahini Dip (protein meal)

Blend 1 large avocado with $^{1}/_{4} - ^{1}/_{2}$ cup tahini and juice of 1 lemon. Add health salt to taste. Fold 2 tbsp of sesame seeds into mixture. Makes a crunchy dip.

Eggplant Pâté with Tahini Sauce (protein meal)

2 medium eggplants
100 ml tahini sauce
20 ml lemon juice (to taste)
5 ml cumin seeds
50 ml chopped parsley
2 spring onions

Bake eggplants at 160 °C for 45 minutes or till soft. Peel when cold. Squeeze flesh to remove as much liquid as possible. Blend with other ingredients till smooth. Season to taste with health salt. Chill and serve with crudités or add some purified water to make a salad dressing.

Cauliflower Dip

1 medium cauliflower
$^{1}/_{2}$ bunch parsley, chopped
1 bottle chili sauce (preservative free)

Steam cauliflower gently for 10 minutes. When cool, purée and add chopped parsley. Add chili sauce. Serve over baked potatoes, use as a dip with pita bread or vegetable crudités, or heat gently and serve over steamed vegetables, rice or millet. Can be used as a sandwich filling.

Eggplant Dip

1 eggplant
60 ml cold-pressed oil
1 tbsp fresh lemon juice
1 tbsp parsley, chopped
³/₄ cup cream
(Soya milk if lactose intolerant)
seasoning to taste

Steam or bake eggplant. When cool blend with remaining ingredients till smooth and add seasoning. Serve with crudités or as a dressing over lightly steamed vegetables or baked potato.

Dressings and Sauces

Traditional dressings tend to be full of oil, preservatives, spices, condiments, bacon bits, onions, vinegar, and added sugar, and I do not recommend that you eat them. You can, however, enjoy the following dressings to your heart's content. If the dressing is made with nuts, remember that it counts as your protein meal and you can only eat it with green vegetables. If it contains no nuts, you could use it with a starch meal and green vegetables. You won't go hungry.

Honey Dressing

2 tbsp raw honey
¹/₂ cup lemon juice
¹/₄ tsp lemon pepper
¹/₄ tsp mustard (optional)
1 tsp health salt
1 cup cold-pressed oil (any flavour)

Combine all ingredients in blender except oil. Add oil to blender a little at a time, until mixture is well blended. Serve over any salad.

Mushroom Dressing

¹/₂ – 1 punnet mushrooms
¹/₂ – ²/₃ cup cold-pressed olive oil
¹/₃ cup fresh lemon juice

Finely slice mushrooms. Blend lemon juice and cold-pressed olive oil. Add sliced mushrooms by hand to dressing. Add seasoning to taste. Pour over salad of your choice.

Mexican Pepper Mayonnaise (protein meal)

¹/₂ cup tahini
1 large lemon, squeezed
¹/₂ cup purified water
1 tbsp finely chopped spring onion
2 tbsp finely chopped red pepper
¹/₂ tsp mustard
¹/₄ tsp vegetable stock powder

Combine tahini and lemon juice in blender. Add water, a little at a time to get desired consistency. Add red pepper, spring onion, mustard and stock powder and blend well. Pour over a green salad.

Mustard Dressing

¹/₂ punnet mushrooms, finely sliced
1 spring onion, finely diced
2 tbsp cold-pressed olive oil
1 tbsp fresh lemon juice
1 tsp mustard (ready made)
1 tsp vegetable salt
¹/₂ tsp lemon pepper
¹/₂ tsp raw honey (optional)

Place all ingredients in blender and blend well. Keep in a glass bottle in the fridge. Always shake well before using. This is delicious over lightly steamed vegetables, eg broccoli or cauliflower.

Tahini Mayonnaise (protein meal)

1 cup tahini
1 cup purified water
1 tsp chopped spring onion
1 tsp vegetable salt
1/4 tsp garlic and herb seasoning
1/4 cup lemon juice

Blend above ingredients together. Pour over any salad of your choice.

Mustard Cream Salad Dressing

2 tbsp freshly squeezed lemon juice
1/4 cup cold-pressed olive oil
1/2 tsp thyme
1/4 tsp origanum
1 tbsp mild mustard (ready made)
1/2 cup sour cream

If using fresh cream add 1 tsp lemon juice to sour it. Blend lemon juice, olive oil and herbs together. Add mustard and sour cream and mix by hand. Pour over salad. Toss well to blend flavours. This is a good alternative to cheese or mayonnaise.

Cashew Cream (protein meal)

110 g raw cashews
purified water

Soak cashews for 4 – 24 hours in enough water to cover completely. Blend nuts together with water. Add lemon juice if desired. Add a little at a time to taste. Pour over lightly steamed neutral vegetables or use as a dressing over your favourite salad.

Soya Sauce Dressing

150 ml cold-pressed olive oil
1 tbsp soya sauce (MSG free)
1 – 4 tbsp fresh lemon juice (optional)
seasoning

Combine all ingredients. Taste first, before adding seasoning. Keeps well in a glass bottle in the fridge. Always shake well before serving.

Creamy Avocado Dressing

1 ripe avocado, peeled and mashed
1 cup soya milk
1 tbsp soya sauce
pinch origanum

Mix all ingredients together. Delicious over steamed broccoli. You can also use for other vegetables.

Mexican Guacamole

2 avocados
1 lemon or grapefruit
1/2 spring onion
kelp to taste
vegetable salt to taste
1/4 small red or green cabbage
1/4 small broccoli
2 stalks celery
fresh parsley
2 tomatoes

Mash avocados. Juice grapefruit or lemon. Blend juice, avocado, spring onion, kelp and vegetable salt in blender. Finely slice cabbage and celery. Chop broccoli, parsley and tomatoes. Add to avocado mixture and blend well. If you want to use as a filling for lettuce leaves, mix vegetables by hand. Use as a dip, or dressing, or as a spread on sandwiches.

Avocado-Orange Dressing

1 avocado
1/2 cup freshly squeezed orange juice
2 tbsp freshly squeezed lemon juice

Slice avocado in half, remove seed and scoop out avocado pulp. Place in blender with orange and lemon juice, and blend until smooth. Serve as a salad dressing or add to acid fruits. You can also add lettuce and/or celery to the acid fruits.

Carrot-Avocado Dressing

1 cup carrot juice
2 avocados

Blend carrot juice with avocados (add a little juice at a time so that you don't add too much). The amount of carrot juice required depends on whether you want a dip or a salad dressing. You can also add either chopped celery, beetroot, sweet potato, cucumber, red pepper, lettuce or cabbage to the carrot juice to give a different flavour. (If adding starch vegetables don't have with a protein meal.)

Avocado Dressing and Fresh Basil

1 large or 2 small avocados
1 – 2 tomatoes, sliced
purified water
fresh basil to taste

Cut avocados in half and remove seeds. Scoop out pulp and put in blender. Add sliced tomatoes, purified water and basil. Blend to desired consistency, retaining the pinkish colour.

Tomato-Avocado Dressing

1 large avocado with seed removed
1 large tomato, halved
1/2 red pepper, finely chopped
2 spring onions, finely chopped
1 tsp lemon juice
1 tsp vegetable salt

Scoop out avocado pulp and mash well. Blend 1/2 tomato, 1 spring onion and red pepper with lemon juice and seasoning. Add to mashed avocado and mix well. Add remaining finely chopped spring onion and tomato.

Carrot Juice Dressing (protein meal)

1/2 cup raw almonds (nuts or seeds of your choice)
1/2 cup fresh carrot juice

Using a blender or food processor, blend almonds first, then add carrot juice. Vary the amount of carrot juice according to the thickness of dressing required. Serve as a salad dressing, as a topping over steamed non-starchy vegetables, or as a dip for raw vegetables.

Beet Nut Dressing (protein meal)

1 cup almonds
1 cup raw beetroot
1 1/4 cups fresh carrot juice
4 tbsp freshly squeezed lemon juice

Peel beetroot and cut into small chunks. Grind almonds to fine powder in blender. Add chopped beetroot, carrot juice and lemon juice to blended almonds. Blend until smooth and creamy.

Cucumber-Celery Dressing

1 medium cucumber, peeled
2 small or 1 medium tomato
2 stalks celery

Chop all ingredients, place in blender and blend until smooth. Add avocado if desired.

Green Gravy

2 carrots, peeled and chopped
2 stalks celery, coarsely chopped
1 bunch spinach
2 medium tomatoes
1 tbsp fresh basil (optional)

Put all ingredients in blender or food processor and purée until finely blended.

Quick Barbeque Sauce

1/3 cup preservative-free tomato sauce (home-made if possible)
1/3 cup chutney (preservative free)
1/3 cup soya sauce

Blend all ingredients together. Keep in a container in the fridge. Serve over pasta with stir-fried vegetables.

Tomato Dressing

300 ml fresh tomato juice
1 tbsp fresh lemon juice
1 tbsp soya sauce
2 tbsp cold-pressed olive oil
vegetable salt to taste
lemon pepper to taste

Blend all ingredients well.

Creamy Tomato Dressing (protein meal)

2 tbsp raw, unsalted cashews
1 – 2 fresh tomatoes
purified water
1 lemon

Combine cashews and enough water in a blender to make a thick consistency. Add chopped tomatoes and blend till smooth. Squeeze sufficient juice from lemon to add a hint of flavour.

Cucumber-Nut Dressing (protein meal)

2 large cucumbers, peeled and diced
4 tbsp raw almonds or cashews
4 tbsp freshly squeezed lemon juice
fresh parsley, chopped (optional)
1 celery stalk

Blend nuts with cucumbers and enough purified water to achieve desired consistency. Add celery stalk and blend well. Add freshly squeezed lemon juice. Add chopped parsley for colour.

Tomato Basil Dressing

1 – 2 tomatoes
purified water
fresh basil
lemon juice

Blend tomatoes with water to desired consistency. Squeeze enough lemon juice to add a slight lemony flavour. Add sufficient chopped basil to impart a hint of its taste.

Italian Pesto

³/₄ cup pine nuts
1 handful fresh basil leaves (no stalks)
¹/₃ cup cold-pressed olive oil
2 tsp dried origanum
1 small garlic clove (optional)

Grind nuts in blender. Slowly add oil. Add basil, garlic and origanum. Blend well.

Soups – Cold (No Cooked Ingredients)

I have included some raw cold soups as well as heart-warming soups for wintery days and nights. Remember, always eat a raw side salad before you eat anything cooked.

Creamy Avocado-Cabbage Soup

1 head cabbage (use cabbage that is sweet)
3 avocados
parsley, alfalfa sprouts and red pepper for garnish

Juice cabbage. Peel avocados, remove seed and quarter. Put cabbage juice and avocado quarters into blender, and liquidise on high speed until creamy and smooth. Pour into soup bowls and garnish with a fresh sprig of parsley, alfalfa sprouts, and a red pepper ring or some diced red pepper. Serves six.

Gazpacho

6 ripe tomatoes
1 cucumber, peeled and chopped
¹/₂ cup diced celery
1 sweet red pepper, chopped
¹/₂ cup chopped parsley
3 tbsp fresh lemon juice
1 cup chopped chives (optional)

In food processor blend 3 ripe tomatoes, ¹/₂ cucumber, ¹/₂ sweet red pepper, ¹/₄ cup parsley, celery and lemon juice. In separate bowl, combine 3 chopped tomatoes, ¹/₂ cucumber, ¹/₂ sweet red pepper, ¹/₄ cup parsley, and chives. Add to blended mixture by hand. Chill and serve.

Carrot Soup

6 carrots
¹/₂ stalk celery
2 sprigs parsley
1 avocado

Scrub and prepare carrots for juicing. Juice 5 carrots and pour juice into blender. Wash celery and parsley, add to blender, and liquidise on high speed together with carrot juice. Halve avocado and remove seed. Add pulp to blender. Liquidise until smooth and creamy and pour into soup bowls. Grate remaining carrot. Stir into soup bowls and serve. A few lightly steamed peas may be mixed in, if desired. Excellent as a meal in itself or served with a vegetable salad. Serves 1.

Creamy Tomato Soup (protein meal)

8 red tomatoes
110 g cashews
2 red bell peppers
8 celery stalks
sprigs of parsley for garnish

Blend 7 tomatoes with cashews to make the soup. Dice red peppers, celery and remaining tomato. Pour soup over diced vegetables and garnish with sprigs of parsley.

Raw Beetroot Soup

2 cups finely grated beetroot
2 cups tomato purée
1 ripe avocado

Blend all ingredients in blender. Serve with small potatoes. Add sour cream/soya milk, if too thick.

126

Carrot-Avocado Soup

1 avocado
2 cups freshly juiced carrots
1/2 cup juiced celery
2 tbsp chopped tomato
2 tbsp chopped red pepper
2 tbsp chopped cauliflower
2 tbsp chopped celery

Blend avocado, carrots and celery juice in blender or food processor until creamy and smooth. Pour blended mixture into large soup bowl. Add chopped tomato, red pepper, cauliflower and celery. Serve immediately.

Chilled Avocado Dill Soup

2 large ripe avocados (Fuerte are best)
1 large English cucumber, peeled
2 spring onions
2 1/2 cups vegetable stock
3 – 4 tbsp freshly chopped dill
1/2 tsp raw honey
1/2 to 1 cup sour cream (use soya milk if lactose intolerant)
vegetable salt to taste
parsley for garnish

Blend all ingredients together. Mix in cream carefully by hand. Refrigerate for a few hours. Garnish with parsley.

Zucchini-Pea Soup

3 medium zucchini (baby marrows)
2 cups fresh peas
1 1/2 cups purified water
2 tbsp spring onions, diced
1/2 cup celery, diced
1 tsp fresh basil leaves, chopped

Grate raw zucchini to yield 3 1/2 cups. Blend zucchini, peas, diced spring onions, and purified water in blender until smooth. Use water as required, to obtain desired consistency. Pour into soup bowls. Mix in diced celery and chopped basil leaves. Serves two.

Soups – Hot (Cooked Ingredients)

Chunky Vegetable Soup

10 tomatoes, peeled and chopped
1/4 cup chopped onion
1/2 cup chopped zucchini (baby marrows)
1/2 cup sliced green beans
1/2 cup chopped celery
1/2 cup chopped broccoli
1/2 cup sliced cauliflower
1/2 cup chopped sweet red pepper
purified water

Place all ingredients in pot/saucepan. Add enough water to cover. Bring to boil. Reduce heat. Cover and cook for 5 to 10 minutes or until vegetables are tender (not too soft). Add seasoning to taste.

Broccoli-Zucchini Soup (protein meal)

1 small head broccoli
2 cups chopped zucchini
1 cup purified water
1/2 cup diced celery
1/2 small red pepper, diced
1/3 cup pine nuts
1 tsp origanum

Cut broccoli into florets. Steam for only 4 minutes. Blend broccoli, zucchini and water from steamed broccoli until smooth. Add more purified water if necessary. Pour into soup dishes. Mix in celery, pepper, and pine nuts. Sprinkle with origanum.

Broccoli Soup (protein meal)

1 large head broccoli
6 stalks celery
3 carrots
120 g sunflower seeds

Steam broccoli or use it raw or, if desired, use ½ steamed and ½ raw. Cut up broccoli and place in large mixing bowl. Juice celery and carrots, and place in blender, with sunflower seeds. Blend on high speed and pour into bowl with broccoli. Stir well.

Avocado Cauliflower Soup

3 cups cauliflower florets
1 large avocado
1 cup tepid purified water
1 cup alfalfa sprouts
1 tsp freshly chopped basil
grated carrot/fresh green peas
and mealies for garnish

Steam cauliflower for 5 minutes. Allow to cool. Seed avocado and cut into chunks. Place cooled cauliflower and avocado in blender with tepid purified water. Add more water if necessary. Blend until smooth. Mix in sprouts and basil. Pour into soup dishes and garnish with grated carrot, fresh green peas, and corn off the cob.

Golden Parsnip Soup

6 small butternuts
4 – 6 parsnips
¼ – ½ cup purified water
¼ cup parsley
¼ cup basil, chopped

Wash butternuts and peel. Cut parsnips and butternuts into small cubes for steaming. Steam cubed butternuts in one pan and parsnips in another, since they require different steaming times. Steam until soft. Place steamed butternut cubes together with parsley and basil in a blender with enough purified water to blend well. Add steamed parsnip cubes, and more purified water if necessary. Blend until smooth. This soup is unbelievably sweet. You could eat this either as a soup or as a sauce over rice, millet or other steamed vegetables. It is delicious!

Cauliflower-Corn Soup (starch meal)

1 small cauliflower broken into florets
¼ cup purified water
1 medium parsnip, grated
2 yellow mealies
½ tsp chopped dill (fresh)
¼ cup chopped watercress for garnish

Steam cauliflower for 5 minutes. Purée cauliflower, grated parsnip and water from steamed cauliflower in blender until smooth. Add more purified water if necessary. Remove from blender. Add mealies and dill. Garnish with watercress. Chill if desired.

Asparagus Soup

(not an ideal combination – but delicious!)
1 cup purified water
1 punnet asparagus
1 cup grated sweet potato
½ cup celery, finely diced
⅓ cup watercress, chopped
½ cup walnuts, chopped (for garnish)

Cut off woody part of asparagus and slice into 25 cm pieces. Steam for 4 minutes. Use steaming water to purée sweet potato and celery in blender. Add asparagus and blend again. Transfer to large soup bowl. Season lightly. Add in watercress. Garnish with chopped walnuts.

Sweet Potato Soup (starch meal)

6 cups sweet potatoes, peeled and chopped
4 – 5 cups purified water
1 cup celery, diced
2 cups yellow mealies cut off the cob
parsley for garnish

Place sweet potatoes, purified water, celery and seasoning in covered soup pot. Simmer over low heat until sweet potatoes are tender. Remove celery and sweet potatoes from stock and blend in food processor. Add yellow mealies to stock. Cook for another 10 minutes. Add blended sweet potato and celery to stock and blend until soup is smooth. Heat and serve garnished with parsley. The thickness of the soup depends on the ratio of water to sweet potatoes. You might have to add more purified water.

Minestrone Soup with Rice (starch meal)

1 packet soup greens, finely diced
1 tin tomatoes, crushed with juice (preservative free)
³/₄ medium cabbage, shredded
1 cup short grain brown rice
1 – 2 tsp vegetable salt
2 – 3 tsp vegetable stock powder
1 – 2 litres purified water
parsley and spring onion for garnish

Place all ingredients in large pot and bring to boil. Lower heat and simmer gently for about 45 minutes or until rice is tender. Adjust seasoning if necessary. Serve in warmed soup bowls, sprinkled with finely chopped parsley, and spring onion.

Curried Pumpkin Soup

2 medium leeks, finely chopped
2 cups pumpkin or butternut, cubed
3 cups purified water
¹/₂ punnet mushrooms, sliced
¹/₂ tsp ground cumin
¹/₂ tsp coriander
¹/₂ tsp cinnamon
¹/₂ tsp ground ginger
¹/₄ tsp mustard (ready-made)
2 tsp vegetable stock powder
juice of ¹/₂ lemon
chopped parsley for garnish

"Stir-fry" leeks, pumpkin/butternut and mushrooms in purified, boiling water until soft. Add seasoning and cook for another 5 minutes. Place in blender and blend thoroughly. Heat before serving. Add freshly squeezed lemon juice and garnish with chopped parsley.

Lettuce Soup (starch meal)

leaves from 1 lettuce
1 carrot, diced
¹/₂ leek, diced
2 cubed potatoes to thicken (optional)
1 – 2 tsp vegetable stock powder dissolved in 1 cup purified water
¹/₂ tsp nutmeg
parsley, finely chopped
4 tbsp cream, soured with lemon juice
seasoning to taste
parsley for garnish

Bring above ingredients (except for cream) to boil and simmer for 20 – 30 minutes. Just before serving, blend together with sour cream. Garnish with parsley and serve.

Steamed Vegetables and Cooked Grains

HOW TO COOK GRAINS:

Always add 1 tsp vegetable salt/1 tsp vegetable paste/2 tsp vegetable stock powder/vegetable soup cubes without MSG to 1 cup of grain of your choice. You can add more seasoning if your taste buds want a saltier taste.

Millet

1 cup millet to 3 – 4 cups purified water
seasoning

Place millet, purified water and seasoning in pot and bring to boil. Simmer gently with lid on for approximately 20 minutes or until soft. Switch off stove and let pot stand with lid on for a further 20 minutes.

Barley

1 cup barley to 3 cups purified water

Cook the same as millet.

Basmati Rice

1 cup rice to 3 cups purified water

Cook the same as millet. Fluff up with fork.

Couscous (pre-cooked form of pasta)

1 cup couscous to 1½ cups hot purified water

Pour hot water over couscous and leave for approximately 10 minutes till water has been absorbed. Steam for 5 – 10 minutes and toss with fork to make it fluffy.

Pasta or Rice Noodles

Boil 1 packet egg-free pasta or rice noodles for approximately 25 minutes or until tender. Pour over any sauce of your choice before serving.

Hot Vegetarian Dishes with Sauces

Tomato and Chili Sauce

2 medium onions, finely chopped
3 tins tomatoes, coarsely chopped (do not drain)
130 g tomato paste
¾ tbsp dried origanum
¾ tbsp dried basil
1 bay leaf
2 tsp raw honey
½ tbsp vegetable salt or more to taste
1 dried, chopped chili for garnish

"Stir-fry" onions in water until transparent. Add rest of ingredients. Bring to boil. Reduce to low heat. Simmer uncovered for 1 hour, stirring occasionally. Add 1 dried chopped chili at the end. Serve over pasta with lightly steamed spinach on top, or use as a sauce over polenta. It is also delicious as a topping for baked butternut.

Vegetable Sauce (starch meal)

1 big zucchini (baby marrow) cut into small chunks
1 sweet potato
1 potato

Bake potato and sweet potato in oven for 45 minutes to 1 hour, or until done. Steam zucchini for 10 – 15 minutes or until a fork will easily poke through the zucchini. Put sweet potato, zucchini and potato in blender with some water from steamed zucchini and blend till smooth. You may have to aid the blending process by stirring the mixture with a spoon. You can thin the sauce by adding more purified water. Be sure to turn the blender off while you do this. Pour blended mixture over cooked grains, steamed vegetables, baked potatoes, steamed mealies or steamed/baked sweet potatoes.

Brown Rice Salad (starch meal)

250 g brown rice
3 spring onions, finely chopped (optional)
1 red pepper, seeded and diced
1/2 head medium cabbage, finely diced
2 yellow mealies, lightly steamed (remove kernels from cob)
3 tbsp parsley, chopped
3 celery stalks, diced
sprouts to garnish
8 tbsp Soya Sauce Dressing*(add more if necessary)

Bring brown rice to boil (1 part brown rice to 2 parts purified water). Simmer for 30 minutes or until water has been absorbed. Transfer rice to bowl and allow to cool. Add remaining ingredients. Toss thoroughly with dressing, garnish with sprouts and serve immediately.

Steamed Rice Casserole (starch meal)

2 cups brown rice
2 cups purified water
6 carrots
250 g Brussels sprouts
3 stalks celery

Bring water to boil. Add rice, cover and lower heat. Simmer for approximately 20 minutes, or until all water has evaporated. While rice is cooking, wash carrots and celery and slice into small pieces. Cut off ends of Brussels sprouts and peel off outer layers. Steam vegetables until soft. Do not overcook! When both rice and vegetables are cooked, mix together in casserole dish and serve hot. This dish is delicious by itself, or you can serve together with your favourite dressing. Serves 2.

Wheat Germ Stuffing

4 heaped tbsp wheat germ
2 tbsp fresh parsley, chopped
4 spring onions, diced
2 mushrooms, sliced
4 fresh tomatoes, chopped
juice of 1/2 lemon
1/2 tsp origanum
2 tbsp cold-pressed oil
sufficient cabbage leaves or vine leaves for stuffing (pour boiling water over cabbage leaves to soften)

Mix all ingredients together. Fill vine leaves or cabbage leaves with stuffing and roll up. Secure with toothpicks. Top with fresh chopped tomatoes. Place in casserole dish. Cover and bake at 180 °C for 30 minutes. Garnish with freshly chopped parsley.

Baked Butternut (protein meal)

1 whole butternut
unsalted butter
chopped fresh or dried thyme
chopped parsley
Parmesan cheese
pumpkin seeds

Halve butternut lengthwise and remove pips. Place in oven dish, cut side up. Sprinkle with thyme and parsley. Bake at 180 °C for approximately 50 minutes. Remove from oven, add blob of butter, pumpkin seeds and sprinkling of Parmesan cheese.

Baked Sweet Potato Crescents (starch meal)

2 medium sweet potatoes
whole-wheat flour (rice flour if gluten intolerant)
40 g unsalted butter
1/2 tsp paprika
1/2 tsp celery salt
1/2 tsp dried origanum

Peel sweet potatoes, and cut into 1 cm slices. Toss crescents in flour and shake away excess flour. Place a single layer on a lightly greased oven tray. Melt butter over low heat in small saucepan. Stir in paprika, celery salt and origanum. Brush mixture over sweet potatoes. Bake uncovered in moderate oven for about 45 minutes or until soft.

Steamed Artichoke Platter

1 artichoke
1/2 sweet red pepper
1/4 cup snow peas
6 Brussels sprouts
4 broccoli florets
4 cauliflower florets
4 baby carrots

Steam artichoke over boiling water for approximately 30 minutes. Cool when cooked. While artichoke is cooking, steam Brussels sprouts in another pan. When Brussels sprouts are half-cooked, add broccoli and cauliflower and steam for about 5 – 7 additional minutes. Do not overcook! When artichoke is cool enough to handle, cut out centre of artichoke and fill with Tahini Mayonnaise* and steamed vegetables. Arrange fresh carrots, snow peas, and strips of sweet red pepper around centre. This is a fabulous main dish. Serves 1.

Polenta Burgers (starch meal)

1½ cups cooked polenta
1 cup mashed potatoes (leave skins on)
1 carrot, grated
2 celery stalks, grated
1 spring onion, chopped
1 tbsp soya sauce (MSG free)
1 tbsp olive oil (cold pressed)
1 tsp vegetable stock powder
2 tbsp tomato purée
vegetable salt to taste
2 tsp curry powder (optional)

Combine all ingredients and make into patties. Place on lightly oiled oven tray. Grill both sides until golden brown. Top with a home-made tomato sauce and serve with a variety of steamed vegetables. Can also be served on a whole-wheat roll with lettuce and tomato.

Spanish Sauce

4 – 5 medium tomatoes, peeled and chopped
1 red pepper, diced
3 spring onions, diced
1 small can tomato juice (preservative free)
1 cup celery, diced
1 tbsp fresh parsley, chopped (and a bit extra to garnish)

Combine all ingredients and cook on low heat for 20 – 30 minutes, adding ¼ cup purified water if needed. Serve over Italian polenta, sprinkled with chopped parsley. Can also serve over any grain of your choice.

Stuffed Butternut

3 small butternuts
2¼ cups purified water
1 cup brown rice
3 ears of corn, steamed (when cool, slice kernels off cob)
2 stalks celery, diced
small handful of fresh parsley, finely chopped
2 avocados, mashed
½ cup celery juice
½ cup red pepper juice

With a very sharp knife and a strong, steady hand, halve butternuts lengthwise and scrape out seeds and stringy fibre. Bake at 180 – 200 °C for 45 minutes to 1 hour, until tender. Bring purified water to boil. Add brown rice, cover and simmer for 45 minutes to 1 hour on very low heat. When rice is cooked, combine with other vegetables (except avocados and vegetable juices) and fill butternuts. Heat through. When ready to serve, add mashed avocados mixed with vegetable juices as a topping. Serves 6.

Stir-fry Marinade

¼ cup cold-pressed olive oil
2 tbsp fresh lemon juice
2 tbsp soya sauce
½ tsp dried rosemary
2 tsp dried origanum
1 tsp dried basil

Marinade must be made beforehand. Place your choice of vegetables in the marinade for a couple of hours. Remove vegetables from marinade and "stir-fry" vegetables in hot pan with a touch of boiling water. Add remaining marinade when vegetables are ready to be served. Can also use this marinade to pour over hot brown rice.

Mushroom Moussaka (protein meal)

1 punnet mushrooms, sliced
2 medium eggplants, sliced into rings
1 – 2 cups tomato purée
250 ml fresh cream
½ cup parsley, chopped
1 cup wheat germ
1 tsp vegetable stock powder dissolved in 1 cup purified water
1 tsp vegetable salt
1 tsp origanum
2 tbsp Parmesan cheese

Steam eggplants for 15 minutes. Combine wheat germ, Parmesan and parsley. In separate bowl, combine tomato purée, origanum, stock powder and salt. Layer eggplant, mushrooms and wheat germ mix in an oven dish (leave some wheat germ mix for topping). Finally, pour over tomato purée mix, and then cream. Top lightly with wheat germ mix. Bake at 180 °C for approximately 40 minutes. **Wheat germ** is high in vitamin E and the B-complex vitamins. It can be used in place of breadcrumbs. The oil in wheat germ can become rancid quickly so it should be kept in the fridge in an airtight container.

Potato Pancakes (starch meal)

500 g hot mashed potatoes (with skins)
freshly ground nutmeg
½ cup whole-wheat flour (rice flour if gluten intolerant)
1 tsp cold-pressed oil (to grease baking sheet)
vegetable salt to taste

Mix potatoes and flour and add seasoning. Shape into small flat cakes. Bake on oiled baking sheet at 180 °C for 10 minutes on each side. Serves 4.

Cauliflower-Cashew Dish (protein meal)

1 head cauliflower, broken into florets
120 g cashew nuts
purified water
alfalfa sprouts
2 broccoli florets

Steam the cauliflower and broccoli until tender. Place in serving dish with alfalfa sprouts. In separate bowl, blend cashews with enough purified water to make a dressing. Pour mixture over cauliflower and broccoli and serve.

Spinach Herb Rice (starch meal)

2 cups brown rice
4 cups purified water
3 – 4 cups mushrooms, sliced
½ bunch baby spinach, chopped
½ tsp basil, chopped
¼ tsp origanum
½ tsp vegetable stock powder

Bring water to boil. Add all ingredients except spinach. Cover and simmer for approximately 30 minutes, adding spinach for last 10 minutes. Serve immediately.

Stuffed Peppers

4 large sweet peppers (red or yellow) with tops and seeds removed
1 cup brown rice
½ cup chopped onions
½ cup chopped carrots
½ cup chopped celery
½ cup chopped zucchini (baby marrows)
1 tsp each of dried origanum, thyme, basil and parsley
2 cups vegetable stock
1 cup chopped, peeled tomatoes

Steam pepper cases for 5 minutes. Set aside. Cook brown rice in another pot. Steam onion, carrots, celery and zucchini until tender. Add steamed vegetables to cooked rice. Add vegetable stock, tomatoes, origanum, thyme, basil, and parsley. Bring to boil. Reduce heat. Cover and simmer for 5 minutes. Fill pepper cases with rice and vegetable mixture. Put filled peppers in an 8-inch baking dish. Add a small amount of purified water to the bottom of the dish. Bake uncovered at 175 °C for 10 – 15 minutes. Serve immediately.

Cottage Pie aux Courgettes (baby marrows)

4 spring onions, sliced
750 g baby marrows, sliced
2 stalks celery, finely sliced
6 tomatoes, skinned and chopped
1 – 2 tbsp tomato purée
vegetable salt
1 tsp vegetable stock powder
750 g potatoes

Heat a little purified water in a pan, and add 2 of the spring onions, the celery and baby marrows. "Stir-fry" for 10 minutes stirring occasionally. Add tomatoes, tomato purée and seasoning. Add stock powder dissolved in a bit of boiling water. Cover and simmer for 5 minutes then turn into an ovenproof dish. Meanwhile steam potatoes. When ready, mash leaving skin on, and add purified water to make a creamy consistency. Add remaining 2 spring onions to mashed potatoes and salt to taste. Spread potato mixture over baby marrow mixture until it covers it completely. Bake at 200 °C for 30 minutes or until golden brown. Serve immediately as a main dish with steamed vegetables.

Chop Suey

1 packet snow peas
¼ head cabbage
1 red or yellow pepper
1 young baby marrow
2 cups cauliflower florets
1 tsp cumin seeds (optional)

Steam vegetables till tender. When ready to serve, add cumin seeds and mix well. Add extra seasoning/dressing of your choice.

Easy Vegetable Curry (starch meal)

4 spring onions, chopped
3 large carrots, sliced
1 cup peas
1 stalk celery, sliced
1 medium turnip, sliced
2 large potatoes, diced
1 – 2 tsp vegetable stock powder
2 tsp mild curry powder
1½ cups purified water
desiccated coconut

"Stir fry" onions in a touch of water. Add curry and vegetable stock powder and stir for a few minutes. Add remaining vegetables and water. Bring to boil, then simmer slowly for 20 – 30 minutes. Dust with coconut and serve.

Baked Polenta (starch meal)

1 cup polenta
2½ cups purified water
1 tsp vegetable stock powder

Bring water to boil, add stock powder and polenta. Keep stirring with a wooden spoon until mixture is boiling, then turn heat down. Simmer for about 30 minutes, stirring regularly. The polenta is ready when the mixture acquires an elastic texture and tears away from sides of pan. Spoon mixture onto lightly oiled baking sheet and grill until brown, turning once.

Basmati Rice with Zucchini Sauce (starch meal)

1 punnet zucchini, sliced
2 cups basmati rice
4 cups water
1 tsp vegetable salt
1 tsp origanum
2 tsp vegetable stock powder

Add rice to water together with vegetable salt. Bring to boil. Stir briefly. Cover tightly and simmer for 15 minutes over low heat. Remove lid. Fluff rice with fork and keep warm. "Stir fry" sliced zucchini in a touch of boiling water. Add 1 tsp origanum and 2 tsp vegetable stock powder to 1 cup water. Add to zucchini. Bring to boil stirring constantly. Reduce heat, cover and simmer for 5 – 10 minutes until zucchini is tender. Spoon over hot basmati rice.

Vegetable Rice Casserole (starch meal)

3 cups brown rice, cooked
1 cup peas
2 cups grated carrots
2 cups green beans, sliced
1 cup mealies (off the cob)
2 cups vegetable stock (use 2 dessert spoons vegetable stock powder to 2 cups water)
1 tsp thyme (optional)

Combine rice, vegetables, and seasoning in medium mixing bowl. Add vegetable stock. Place mixture in covered casserole dish or loaf pan (if you cover dish, it will take less time to cook). Bake at 175 °C for 25 minutes or until all vegetables are tender.

Baked Potatoes with Cream and Mushroom Sauce (starch meal)

2 potatoes
1 punnet button mushrooms
1 tsp whole-wheat flour (rice flour if gluten intolerant)
1 tsp paprika
1 tsp vegetable salt
½ cup sour cream
parsley for garnish

Bake potatoes, set aside and keep warm. Slice mushrooms and "stir-fry" in water for a few minutes. Sprinkle with flour and seasoning and cook a further 3 minutes. Add sour cream and cook until thickened. Cut a deep cross in the centre of each potato. Press the sides together gently to open the cross. Add sour cream mixture and sprinkle with parsley. This sauce is also delicious served with pasta.

Millet Casserole (starch meal)

1 cup millet
1 cup spring onion, diced
⅓ cup red pepper, diced
4 cups purified water
4 tbsp parsley, chopped
1 cup mushrooms, sliced
½ cup celery, diced
1 cup carrots, diced
3 tbsp soya sauce
2 tbsp fresh basil
2 tbsp fresh origanum

Mix all ingredients well. Place in large casserole dish. Bake slowly at 160 °C.

Millet Casserole with Butternut Sauce (starch meal)

2 large carrots
½ butternut
½ small onion (optional)
vegetable salt to taste
1 cup purified water
1 cup millet

Cut carrots into small pieces and steam with butternut until tender. Put carrots, butternut, water, and chopped onion into blender. Blend, then add seasoning to taste. Combine uncooked millet with carrot-butternut sauce in covered casserole dish. Bake in oven for 1½ hours at 160 °C.

Pasta Casserole with Spanish Sauce (starch meal)

1 packet pasta of your choice
4 cups purified water
½ cup sliced cauliflower
½ cup chopped celery
½ cup chopped sweet red peppers
1 cup broccoli florets
Spanish Sauce*

Bring water to boil. Add pasta and cook until soft. Lightly steam cauliflower, broccoli, celery and sweet peppers. Mix vegetables with cooked pasta. Spoon over Spanish Sauce*. Heat and serve.

Baby Marrow Curry

1 punnet baby marrows, cubed
1 tsp mustard seeds (or cumin seeds)
½ tsp lemon pepper
1 tsp spring onion, chopped
100 ml purified water
1 tbsp curry powder
chopped parsley for garnish

Steam marrows lightly. Heat pan and add a little water. "Stir-fry" mustard seeds, lemon pepper, spring onions and curry powder in a little water. Add marrows and some purified water. Cook gently until heated through. Delicious over hot brown rice. Garnish with chopped parsley.

Corn Casserole (starch meal)

6 yellow mealies
2 avocados
3 – 4 turnips
2 stalks celery
sprouts (optional)
lettuce (optional)

Steam mealies and allow to cool. Quarter and peel avocados. Peel and slice turnips. Put avocados and turnips through blender. Remove corn from cob and keep warm. Wash and dice celery and add to corn. Add avocado and turnip mixture to celery and corn and mix thoroughly. Do this only when ready to serve. Serves 2. This is a very chewy casserole dish and can be served in a variety of ways – on a thick bed of sprouts or on big lettuce leaves etc.

Eggplant Patties

1 small eggplant, sliced
2 stalks celery
1 red pepper
1 peeled onion
120 g ground pecans

Steam eggplant. When ready allow to cool. Peel and mash well. Add other vegetables and ground nuts. Make into patties and put on oiled baking sheet. Bake for 30 minutes at 175 °C.

Potato Casserole (starch meal)

3 celery stalks
1 large onion
2 large carrots
3 large potatoes (do not peel)
1 peeled turnip
fresh parsley for garnish

Wash and dice vegetables, and place in steamer. Add 2 – 3 cups purified water to steamer and steam until vegetables are soft. Put all steamed vegetables in food processor and blend till smooth. Put on oiled baking tray, and press down well. Decorate top with fork. Place in an oven for just a few minutes to brown the top. Sprinkle with fresh parsley before serving.

Potato Avocado Blend (starch meal)

4 potatoes cut into cubes
1 baby marrow, cut into cubes
1 beetroot, sliced
2 mealies (kernels off the cob)
1 avocado, mashed
½ cup red pepper, chopped
½ cup carrot, grated
½ cup celery, chopped
2 spring onions, finely diced
seasoning of your choice

First steam potatoes and beetroot for approximately 30 minutes then steam baby marrow, mealies and spring onions for about 10 minutes. Mix celery, pepper and carrot with mashed avocado. Add seasoning. Add avocado mixture to steamed vegetables when ready to serve. (Never heat avocados.)

Legumes – Pulses

HOW TO COOK LEGUMES

Soak in purified water for several hours or overnight in a cool place before cooking (always throw away the soaking water). Soaking softens the legumes and cuts down on the cooking time considerably as well as breaking down some of the starches, thus making them more digestible. After soaking, put in a pot, and add 3 times as much purified water as legumes. Bring to the boil and simmer until tender.

Cooked Legume Dishes

Falafel Balls (transitional)

1 cup chickpeas (garbanzo beans) or 1 cup soya beans soaked overnight
(you could also use 1 cup lentils, soaked for 1/2 hour)
2 large onions
4 – 6 carrots
bunch parsley
small bunch celery
1 cup whole-wheat flour
1/4 cup purified water
vegetable salt to taste
1 tbsp tahini

Blend all vegetables together in food processor. When legumes are cooked, pour off water and blend together with vegetables. Add flour, water, and seasoning. Blend again. Make into balls. You can freeze these balls if you do not want to cook them straightaway. If you want to eat them immediately, lightly oil baking tray, and brush balls with a touch of cold-pressed oil. Bake at 180 °C for approximately 15 minutes or until golden brown. Serve with health or pita bread, and finely chopped salad; drizzle with tahini.

Variation 1

Add coriander and thyme to mixture before making into balls (season as required).

Variation 2

Put balls in casserole dish and pour Barbeque Sauce* over. Bake covered at 180 °C for 20 minutes.

Dahl Stew (protein meal)

1/2 – 1 cup green lentils
1 large cauliflower broken into florets
3 large carrots cut into chunky pieces
1 large onion or bunch spring onions, finely chopped
1 sweet red pepper, chopped
1 sweet yellow pepper, chopped
1 large parsnip cut into pieces
1 cup broccoli florets
pinch of turmeric
2 tbsp vegetable stock powder
2 tsp ground cumin
2 tbsp fresh ginger, finely chopped
1 – 2 tsp mild curry powder
chopped parsley for garnish

Prepare lentils for cooking. Add 1 tbsp stock powder to purified water before cooking lentils. When soft, purée in food processor. "Stir-fry" onion in water with ginger and remaining 1 tbsp stock powder. When soft, add all vegetables except for broccoli. Add remaining seasoning. Simmer until cooked. Add puréed legume mixture to vegetables. Add broccoli and allow to heat through. Garnish with chopped parsley. Serve immediately.

Brown Rice and Lentils (transitional)

1 cup brown rice
1/2 cup brown or green lentils
1 – 2 tsp vegetable salt
cold-pressed sunflower oil or butter to taste

Soak lentils for 1/2 hour in purified water. Throw soaking water away. Combine with rice and salt. Put in pot and add approximately 4 cups of purified water. Bring to boil and simmer until water has evaporated (20 – 30 minutes). Add oil or butter just before serving.

Lentil Casserole (protein meal)

1 cup lentils, soaked
4 stalks celery with leaves
2 sprigs fresh chopped parsley
1 small sweet red pepper, diced
2 cups purified water
seasoning of your choice

Steam lentils for approximately 15 minutes or until almost tender. Add other ingredients and steam for a further 5 minutes. Do not overcook. Add seasoning. You can also add curry powder (1 – 2 tsp – taste first).

Soups with Legumes

Lentil Vegetable Soup (transitional)

2 cups green lentils
10 cups purified water
½ cup chopped carrots
½ cup chopped celery
½ cup chopped green pepper (red or yellow preferred)
½ cup sliced green beans
½ cup sliced cauliflower
½ cup chopped broccoli
½ cup millet
½ cup chopped onions (optional)
3 cloves garlic, crushed (optional)

Soak lentils for 3 hours or overnight. Throw soaking water away. Place lentils in fresh purified water and bring to boil. When water is boiling, reduce heat. Cover and simmer until lentils are completely tender. Add carrots, celery, green, red or yellow pepper, green beans, cauliflower, broccoli, millet, onions and garlic to cooked lentils. Bring to boil again. Reduce heat. Cover and simmer until all vegetables and millet are tender. This definitely could be served as a meal on its own. Remember to eat raw salad first.

Minestrone Soup (transitional)

1 cup chickpeas (garbanzo beans)
10 cups purified water
½ cup whole-wheat pasta
2 cups fresh chopped tomatoes
1 cup chopped onions
1 cup chopped celery
1 cup grated carrots
1 cup chopped zucchini (baby marrows)
1 cup chopped sweet peppers (red or yellow)
1 cup chopped parsley
1 tbsp basil
1 tbsp origanum

Soak chickpeas overnight in just enough water to cover them. Throw soaking water away. Bring chickpeas and 10 cups of purified water to boil. Reduce heat. Cover and simmer for 3 – 4 hours until chickpeas are tender. Add onions, celery, carrots, zucchini, sweet peppers, whole-wheat pasta, basil and origanum. Bring to boil again. Reduce heat. Cover and simmer for 30 minutes or until pasta is soft. Blend only 1 cup of chopped tomatoes. Add puréed tomatoes and remaining 1 cup of chopped tomatoes to soup pot. Simmer for another 15 minutes. Top with parsley. This is definitely a delicious meal on its own. Remember your raw salad first.

Split Pea Soup (protein meal)

2 cups split peas
1½ cups purified water
4 tbsp tahini

Soak split peas in purified water overnight. Throw soaking water away. Place peas and fresh water in pot. Bring to boil. Cover tightly, lower heat, and simmer for approximately 12 – 15 minutes. Add more water if necessary, and cook until peas are soft. Place peas, an additional ½ cup of water, and tahini in blender. Blend until smooth. This makes a hearty soup, a delicious sauce or a tasty dip. You can substitute other legumes for the peas, eg lentils.

Tofu

Tofu is made from soya beans. It is also known as soya bean curd, and is available at most health stores. If you are lactose intolerant, tofu is the answer. You can use it in place of cheese. As it is high in both starch and protein, you should have it with neutral vegetables. Those who are just starting out on my programme, could use tofu as a spread on bread. I am not concerned with food combining when it comes to children. This is really a wonderful food to give them. Always keep tofu covered in water in the fridge and change the water every day. It will keep in the fridge for up to 4 weeks. To prepare tofu, drain and rinse well under cold purified water. Split tofu into 2 parts, press out any excess water with paper towels and pat dry. This is very important. The tofu is now ready to use. You can freeze tofu. This changes its texture, but not its nutrient value.

Tofu Cubes (variations)

- Cut tofu into cubes. Put into a covered glass dish. Season with origanum, health salt or soya sauce (start with 1 tsp and taste – you can add more if necessary). Cover with cold-pressed olive oil and leave in the fridge to marinate.
- Cube tofu. Add lemon juice to taste and 1 tsp of raw honey, 1 tsp of soya sauce and 1 tsp of origanum. You can blend the ingredients and use as a dressing over vegetables, as a dip with vegetable crudités, or as a spread on health bread. Not an ideal combination, but acceptable for those on a transitional pattern of eating.

Tofu Dip

1 tub tofu
1 tsp health salt
1 tsp garlic and herb seasoning
$^1/_3$ cup cold-pressed oil
$^1/_4$ cup fresh basil, chopped

Blend all ingredients together until thick and smooth. You can use this in a lasagne dish in place of ricotta if lactose intolerant. Makes $2^1/_2$ – 3 cups.

Tasty Tofu Strips

Slice tofu into thick strips. Sprinkle both sides with tamari sauce (don't add too much). Place on lightly oiled baking sheet. Bake at 175 °C for 20 minutes.

Tofu Mayonnaise

1 cup tofu
$^1/_4$ cup purified water
1 tbsp lemon juice
1 tbsp tahini
$^1/_4$ cup chopped fresh dill
1 tsp cucumber, chopped
1 tsp vegetable salt
1 sprig dill for garnish

Combine tofu, water, lemon juice, salt and tahini in blender. Mix in chopped dill, and cucumber. Chill before serving. Toss with shredded cabbage or any salad of your choice. Garnish with a sprig of dill.

Tofu Salad Dressing

120 g tofu
juice of $^1/_2$ lemon
4 – 6 tbsp cold-pressed oil
1 tomato, chopped
2 tbsp parsley, chopped

Blend all ingredients well. Season with vegetable salt. Makes $1^1/_2$ cups.

Tofu Spinach Dip

300 g tofu
1 cup cooked spinach
1 tbsp lemon juice
2 tbsp spring onion, chopped
1 tsp garlic and herb seasoning
1 tsp health salt

Purée all ingredients. Serve with pita bread (transitional) or vegetable crudités.

Tofu Falafel (transitional)

2 cups uncooked brown rice
2 tbsp tamari sauce
1 kg tofu, mashed
4 cups purified water
2 cups ground almonds
2 cups wheat germ

Cook rice in water till soft (45 minutes). Mix with other ingredients and make into small, flattened patties. Grill till brown on both sides and serve in pita bread with cucumber, lettuce, grated carrots and sprouts.

Vegetable Chow Mein (transitional)

3 cups celery cut into thin diagonal slices
2 cups onions, thinly sliced
2 cups mung bean sprouts
1 cup mushrooms, sliced
1 cup tofu, cubed
$\frac{1}{4}$ cup peas
2 tbsp parsley, chopped
$\frac{1}{4}$ cup purified water
$\frac{1}{2}$ tsp vegetable salt
$\frac{1}{2}$ tsp vegetable stock powder
$1\frac{1}{4}$ cups purified water or liquid from steamed vegetables
$\frac{1}{4}$ tsp kelp
$1\frac{1}{4}$ tbsp potato or rice flour to thicken

Put all vegetables in large pot (except peas and parsley) with $\frac{1}{4}$ cup water, vegetable salt and stock powder. Steam for about 15 minutes with lid tightly on. Then add peas and parsley for colour. Make sauce from $1\frac{1}{4}$ cups purified water or liquid from steamed vegetables. Heat liquid. Add kelp and stir in flour off the stove. Put back on stove and stir until thick. Pour sauce over steamed vegetables or over cooked fluffy brown rice (transitional). Add cubed tofu.

Scrambled Tofu

1 block tofu cut into cubes
1 tsp cold-pressed oil
$\frac{1}{4}$ tsp turmeric (optional)
$\frac{1}{2}$ tsp kelp, soya sauce or health salt
1 tsp vegetable stock powder
$\frac{1}{2}$ tsp mixed herbs

Mash tofu. Add remainder of ingredients. Heat pan and scramble ingredients. Serve on toasted health bread (transitional) or with steamed vegetables.

Tofu Yoghurt (transitional)

360 g tofu
1 frozen banana and 1 fresh banana
1 tsp raw honey
$\frac{1}{4}$ cup fresh apple juice

Blend all ingredients together until creamy. You can add other fruits, eg strawberries, cherries etc. You will then have fruit flavoured yoghurt. Chill in freezer for 30 minutes and serve with raisins and sunflower seeds.

Breads and Sandwich Fillings

It is preferable to make your own bread. Shop bread contains preservatives, eg calcium propionate, which is known to cause gastrointestinal problems and can be a contributor to migraine headaches. Some health stores stock yeast-free, egg-free, dairy-free and wheat-free bread.

Breads

Gluten-free Bread

$\frac{1}{2}$ cup polenta
$\frac{3}{4}$ cup soya flour
1 tsp vegetable salt
2 tbsp cold-pressed oil
2 tsp raw honey
1 cup purified water
1 tsp baking powder (use one which does not contain aluminium)

Mix all ingredients together. Place in greased flat baking tray. Bake at 180 °C for 35 minutes. Cut into squares and use for dips. This bread contains no yeast, and thus does not rise very much.

Corn Bread

$\frac{1}{4}$ cup soya flour
$\frac{1}{2}$ cup purified water
1 tsp tahini
1 tbsp cold-pressed oil
$1\frac{1}{2}$ cups polenta
1 cup water

Mix first 4 ingredients together. Then add last two ingredients. Mix well. Pour into greased loaf tin or into greased muffin pans. Bake at 205 °C for 45 minutes.

Quick and Easy Health Bread

7 cups stone-ground whole-wheat flour
2 tsp vegetable salt
2 tsp raw honey
1 packet instant dry yeast
± 3 cups warm purified water
$\frac{1}{2}$ cup mixed seeds (optional)

Combine flour with yeast in large bowl. Add salt. Dissolve honey in 1 cup of purified water and add to mixture in bowl. Slowly add remaining water until dough is of a sticky consistency. Add some of the seeds. Divide dough in half and place dough in 2 greased loaf tins. Sprinkle remainder of seeds on top. Cover with a blanket and allow dough to rise in a warm place for approximately 20 minutes. It should rise to the top of the tins. Bake both tins at 200 °C for 1 hour.

Sandwich Fillings

As you cannot mix protein and starch together, your usual cheese and chicken sandwich is taboo. I have put together a variety of sandwich fillings which should tempt your taste buds. Look at the dip recipes. You can also use them as fillings for sandwiches.

Fruit Spreads

Use 250 g of dried raisins, dried dates, figs, peaches, apricots, or bananas (sulphur dioxide free). You can mix 2 varieties. Add purified water to cover and soak overnight. Blend the following day with some of the soaking water to make a jam-like consistency.
- Blend some chopped celery and 1 banana with above OR
- Blend 1 banana and 1/4 cup ground macadamia nuts with above.

Nut Spread

Mix 125 g of macadamia nuts and a little purified water to make a smooth paste. You can also serve this as a topping over Banana Ice Cream.*

Vegetable Spread

Mash cooked peas, seasoning and a little chopped mint.

Avo with a Difference

1 cup celery
2 cups carrots
1/4 cup cabbage, sliced
2 ripe avocados
juice of 1/2 lemon

Put all ingredients into blender. Add seasoning to taste. Spread on bread with lettuce and tomato.

Mushroom Pâté

2 spring onions, chopped
1 stalk celery, chopped
1/4 cup mushrooms, sliced
1 avocado
fresh lemon juice and vegetable salt to taste

Put all ingredients into blender and make smooth paste. Add fresh lemon juice and seasoning to taste. Spread on bread, layered with lettuce and sprouts.

Macadamia Nut Spread (quite rich – don't have on a regular basis)

1 avocado
1/4 cup ground macadamia nuts
1 cup grated cabbage
1/2 tsp chopped parsley
fresh lemon juice and vegetable salt to taste

Put all ingredients into blender. Blend till smooth. Add fresh lemon juice and seasoning to taste. Spread on bread with lettuce, tomato and cucumber.

Ricotta Cheese (transitional)

Cover a slice of bread with lettuce, tomato and cucumber and spread on a layer of ricotta cheese (low in protein). Add seasoning and enjoy!

Tofu Mayonnaise Spread

Spread delicious Tofu Mayonnaise* mixed with lettuce, tomato, cucumber and sprouts on bread.

Herbed Butter

500 g unsalted butter (melt at room temperature)
1 tsp health salt
1 cup cold-pressed oil
2 tsp parsley
2 tsp dried basil
1 tsp origanum
1 spring onion

Blend all ingredients together till smooth. Store in a tub in the fridge and use as a spread on bread or rice cakes.

Marinated Dried Tomatoes

Pour boiling water over dried tomatoes. Leave to soften for 1/2 hour. Remove from water. Cut into pieces. Place in glass dish and pour in just enough cold-pressed olive oil to cover. Add fresh lemon or fresh grapefruit juice to taste. Add 2 tsp origanum and leave to marinate. Keep in the fridge and use in salads or as a sandwich filling. Drain the oil from the tomatoes, if used as a sandwich spread.

Ice Creams

Ice cream can be made from completely healthful ingredients and taste absolutely delicious. Making super, delicious, creamy, wholesome ice cream requires a good blender eg **VitaMix®** or **Magimix®** and a variety of frozen and fresh fruit. These ice creams are made without harmful chemicals, such as stabilisers, emulsifiers and flavourings. Read the ingredients on your usual ice cream container and see what you are about to eat.

Strawberry-Banana Ice Cream

frozen bananas
fresh strawberries

Make this delightful frozen treat the same way as Banana Ice Cream (see below). Wash, de-stem and freeze the best fresh strawberries you can find. Put 3 or 4 frozen strawberries into the blender along with each frozen banana half. Out comes a fantastic pink frozen custard.

Banana Ice Cream

I use overripe bananas, but they must be firm inside and not mushy. Peel bananas, cut them into thirds and place in plastic bags, one layer deep. Seal the plastic bags with twisters and place in the freezer. The purpose of only one layer is to prevent the bananas from freezing into a lumpy mass which makes them difficult to remove singly. You can add other fruit to banana ice cream. You can put the fruit through the blender along with the frozen bananas or you can cut it up or blend it before making your ice cream. You can also serve fruit as a topping, eg macerated dates or other dried fruit, soaked and blended, or just kept whole. Remove the frozen bananas from the freezer. Put a few at a time into the blender and blend till frothy and creamy.

Frozen Layered Banana-Mango Pie

25 ripe frozen bananas
4 mangoes
peach slices
blueberries

Blend mangoes in blender to make mango sauce. Keep this in separate container. Put frozen bananas through blender. Put some of blended frozen bananas in large Pyrex dish. Layer mango sauce on top of bananas. Put the rest of blended frozen bananas on top of mango sauce. Garnish top with peach slices and blueberries. Freeze till ready to eat.

Banana Apple Supreme

frozen bananas
dried apples
fresh bananas
fresh apples or grapes

Wash fresh apples and cut into cubes or use seedless grapes. Peel and slice fresh bananas and toss all fresh fruits together in bowl. Feed frozen bananas and dried apples through blender alternately, using bananas to push dried apples through. Place frozen banana apple ice cream over fruit mixture. Serve immediately.

Party Foods

The following party foods will appeal to both children and adults. These heavenly tasting recipes are great to have on hand during the holidays. They are great for special occasions and your friends (young and old) can enjoy these wonderful foods whenever they drop in. These dishes will also be a big hit at parties.

Banana Pudding (transitional)

1 – 2 bananas
spoonful of raw, unsalted tahini
one or more of the following:
Mulberries, strawberries, blueberries, raspberries, grapes,
diced apricots, nectarines, apples, pears, kiwis,
and soaked raisins

Mash bananas and add tahini. Stir until smooth. Add berries or diced pieces of fruit to mixture to taste. Serves 2.

Banana Party Pie

20 bananas
1 kg pitted dates
500 g dried apricots
1 kg unsweetened desiccated coconut
4 papinos or mangoes or
5 large persimmons or
1 cup dried or fresh apricots

Soak all dates and apricots in purified water for 1 – 2 hours. Blend dates and apricots in blender without water. Add enough coconut to make a spreadable base. Spread out onto bottom of dish. This serves as the crust. Slice 12 bananas until they are piled three layers high in the dish, on top of the crust. In a blender or food processor, blend 8 bananas with 2 papinos (or 3 mangoes or 3 persimmons or ½ cup dried or fresh apricots). Use a small amount of the soaking water if using dried apricots. Pour this creamy mixture over sliced bananas and "seal" it with a sprinkling of coconut. To decorate, use slices of apricots, papino, mango and persimmon, in an interesting design. Leaves of broccoli are very beautiful and fresh flowers may also be added for decoration. Serves 15.

Date-Coconut Pie

1½ cups desiccated coconut
⅓ cup purified water or home-made fruit juice of your choice (I prefer apple or pear)
3 large bananas
⅔ cup pitted dates
⅔ cup shredded coconut (for the topping)
⅓ cup pitted dates, sliced

Moisten 1½ cups freshly grated coconut with some water and then pat the mixture into the pie plate for the crust. Chill the crust for an hour or so. Blend the bananas and the ⅔ cup of pitted dates in a little water or fruit juice. The mixture should be quite thick. Pour the pie filling onto the crust. Top the pie with the ⅔ cup of shredded coconut and the ⅓ cup of sliced dates. Chill for at least 2 hours before serving.

Pineapple-Granadilla Sorbet

1 whole pineapple
4 granadillas or 1 punnet strawberries
½ cup flaked almonds

Blend pineapple until smooth. Pour into container and freeze until semi-hard. Remove from freezer and stir well. Fold in granadilla pulp (or sliced strawberries) and almonds. You can freeze overnight or eat immediately without freezing.

Carob Pears

4 ripe pears
1 cup carob, melted
¼ cup desiccated coconut
1 tbsp raw honey

Remove thin layer of peel from pears, leaving stalks on. Cut a thin slice off base to allow to stand upright. Put honey in pan with just enough boiling purified water to cover. Mix together. Brush over pears. Spoon melted carob over pears, and immediately sprinkle with coconut. You must work quickly or the coconut will not stick to the carob.

Macadamia Nut Pie

Crust:

Blend ½ cup macadamia nuts (not too fine) with 125 g pitted dates. Line Pyrex dish with this mixture.

Filling:

Blend 8 ripe bananas with 125 g pitted dates. Mix 1 tbsp agar-agar in ¾ cup purified boiling water. Stir dissolved agar-agar into blended banana mixture and pour over crust. Allow to set in refrigerator overnight before sprinkling some macadamia nuts on top.

Frosted Pears

10 dates, pitted and soaked
juice of 1 lemon
8 pears (can use mangoes or papinos)
1 ripe banana
up to ½ cup purified water

Blend dates, banana and 1 tsp of the lemon juice until smooth, adding a little water if necessary. Mixture should form peaks when spoon is lifted out of it. Cut pears into cubes. Dip into remaining lemon juice to preserve colour and drain off excess liquid. Place cubed pears or mangoes/papinos in dish and fold in blended mixture. Serve immediately.

Date-Coconut Balls

2 cups pitted dates
1 cup shredded coconut

Soak dates in just enough purified water to cover, for approximately 2 hours. Blend dates, using some of soaking water and $1/4 - 1/2$ cup of coconut. Mixture must be firm. Roll into balls and dust with remaining coconut. You can refrigerate or freeze.

Peanut Butter/Tahini Balls (transitional)

6 dried figs
8 pitted dates
1 cup raisins
$1/2$ cup unsalted raw peanut butter or tahini
1 cup desiccated coconut

Put dried fruit through food processor. Mix with peanut butter/tahini sauce. Shape into balls and roll in coconut.

Carob Delights

1 cup macadamia nuts
$1/4$ cup carob powder
$3/4$ cup raw honey
$1/2$ cup rolled oats
1 cup desiccated coconut

Blend above ingredients together. Shape into balls and roll in coconut to cover.

Stuffed Dates

mejool dates
macadamia nuts

Remove seeds from dates. Stuff mejool dates with halves of macadamia nuts. Children love this, and it also makes a delicious holiday confectionery, when arranged on a pretty glass plate.

Apple on a Stick

apples
dates (soaked in enough purified water to cover)
macadamia nuts

Wash apples and remove stems. Push an ice cream stick through the middle of the apple for a holder. Purée dates with soaking water. Cover apple with puréed dates. Coarsely grind macadamias. Roll date-covered apples in nut mixture. You can also coat apples in melted carob.

Fig Cookies

1 cup dried figs
$1/2$ cup seedless raisins
$1/2$ cup macadamia nuts
desiccated coconut

Blend figs, raisins and macadamia nuts. Make into small balls and roll in coconut.

Carob Treats

Melt 100 g carob in double boiler. Mix melted carob with enough muesli and coconut to make a sticky ball. Fill small cookie cups or press into a tin. Leave to set, then cut into squares.

Fun-filled Dates

Mejool dates
1 cup desiccated coconut
1 cup macadamia nuts
soaked, dried pears

Blend macadamia nuts roughly with coconut and pears. Don't use soaking water. Remove seeds from dates and fill with mixture. Enjoy!

Peanut Butter Fudge (transitional)

$1/2$ cup raw peanut butter
$1/2$ cup tahini
$1/2$ cup desiccated coconut
$1/4$ cup carob powder
$1/2$ cup raw honey or 1 cup macerated dates
$1/2$ cup purified water
1 cup nuts of your choice or 1 cup raisins

Place all ingredients in bowl except carob powder and water. Boil carob powder in water, stirring for 5 minutes until a smooth paste forms. Add to ingredients in bowl and mix well. Press into square pan. Refrigerate. Cut into squares when firm.

Fruit Chewies (ideal for children's lunch boxes)

1 cup dried bananas
8 dates without seeds
$1/2$ cup dried figs
1 cup raisins

Place all ingredients in food processor and blend into a big ball. If mixture is too moist, add more dried bananas. Roll mixture into small balls. Children really enjoy these.

Date Slices (transitional)

250 g chopped dates or dried apricots
(soak in enough purified water to cover)
grated rind of $^{1}/_{2}$ lemon
225 g whole-wheat flour
100 g oats
75 g raw honey
150 g melted butter (unsalted)

Put dates (or other chopped, dried fruit), soaking water and lemon rind in a saucepan. Heat gently, stirring occasionally until mixture is soft. Combine with remaining ingredients. Mix well. Put into shallow baking tray and press down well. Bake at 200 °C for about 20 minutes. Cool in tin and cut into slices. Makes 16 slices.

Carob Chip Cookies (transitional)

175 g unsalted butter
225 g whole-wheat flour
120 g raw honey
pinch salt
1 free-range egg
80 g chopped carob (chop into chips)

Rub butter into flour until mixture resembles fine crumbs. Add honey, salt and egg, and mix well. Stir in carob chips and mix to a soft dough. Chill dough for $^{1}/_{2}$ hour, then roll out on a lightly floured surface to a thickness of 6 mm. Use cookie cutter and place individual cookies well apart on lightly greased baking sheet (tray). Bake in oven at 180 °C for 10 – 12 minutes or until golden brown. Cool slightly then transfer to wire tray. Makes 15 cookies.

Fruit Fudge Squares (transitional)

2 cups whole-wheat flour
$^{1}/_{2}$ cup soya flour
$1^{1}/_{2}$ cups sunflower seeds, finely ground
2 tbsp raw honey
4 tbsp almond oil
$1^{1}/_{2}$ cups currants
$^{3}/_{4}$ cup ground almonds or pecans

Mix first 5 ingredients together. Divide into 2 halves. Sprinkle half mixture in glass baking dish and press to cover bottom of dish. Mix remaining ingredients together and spread mixture over bottom layer of dish. Sprinkle remaining half of mixture on top and press down. Chill for 1 hour. Cut into squares and serve.

Carrot Cake

500 g pitted dates
500 g carrot pulp from juicing
(1kg carrots makes about 500 g pulp)
500 g grated coconut
4 tbsp honey
macadamia nuts for garnish

Juice carrots (juice can be used to moisten mixture if necessary). Put dates and carrot pulp (from juice) in blender. Add 250 g coconut. Blend together. Press half mixture into a pan. Put aside 3 tbsp coconut for topping from remaining coconut. To remaining coconut, add 4 tbsp honey and blend by hand. Spread evenly over first layer. Add remaining half of mixture and press firmly in pan. Sprinkle with the 3 tbsp of plain coconut and press firmly. Garnish with macadamia nuts. Cover with wax paper and put in fridge.

Strawberry Granita

5 cups strawberries
$^{1}/_{2}$ cup honey
$1^{1}/_{3}$ cups purified water
$1^{1}/_{2}$ tbsp fresh lemon juice

Purée strawberries in blender. Place honey and water in saucepan over moderate heat and stir until dissolved. Bring to boil and continue to boil for 5 minutes. Cool to room temperature then stir in puréed strawberries and lemon juice. Pour mixture into ice cube trays and freeze granita until solid. Remove cubes and crush in blender. Spoon into tall glasses and serve immediately with a spoon.

Carob Truffle Bars (gluten free)

2 cups rice cakes, broken up
$^{1}/_{2}$ cup unsalted butter
3 tbsp raw honey
3 level tbsp carob powder
1 cup raisins
240 g melted carob

Crush rice cakes in blender. Melt butter, honey and carob powder in pot over low heat, stirring continuously. Add crushed rice cakes to raisins. Mix thoroughly. Press mixture into 8-inch square dish. Cover with melted carob. Refrigerate until cold. Cut into squares and serve.

Carob-coated Fruit

Melt carob chunks in double boiler. Coat strawberries, frozen bananas, frozen pineapple slices etc. Refrigerate. You can also use melted carob in place of hot chocolate sauce over banana ice cream.

Raw Apple Pie

2 cups shredded coconut
500 g dates
1 cup macadamia nuts
grated Golden Delicious apples to fill shell
apple juice to moisten ($1/4$ – $1/2$ cup)
cinnamon to taste

Blend coconut, dates and macadamia nuts together. Press into a pie dish to make a shell. Mix grated apples, juice and cinnamon together. Pour into shell and refrigerate. Delicious with blended bananas and raisins or dates.

Tropical Jelly

$1/4$ cup lemon juice
4 tbsp raw honey
1 cup purified water
1 tbsp agar-agar
$1/2$ cup diced pineapple
$1/2$ cup fresh granadilla pulp
sprig of mint for garnish

Mix together water, honey and lemon juice. Stir in agar-agar. Bring to boil for 2 minutes, stirring constantly. Cool. Add fruit. Chill until set. Garnish with sprig of mint and serve. Do not leave overnight as jelly tends to separate.

Honey Fingers (transitional)

1 cup puffed rice
1 tbsp each raw honey, tahini and chopped nuts
a few chopped dates

Mix all ingredients together, roll into balls, and chill well. Delicious served with whipped banana ice cream.

Carob and Pineapple Blend

Cut off top and hollow out pineapple. Cut pineapple into pieces. Blend with strawberries, mangoes or granadillas. Pour blended mixture into pineapple shell. Top with melted carob.

Carob Fudge

$1/2$ cup honey
$1/2$ tsp vanilla essence (tartrazine free – this is very concentrated)
$1/4$ cup carob powder
$1/2$ cup chopped almonds

Mix honey and vanilla essence together. Add carob powder and nuts. Press into flat dish and chill. Cut into squares and serve.

Carob-Apple Brownies

1 cup chopped dates
1 cup grated apple
$3/4$ cup cold-pressed sunflower oil
$1/2$ cup sunflower seeds
2 cups rolled oats
$3/4$ cup carob powder

Combine dates, apple and oil. Mix well. Add other ingredients. Let stand for 10 minutes. Press mixture into slightly greased pan. Bake at 180 °C for about 25 – 30 minutes. Cut into squares when cool, and drizzle with melted carob chunks if desired.

No-nonsense Fruit Crumble (transitional)

4 cups blueberries, sliced apples or pears
$2/3$ cup whole-wheat flour
$1 1/2$ cups rolled oats
2 tbsp fresh lemon juice
$1/2$ tsp cinnamon
$1/2$ cup cold-pressed oil

Arrange fruit in casserole dish. Sprinkle with lemon juice and cinnamon. In a separate bowl, combine flour, rolled oats and oil. Mix until crumbly. Spread over fruit. Bake at 180 °C for 40 minutes. Add raisins for a nice variation.

Nut Cake

250 g macadamia nuts
350 g dried fruit (sulphur dioxide free)

Blend macadamia nuts with dried fruit in blender. Knead well and shape into little balls. Put in fridge to set. Children love these.

Party Bananas

4 ripe bananas
$\frac{1}{2}$ – 1 cup coarsely ground macadamia nuts
raw honey

Peel bananas. Skewer onto kebab sticks, roll in honey and then in chopped nuts. Freeze until hard. Another option is to dip bananas into melted carob and then roll in coconut, chopped nuts, or finely chopped dates, or all three!

Nutty Clusters

600 g carob chunks
1 cup dried peaches or apricots, chopped
1 cup pitted dates, chopped
1 cup sultanas
$1\frac{1}{2}$ cups broken macadamia nuts

Melt carob chunks. Add all ingredients to hot carob and mix well. Place mixture in a baking tray and press down. Allow to cool and cut into squares. Makes 32 squares.

Rice Biscuits

$\frac{3}{4}$ cup seeded dates
$\frac{1}{4}$ cup organic brown sugar or raw honey
225 g unsalted butter
$3\frac{1}{2}$ cups puffed rice
coconut for topping

Melt unsalted butter and dates in a pot. Add puffed rice and sugar or honey to the melted mixture. Mix well. Place mixture in a baking tray and press down. Sprinkle coconut on top. Allow to cool and then cut into squares. Makes 32 squares.

Rice Biscuits with Carob

Prepare previous recipe. Before cutting into squares melt 600 g carob and pour over rice biscuits. Spread evenly with spatula. Allow to cool and cut into squares. Makes 32 squares.

Carob Raisins/Dates/Macadamia Nuts/Puffed Rice

Melt carob and add either raisins, dates, chopped macadamias or puffed rice. Coat well with melted carob. Use a teaspoon and spoon into little cookie cups. Put straight into freezer to set. When set, remove from freezer and keep in fridge during the summer.

Oatees (transitional)

1 cup rolled oats
$1\frac{1}{2}$ cups dates, chopped
$\frac{1}{4}$ cup sunflower seeds
$\frac{1}{4}$ cup raw honey
$\frac{1}{4}$ cup desiccated coconut

Put all ingredients into food processor except coconut, and blend until a sticky ball is formed. Remove from blender and make into balls. Use 1 full tablespoon of mixture for each ball. Roll in desiccated coconut.

Nutty Surprises

$\frac{1}{2}$ cup pitted dates, chopped
$\frac{1}{2}$ cup dried peaches or apricots
$\frac{3}{4}$ cup macadamia nuts, chopped
$\frac{1}{4}$ cup raw honey
$\frac{1}{4}$ cup desiccated coconut

Put all ingredients into food processor except coconut, and blend for 5 minutes. Do not over-blend – macadamia nuts must not be finely chopped. Make into balls. Use 1 full tablespoon of mixture for each ball. Roll in desiccated coconut. Makes 12 balls.

If you have enjoyed these delicious meals then try vegetarian cookbooks for more ideas, and adjust these recipes to suit your lifestyle.

PART 5

Selected Issues

Fasting – The ultimate physiological rest

Appropriate fasting is one of our greatest healing tools. We must learn to use it wisely
ANNEMARIE COLBIN

It is well known that when people become ill, the desire for food diminishes. Animals in the wild and many domestic animals abstain from food when sick or injured. Fasting is the fastest and most natural way to regain health. When the fast is over, you should not indulge in your previous unhealthful living and eating practices. Disease results from undesirable living habits such as over-indulgence in the eating of animal products, refined foods, the use of drugs (including tobacco, alcohol, coffee etc), a lack of adequate sleep or exercise, psychological stress, and from hereditary factors.

WHAT IS FASTING?

Fasting is the abstinence from all food as well as sensory, emotional and physical activities for a period of time. This allows the body to redirect its energies from the task of digestion and assimilation to the task of purification and repair. It is definitely necessary to rest your internal organs periodically. You will find that digestion, assimilation, absorption and elimination are all dramatically improved after a fast.

"Therapeutic fasting is not a mystical or magical cure. It works, because the body has within it the capacity to heal when the obstacles to healing are removed. The common medical practice of giving drugs (which are all toxic) to treat the ill effects of retained toxins, is a misguided approach, illustrative of the overall inadequacy of today's health care system. When a fast is done under correct supervision, patients can eventually be taken off their drugs when they learn how to adapt to healthful eating patterns and lifestyle practices that are much more effective"
(Source: Fuhrman, Joel – Fasting and Eating for Health)

During a fast only purified or distilled water should be taken. I have at times (depending on an individual's condition) added fresh lemon juice or a slice of lemon to the water. This usually gives the drink a zest. It is also a good measure to ensure that you drink sufficient water; you have to guard against dehydration. The fresh lemon, which is of a very low caloric value, will not hinder your progress. Some individuals while on a fast may develop an "acid stomach". Raw celery juice freshly made is an excellent alkaliniser. Many people feel much more comfortable after taking the celery juice, especially if they have stomach discomfort. I do recommend these exceptions in special circumstances because I feel that your wellbeing must always be a priority in bringing about health. Most people do not overcome all health problems in just one fast, especially if the fast is not long enough. Some people, however, are not in a position to fast because they either have to go to work and are not able to rest, or they cannot afford to visit a fasting clinic. These people can still improve their health by following the other programmes recommended in this book.

WHAT HAPPENS TO THE BODY DURING A FAST?

When you go without food, the functioning tissues still receive nutrients. The surplus of stored material in the body is used for this purpose and the fast does not suspend metabolism, but rather increases its efficiency. Under the conditions of a fast the body will first burn up the glycogen reserves of the liver and muscles for its energy. These reserves are generally exhausted in only a few days. The body uses the most efficient fuel of all – its own fat reserves in and around every cell and blood vessel in the body. After 2 – 3 days of fasting the body then begins autolysing (breaking down) growths such as tumours, cysts etc.

If you fast for longer than 3 days, you should fast under supervision. I do not claim that fasting "cures" disease but it does enable the organism to heal itself.

Under the conditions of a fast the body can get rid of plaque in the arteries, stones in the gall bladder and kidneys, and ossification materials in the feet, back and joints. You will find that if a prolonged fast is specifically undertaken for circulatory problems, any digestive and arthritic problems you may also have, will be a thing of the past along with your circulatory problems. All the processes of the body continue at a reduced rate during the fast, with the exception of the functions of

organs of elimination which are greatly accelerated during this time. During the fast the essential organs and tissues of the body remain intact and no cells are lost.

Cells are replaced daily but after a fast they are more vital. During a fast, healing and rebuilding takes place in all areas.

You may find you need extra blankets and warm clothing during a fast, as you might feel cold, even if the temperature is 30 °C. Sleep patterns vary in fasters. In the beginning you will sleep longer than usual, perhaps as much as 12 to 18 hours the first day, then after a week of fasting, you may sleep as little as 3 to 4 hours a night. This is because you are not forcing the body to metabolise (break down) food. The heart, nervous system, lungs and other vital parts remain intact, and calcium is not robbed from the bones and teeth, while fasting.

Bowel movements usually cease during a fast. There may be a bowel movement or two after the fast begins, but not usually. On **rare** occasions, people could have bowel movements well into the fast.

If this is your first fast you may experience headaches or other symptoms. A small percentage of people may experience some vomiting. This is normal. The body is simply trying to release poisons. Various drugs taken in the past are usually tasted in the mouth during a fast. The more severe your reactions, the greater the need for the fast.

THE BENEFITS OF FASTING

- **Fasting** helps you make the transition to healthful living much easier to handle. You may find it difficult to stay on the pattern of eating I recommend, but by initially fasting, you will rid the palate's desire for incorrect foods. When eating is resumed, healthful foods will often taste delicious and bad habits will have much less appeal.

- **Fasting** speeds up the healing process. Symptoms that would take months or years of proper living to eliminate, can sometimes be eliminated much more quickly by fasting.
- **Fasting** is extremely effective in bringing down high blood pressure, elevated blood levels of cholesterol, triglycerides, uric acid etc.
- **Fasting** is an efficient method of overcoming dependence on recreational drugs such as coffee, tobacco and alcohol.
- **Fasting** stops the intake of foods that decompose in the intestines and further poison the body.
- **Fasting** empties the digestive tract and disposes of putrefactive bacteria.
- **Fasting** re-establishes normal physiological chemistry and normal secretions.
- **Fasting** restores the youthful condition of the cells and tissues and rejuvenates the body.
- **Fasting** clears and strengthens the mind – you become more mentally alert.
- **Fasting** promotes the breaking down and absorption of deposits, "diseased" tissues and abnormal growths.

FASTING IS THE BEST MEDICINE FOR THE FOLLOWING CONDITIONS

- Obesity
- Colds, flu, diarrhoea and fever
- Toxic saturation eg puffy eyes, mucus expectoration, bad breath, swollen ankles and fingers
- Partial or total exhaustion
- Depression
- Chronic medical conditions such as asthma, bronchitis, sinusitis, tinnitus, acne, allergies, arthritis, tumours etc
- Mental problems

- Addictions
- Injuries.

FASTING IS PROHIBITED UNDER THE FOLLOWING CONDITIONS

- **Pregnant and lactating (breast-feeding) women** Women over 2 months pregnant and those breast-feeding should not fast for longer than a day. Fasting adversely affects foetal development. In the nursing mother, the milk supply starts decreasing from day 1 of the fast. If a nursing mother feels she needs a mild cleanse, a day or two on raw fruit and vegetable juices is advisable. Consult a nutritional counsellor.
- **Liver induration** (hardening of the liver).
- **Irregular heartbeat** You should rather skip a meal or do a juice fast, or eat mono fruit meals. Consult a nutritional counsellor or medical doctor trained in fasting.
- **Diabetes** You should rather go onto properly combined meals as well as an abundance of raw foods. Insulin intake could be reduced by your doctor on such a programme. Consult a nutritional counsellor or medical doctor trained in fasting.
- **Cancer**
- **Fear of fasting** This is one of the foremost contra-indications to fasting. Some people have a deep-seated dread of going without food.
- **Emaciated individuals** People who are normally very thin should not fast but should go on a restricted pattern of eating, ie fresh juices or small fruit meals. Consult a nutritional counsellor. These individuals usually "eat like horses" but do not gain weight because of a metabolic problem, ie they are unable to digest or assimilate food properly. They should also do some exercises which involve weight resistance.

151

Initially, emaciated people lose weight on a restricted pattern of eating and then start gaining weight properly.

RULES ON FASTING – WHY A FASTING INSTITUTION IS ADVISABLE

The most important advice I can give you about fasting is: **do it right** or **don't do it at all!**

I insist that you do not fast for more than a day or two without professional supervision, because of the increase of toxins in the lymph and bloodstream that occurs during the fast.

Another problem is that most people have diseases which are not detectable by clinical methods alone and they need supervision.

Going without food is not the danger of fasting. The danger of fasting is that seriously ill people and the elderly are far more physiologically fragile than they may realise. There is always the possibility that the physiology may begin to fail. Crises can occur quite suddenly. Trained professionals are aware of the significance of symptoms, vital signs, attitudes and other criteria.

As a fast progresses, the body may reach a level where it cannot adequately mobilise essential nutrients. At this point it becomes necessary to resume eating and this has to be done very carefully.

Fortunately the body gives the trained professional plenty of warning when refeeding is necessary. People should go off their medication and vitamins while fasting, and medical doctors trained in this field have the necessary expertise. In addition, these medical doctors are able to evaluate the appropriateness of various medical treatments that might have to be given.

It is important that the individual be monitored. The primary purpose of this is to keep a close check on the individual's vital organs eg kidneys, liver etc.

Certain changes take place during the fast and these have to be assessed, such as changes in temperature, pulse, blood pressure, blood sugar level and nitrogen balance. The individual is thus assured of being carefully looked after. It is for this very reason that a fasting institution is advisable.

A good fasting institution is equipped with various facilities which aid in the rapid removal of toxins, especially via the skin. These facilities are known as hydrotherapy treatments eg massage, sweat therapy etc.

These treatments should all be followed by a cold shower. It is one of the most invigorating experiences. *Dr André Sinden* of Hoogland Hydro in Pretoria suggests you adhere to the following routine, changing the choice of treatments on a daily basis.

- *EXERCISE (gym, walking, running and swimming)*
- *MASSAGE (hand massage, Jacuzzi, and sitz bath)*
- *HEAT (sauna, Turkish/steam baths, hot tub)*
- *COLD (shower, cold swim)*
- *REST (relaxation, sleep, meditation).*

At a fasting institution you will be getting complete rest and a supportive environment in the company of others, doing the same thing, and this reassures you that fasting is safe.

An "in-patient setting" is designed to support a patient during a fast, even though the individual may feel that he is coping well. At home, relatives are not always supportive and there are always doubts and negativism, which interfere with the patient's desire to relax and achieve a good fasting result.

At the institution you are encouraged to read books on fasting and educational material designed to improve your eating pattern and lifestyle after the fast.

You will also be encouraged to rest extensively, because of the diversion of energies used for detoxification. You **are** going to feel tired.

You might find that while fasting your mind becomes befogged at times, especially if there is heavy "cleansing", and your breath could be foul. You need to be continually reassured that "all is well".

You are encouraged to drink water throughout the day to keep urination up to a normal level. It is definitely not necessary, however, to drink **large quantities** of water (listen to your body) as this may overwork the kidneys and interfere with the elimination of toxic material. The kidneys and the lungs are the 2 primary elimination outlets during the fast. The liver and the skin also play a role in the disposal of waste products. All this can be very frightening, and being at a fasting institution definitely gives you "peace of mind".

PREPARATION BEFORE A FAST

The important issue here, is that you must plan ahead for the fast.

- You have to withdraw from your normal activities, ie work etc and take a complete rest.
- If you haven't been eating the way I suggest for a least 2 months prior to the fast, I suggest you eat raw foods, ie mainly fresh fruit, raw vegetables, nuts and seeds for 2 weeks before the fast. If you are not a vegetarian, you could include chicken or fish twice a week with steamed neutral vegetables.
- Do not consume any dairy products.
- For the 3 days prior to the fast, eat only fruit, correctly combined, for breakfast, lunch and supper. Add lettuce and celery to your fruit meals.
- You could drink fresh fruit and vegetable juices instead of fruit; do not drink more than 1 litre per day. Remember: vegetable juices can only be consumed after 12.30 pm.

Eating like this before the fast lessens the possibility and/or intensity of any withdrawal symptoms. The fasting institution you choose will advise you on what to eat before visiting the clinic.

Dr André Sinden of Hoogland Hydro in Pretoria advocates another approach in preparation for a fast, especially if you are doing a 1 day fast: *"On the day before the fast, you should indulge in the foods you have missed most, especially if you follow a 'healthy diet' for 6 days of the week; you should eat a 'high fat meal'. The reason behind this is that fat is taken in to stimulate the formation of fat breakdown enzymes and to thus ensure their availability on the fasting day to liberate energy from fat sparing protein (muscle and organs)."*
(Source: Sinden, André – Health Won)

A high fat intake prior to the fast will ensure greater fat loss on the fasting day, leaving the body with a larger percentage of muscle tissue. *Dr André Sinden* suggests you fast once a week for 36 hours on water only. If you take vitamins, do not take them on the day of your fast. If on medication, do not fast without consulting a nutritional counsellor first.

SHORT FASTS

If you are not on prescription drugs and there is no established serious disease, you can undertake a short fast of 3 days. Remember always to contact a nutritional counsellor to get support. If you don't really feel like fasting for so long, you could skip a meal or two, or fast for 24 – 36 hours, eg from 7 pm on Monday evening to 7 pm on Tuesday evening or till Wednesday 7 am. This is also of great benefit to the body. When breaking the fast, the first food eaten must be either freshly squeezed fruit juice prepared at home or fruit only.

I must emphasise that if short fasts are taken too frequently, they can cause enervation and exhaustion, as well as nutritional deficiencies. A regular 1 day a week fast is not included in this rule.

However, short fasts are necessary in the following circumstances:

- when you have a fever, diarrhoea or a cold
- if you have eaten some food that disagrees with you (skip the next meal or meals until you feel better)
- if you are tired or under great stress and/or emotional strain.

BREAKING OF THE FAST

Great care should be exercised in the breaking of a fast. Correct eating is important in order to re-establish intestinal flora and digestive secretions. You must consult a nutritional counsellor.

AFTER A 3 DAY FAST

- Break the fast on freshly squeezed fruit juices prepared at home (orange juice is preferable). You can drink 240 ml every 3 hours or 120 ml every 2 hours, throughout the day. Drink juices at room temperature.
- Eat only fruit the following day (as much as you want).
- The next day you should only eat raw food eg fruit and vegetable salads. Before eating "other foods" consult a nutritional counsellor.

AFTER A 10 DAY FAST
(always consult a nutritional counsellor)

- Drink home-made freshly squeezed juice only for 2 days.

- **1st day:** 90 – 120 ml every 2 hours – 50% water and 50% juice, decreasing the water dilution as the day goes on. By the end of the day you can have full strength fruit juice.
- **2nd day:** 180 – 240 ml full strength fruit juice every 4 hours.
- **3rd and 4th days:** one kind of fruit only throughout the day.
- **5th day:** fruit in the morning (one kind) and a raw vegetable salad at lunch and supper. Do not use any seasoning or dressing. You can add an avocado blended with tomatoes as a dressing.
- **6th day:** eat fruit correctly combined till 1 hour before supper.

Supper: raw vegetable salad and 1 avocado pear

OR

raw vegetable salad and a $1/2$ cup of nuts (unsalted and unroasted – no peanuts).

- **7th day:** breakfast and lunch the same as for the 6th day.

Supper: if you had nuts on the 6th day then have avocado pear on the 7th day or vice versa. You can now add steamed neutral vegetables. Do not have steamed vegetables every single night; alternate, ie one night raw and the next night cooked.

AFTER A FAST OF 2 WEEKS OR LONGER
(always consult a nutritional counsellor)

- **1st and 2nd days:** diluted fresh fruit juices, prepared at home, ie 30 – 50% fresh fruit juice diluted with purified water every 2 hours, ending up with full strength fruit juice or 60 – 90 g of watermelon chewed slowly every 1 – 2 hours.
- **3rd – 5th day:** fresh fruit for 3 days (juicy fruits are preferable).
- **6th and 7th days:** small raw salad.
- **8th and 9th days:** add 1 avocado pear to the

small raw salad.

- **10th day:** add $1/3 - 1/2$ cup of nuts to a large raw salad.
- **11th – 16th day:** eat raw foods only. Do not have nuts and avocado on the same day.
- **17th day and thereafter:** add steamed vegetables, on alternate days. Always include more raw than cooked foods in your daily pattern of eating.

The most important part of fasting is eating the correct foods after the fast. You don't want to undo all the good that has been achieved.

THE ALTERNATIVE TO A WATER FAST

For those who have to go to work and cannot take a complete rest I suggest **JUICE FASTING** or eating **Fruit only** for all meals. This will also help in eliminating toxins, although not as effectively as a water fast.

Juice Fasting is excellent for those people who find it difficult to digest whole raw foods.

- Drink no more than 1 litre per day, ie 250 ml, 4 times per day.
- Always sip the juice and drink it slowly.

This allows for better assimilation.
- Do not use commercial juices. They are heated during canning or bottling, which results in vitamin and mineral loss. In addition, they are often sweetened with refined sugars and chemicals.
- I suggest you have 2 x 250 ml fruit juice prepared at home during the early part of the day and 2 x 250 ml fresh raw vegetable juice later on in the day.
  Vegetable juices are very high in chlorophyll, calcium, iron and many other minerals. Drink carrot juice only 3 times per week. If consumed in large quantities, it can colour the skin and cause carotenemia. This is an indication that the liver is unable to tolerate it.
- If you feel like a "clean out" regularly, I suggest **Mono Fruit Diets** (one kind of fruit at a meal) for 2 or 3 days.

Remember, you should not revert to bad eating habits after using these methods (water fasting, juice fasting, mono fruit diets). Always consult a nutritional counsellor who will guide you in your choice of a fasting programme.

What to eat while pregnant and breast-feeding

A healthy body tomorrow begins with a healthy diet today – in childhood
SUZANNE HAVALA

This section is intended to provide parents with information that will ensure that their children get the real benefits of eating correctly.

By learning how to meet the dietary needs of your children, you will give them a healthy start in life. Parents need to be good role models for their children. One thing that will never work is trying to put a child on a strict diet while the parents continue to eat the same amount of fat-producing foods they normally eat.

Children imitate the eating patterns and habits of those whom they respect and love. When parents are willing to make changes for themselves it is much easier for the children to follow. If they see you eating and enjoying wholesome foods, they will then have good role models to follow.

Most people seem to be more concerned about the type of petrol they put in their car than they are about the food (chemicals) that they put in their bodies. Your car gets traded in about every 4 years; your body is yours for life – healthy or sick! – you make the choice.

If you start your children on the right pattern of eating from day one, it is much easier. If you haven't done this and want to make the changeover to healthier foods, it is more difficult, but worth it.

A DIET FOR PREGNANT AND BREAST-FEEDING WOMEN

The pattern of eating of pregnant women has a profound effect on the health of the growing child inside the womb. The developing foetus will be made from the food that the mother consumes while carrying the child. If the mother eats correctly, she is assured of an easy delivery, contented and calm babies who sleep well, toddlers who are not wild and cranky, and children who do not have constant earaches, colds and runny noses.

Conception should really not be considered if you have any major illnesses or are in a run-down state physically, as some serious health problems often develop after pregnancy.

The programme that I advise in this section is for both pregnant and breast-feeding women.

You should avoid red meat, dairy products (butter being the exception), tobacco, sugar, caffeine and alcohol. These are definitely not ideal foods to consume, especially while pregnant and breast-feeding.

In order to avoid the feeling of nausea while pregnant eat only fruit, correctly combined, throughout the morning. If you experience **severe** morning sickness, I suggest you drink only fresh fruit and vegetable juices for 3 days. Do not include any other foods. As vegetable juices have a high vitamin and mineral content, pregnant and breast-feeding women should drink at least 1 – 2 glasses in between meals on a daily basis. If you are drinking fresh fruit juices try and include celery and lettuce; do not add any melons.

This increases the calcium, iron and B vitamin content that is so important during pregnancy and nursing. Include in your daily programme $1/4 - 3/4$ cup of raw, unsalted nuts and seeds as your protein meal (no peanuts). You can eat free-range chickens or fish 4 times per week (if you want animal protein). During the rest of the week, include the nuts and seeds. They contain as much protein as fish, and have more calcium than milk.

You can snack on fresh or dried fruit (sulphur dioxide free) or celery sticks. Limit your quantities of dried fruit to $1/4 - 1/2$ cup per day. Eating more natural fresh foods is the healthiest way to go.

Pregnant and breast-feeding women often have cravings: If you crave sweet foods, your body needs glucose in the form of fresh fruit and dried fruit. If you crave something savoury, I suggest you use cold-pressed oils over your salads and eat raw nuts, seeds, avocados, olives in brine and yellow mealies. These foods contain all the essential fatty acids so needed by pregnant and breast-feeding women.

If at least 75% of your diet consists of raw fruit and vegetables, you will be getting sufficient calcium as well as an excellent source of water, and soluble fibre, which will keep you "regular" throughout your pregnancy. As calcium needs vitamin D (sunlight) in order to be absorbed efficiently, you should spend at least 20 – 30 minutes each day in the sun (before 9.30 am and after 3.30 pm).

You must also include a gentle, regular exercise programme. This is very important in helping the body retain its calcium levels. The mineral iron is very important during pregnancy and lactation. It is easily available on a diet of raw fruit and vegetables. The high levels of vitamin C in fruit and vegetables help the body to utilise iron very easily from plant sources. If you are really concerned about which foods contain a great deal of iron, then choose yellow fruits, oranges, raisins, currants, leafy green vegetables and yellow vegetables. Remember, all fruits and vegetables contain some iron.

Another important substance for pregnant women is folic acid, a constituent of vitamin B complex found especially in green vegetables. Again, if your diet contains at least 75% raw fruit and vegetables, you will be assured of obtaining sufficient folic acid.

SUMMARY

I suggest you follow my Maintenance Programme with the following minor adjustments: Always eat 2 protein meals every other day. One of the 2 protein meals must be $1/2$ a cup of nuts or seeds. On the days in between eat 1 protein meal – this must be $1/2$ a cup of nuts or seeds (plant protein).

Always consult a nutritional counsellor for advice.

HOW TO FEED BABIES

The recommended food for infants is mother's milk. It contains everything the baby needs. Breast milk provides not only the best nutritional support but also immunological, digestive and psychological support for your infant. It is better than any man-made formula.

The mother's dietary intake, however, is of great importance as this determines the quality of the milk. Babies on formula, especially a cow's milk based formula, usually develop some sort of mucus congestion which affects sinuses, lungs, bronchial tubes, throat and ears, as well as causing allergies. Breast-fed babies may have these problems, but they are far less frequent or intense. If a breast-fed baby has mucus problems, it is usually due to the incorrect diet of the mother, and the adverse effect of this diet on her milk.

If, for whatever reason, the mother is unable to breast-feed, the best substitute is equal parts of raw goat's milk and purified water. As the baby gets used to this, slowly increase the goat's milk and use less water. If the baby gets colic or diarrhoea, the goat's milk is too concentrated and you need to add more water. Make sure that the goat's milk is from a farm where the goats have been tested for brucellosis and TB. The next choice is a soya-based infant formula ie soya which is scientifically formulated for babies and not the normal soya milk from health stores. Do not use blended fruit and nut milks as a replacement for breast-feeding or for formula. They do not provide adequate infant nutrition. They can however be used as an additional food or drink, or if the infant is experiencing diarrhoea or mucus problems.

I do not recommend cow's milk based formula or fresh cow's milk for infants. It not only causes mucus problems, but can upset the baby's mineral balance as it is too high in calcium. It is also very high in protein and this can cause digestive problems such as diarrhoea, colic and constipation.

HOW OFTEN SHOULD INFANTS BE FED?
Babies should generally only be fed every 3 to 4 hours. This allows for complete digestion. It is very important not to overfeed babies. The most common symptom of overfeeding is colic, excessive spitting up and sometimes projectile vomiting. Often when a baby cries, it just wants to be held or have a nappy change. A mother should be aware of her baby's needs.

WHY SOME BABIES NEED TO BE FED MORE OFTEN
If infants need to be fed more frequently (especially if breast-fed), this is often as a result of the poor quality of the mother's milk. Mothers must then improve their diet. If there is a lack of milk production, mothers should drink more water and consume more fresh fruit and vegetable juices. If the baby loses weight or fails to gain weight, this is a sign that the baby needs frequent feeding.

WHEN TO INTRODUCE SOLIDS
There is really no rush to introduce other foods. Solids, fed to babies at an early age, often lead to allergies later on. The presence of teeth is nature's way of saying it is time to begin adding solids. If there are no teeth, the infant is really not ready for other foods and mothers should continue with breast milk or formula only.

The baby's body begins to manufacture the digestive enzyme ptyalin, used for the breaking down of starches such as cereals, only much later. The indigestion and catarrh that result from eating cooked starches (cereals) serve as starting points for the evolution of a whole series of diseases. Cereals are best omitted from the diet of infants for this very reason. No starch and especially no cereals should be given to a child before the age of 12 months. The best time to begin adding cereals is really when the baby can chew them. Babies need to have just 4 – 6 teeth to begin eating solids other than cereals.

WHAT SOLIDS TO BEGIN WITH

Raw fruit is the ideal food to begin feeding. Fruit is also sweet and the baby will be attracted to it naturally.

Dr Joel Robbins says "fruit is the easiest food to eat, digest and assimilate and has the greatest nutritional value for the growing baby."
(Source: Robbins, Joel – Pregnancy, Childbirth and Children's Diet)

Begin with 1 – 2 teaspoons of 1 kind of soft fruit, such as bananas, peaches, apples, pears, nectarines, mangoes, strawberries, grapes with seeds and skins removed, and soaked dried fruit (sulphur dioxide free). When giving a particular fruit for the first time, observe how well it is tolerated before adding another kind of fruit. You must give the baby's digestive system a few days to get used to each new food. If the baby is not interested in eating solids the first few times, shelve it for a week then try again. Some babies are not really interested in solids until much later. If they appear healthy, there is no need to worry.

Recipes to help you:

Blended Banana:
1 banana
2 – 3 tbsp distilled/purified water
Mix ingredients in blender until smooth.

Blended Fruit and Banana:
$1/2$ – 1 banana together with soft mushy fruits
2 – 3 tbsp distilled/purified water or freshly squeezed juice (prepared at home)
Add all ingredients to blender and blend until smooth.

Apple Sauce:
1 apple, juiced
2 apples, peeled and cut
1 banana
Add all ingredients to blender and blend until smooth.

All foods should be prepared and fed immediately. The longer you wait after the fruit has been peeled and liquidised, the greater the oxidation and the loss of vitamins. The baby can snack on dried fruit. It is excellent for teething and provides something to chew on. You could also use raw carrots and celery sticks. Cut the celery sticks into thick slices, so that the baby can hold them comfortably. Avoid acid fruits such as oranges, grapefruit, and pineapple, and vegetables such as tomatoes, as they tend to cause nappy rash.

Each time a new food is introduced into a baby's diet, always watch for the following signs: undigested food in the stool, nappy rash (often associated with new food), diarrhoea, colic, constipation, skin or other allergy-type reactions.

If any of these signs appear when a new food is given, consider that too much of that food was fed.

You should simply cut back the amount of food given. If the reactions still continue, they are an indication that the baby's digestive system has not "woken up" to that food.

The next food to introduce is **vegetables**, which are high in calcium and iron. Fruit alone does not contain all the nutrients, necessary for proper nutrition. Let the baby suck on or chew on raw vegetables such as carrots, celery, red peppers, and cucumbers between meals, so that he becomes used to eating whole raw food. It is advisable to give vegetable juice at 4 pm. Carrot juice should be the primary juice; other vegetables should be added in limited quantities. Fresh apple juice may be mixed with the carrot/vegetable juice to sweeten it.

WHAT KIND OF PROTEIN FOOD SHOULD BE FED TO BABIES?

You should make **nut butters** from raw, unsalted, unroasted nuts, for example, almonds, cashews etc. These must be refrigerated soon after being made. You must taste the nut butters daily as they go off rather quickly. Peanut butter is not to be used at all. You can add celery, steamed vegetables, or any fruit (except melons) to the nut butters. These foods will aid in the digestion of the nuts. Nut butters should only be given from about 7 months.

Another good source of protein is the avocado pear. All you need to do is to mash half an avocado or less and feed it to your baby. Start off with 1 – 2 teaspoons mixed with fruit. Avocados can be added to fresh fruit or raw vegetables. If using with lightly steamed vegetables, warm the vegetables first and then add the avocado. **Never heat avocado.**

NUT BUTTER AND NUT MILK RECIPES
Almond Butter

Pour boiling water over almonds, leave them to soak for about 1 hour and then skin them. Add skinned almonds to a blender, blend well, then add some purified water to make a paste. Start off with 1 teaspoon of nut butter in your baby's food.

Banana Milk

Add ripe bananas to a blender. Add sufficient purified/distilled water to make a "milk" consistency. Never use banana milk in place of breast milk or formula. You can, however, use it in addition to the above especially if the infant is underweight.

Cashew Milk

$1/4$ cup raw cashews
1 cup distilled/purified water

Put cashews and water in a blender. Blend at high speed for 2 – 3 minutes until a thick white milk is formed. The nut milk will need to be strained through a muslin cloth, so that the baby can drink from the bottle.

Almond Milk

$1/4$ cup raw almonds
1 cup distilled/purified water

Blanch almonds first, then blend the same way as the cashew milk.

SUMMARY

This is the recommended pattern of eating. If you have any questions consult a nutritional counsellor. For each age group you add the food for the previous age group, plus the new foods.

Newborn

Breast milk, goat's milk, goat's milk powder or formula (not milk based) ie soya, every 3 – 4 hours.

2 – 3 months

First add fruit juices, then vegetable juices. Strain the juice and dilute it with 50% purified/distilled water. Gradually decrease the amount of water as the baby gets older.

4 – 6 months

You can add mushy (soft) raw fruits. Always feed the fruit first, then give the milk $1/2$ – 1 hour later.

7 months

Avocado, cooked green vegetables, sprouts, blended raw salads and nut butters.

8 months

Cooked starch vegetables, eg carrots, sweet potatoes, pumpkin, squash etc. You can add tahini sauce.

12 months

Cooked starchy foods, eg potatoes, millet, brown rice, and rice cereals.

14 months

Legumes eg tofu. You can give free-range

chicken or fish at this stage, if you as a family are not vegetarians.

15 – 18 months

Bread and pasta. **Do not give these foods till the baby is at least 1 year old.**

GENERAL RULES FOR FEEDING BABIES

- Never encourage or force the baby to finish a meal. This leads to trouble later on in life. The baby will let you know when he has had enough, by turning his head away, clamping his mouth shut or spitting the food out. Take his word for it!
- Avoid all foods that contain sugar or artificial sweeteners.
- If a particular food seems to cause a reaction, eg a skin rash, sore bottom or mouth sores, eliminate that food for 1 week and then try again. If it has the same effect when added again, discontinue it for at least 4 months.
- Don't give teething biscuits, crackers and pretzels as snacks, as they are "white starch" products with little food value. Use celery or carrot sticks.

HOW TO FEED CHILDREN PAST THE TODDLER STAGE

Children have special needs; they are not "little adults". A pattern of eating that may be perfectly adequate for you as a parent, may not be at all adequate for a child.

Children are growing all the time. They have faster heartbeats, a more rapid respiration, higher body temperatures and a faster metabolism than adults. In general, it takes more care and precision to plan diets for children than it does for adults.

I suggest you always feed children lots of fresh fruit and vegetables. In addition, children must consume a sufficient amount and variety of the right "concentrated foods"

other than fruit, and vegetables as they need relatively more calories than adults. Because their stomachs are small they should not fill up on fruit and vegetables only, as they may not have enough room to eat other foods. Don't be concerned if your child is eating more "concentrated food" than you would. He/she needs it. The "concentrated foods" I am referring to are: whole grains, legumes, avocados, nuts and seeds.

These foods have the most calories per unit of volume in a vegetarian diet. If a child does not get enough calories it could result in the following: below average weight, listlessness, low resistance to infections, and constant hunger. This often applies to the child who always wants to eat, rather than play. He/she is not getting a balanced diet.

HOW TO TRAIN CHILDREN TO EAT CORRECTLY

You should start to clean out all the junk food in your house, and fill it with a variety of health-promoting foods. The family plays a very important part in forming correct, lifelong eating habits.

In order to train children to enjoy these foods you should involve them in selecting healthy foods and encourage them to take part in cooking the food.

You should also explain in a language that the child can understand, how and why you are changing his diet. Praise him when he makes good choices and express disappointment when he eats the incorrect food.

Don't be rigid in your approach – exceptions can be made occasionally. You should have a set of rules and not be scared to say no when you know it is for the benefit of the child.

Children are generally finicky eaters so never force the child to eat food he doesn't like. Wait till the next meal and offer it again – if the child doesn't like it don't force him. Patience and time is what is needed here. Eventually, when the child gets off sugars you will find he will be less bad tempered.

It is important that the family sit down together for the meal. They should all eat the same type of food, so no one is really going to feel deprived. Start children with a small raw salad first and leave room for the concentrated foods eg potato, rice, pasta etc.

It is difficult to change an eating pattern and lifestyle overnight. You can motivate the children to eat the right food for perhaps 5 nights a week and perhaps 2 nights a week you can allow them to eat exactly what they want, eg pizzas, hamburgers etc.

Don't make the mistake though of using food as the "special treat" and say for example, "if you eat all your vegetables you will be allowed ice cream". The vegetables seem to be the "punishment" and the ice cream the "reward". This is not the right way to teach children about food.

A deviation from the correct diet 1 or 2 nights out of 7, will not stop the cleansing/healing process. It just slows it down a bit. In time, as the body cleanses, children will find those "wrong foods" less appealing.

Don't make eating a chore. Children must never be made to feel they are being deprived. I am aware that children and sweets seem to be inseparable.

I would prefer you used healthy substitutes like honey, maple syrup, barley malt, dates, carob brownies, and carob snacks.

CHILDREN MUST OBTAIN SUFFICIENT PROTEIN
Children require protein both for main-tenance and for growth. They must eat a variety of foods, especially unrefined plant foods like nuts, seeds, lentils etc on a regular basis. I prefer these foods to animal proteins which contain a lot of fat. If they do eat chicken and eggs, make sure they are free-range. Children as young as 2 years old should have their cholesterol checked. This is very important.

FOOD COMBINING IS TOO RESTRICTIVE FOR CHILDREN
Most children can eat anything they want and not experience digestive distress. Living healthfully involves a great many restrictions in your child's eating pattern, so please don't make these restrictions greater than they have to be.

As long as your child is willing to eat wholesome natural foods, do not be concerned about the way they are combined or the order in which they are eaten. For example, if the child wants watermelon after a meal, do not make an issue out of it. Be grateful that he/she wants watermelon and not ice cream.

FOOD MUST BE MASTICATED VERY WELL
This applies especially to foods such as nuts and starch meals, for example bread and rice. Few children chew nuts till creamy in the mouth. It is better to feed them nut/seed milks and nut/seed butters instead of whole nuts.

Neither children nor adults really chew brown rice very well. It is a fibrous food and if it is not chewed well, the wealth of nutrients in it cannot be used by the body. Teach your children to take small bites and chew each bite well. The rice should have the consistency of rice milk before it is swallowed.

AN ALL RAW DIET IS NOT FOR CHILDREN

I advise adults to eat an abundance of raw foods and less cooked foods. However, where children are concerned, I feel that an adequate diet can be made up of a wide variety of plant-based foods, eg legumes, cooked whole grains, together with raw fruits, nuts and vegetables.

BE WARY OF FEEDING CHILDREN ULTRA LOW FAT FOODS

You must include a moderate amount of nuts, seeds and avocados in your children's eating plan. If you want to cut down on fats rather leave out margarine, mayonnaise etc. Do not fry foods in oil or butter and cut down on animal protein.

Children need fats for the development of their nervous systems and the high calorie content of the right fat is something that most children need. Children who are hungry all the time may need to eat more nuts and seeds.

YOUR CHILD MUST BE ASSURED OF GETTING ENOUGH VITAMIN B_{12}

The body, however, needs very little vitamin B_{12}. Children require relatively more than adults, because their cells are growing and dividing rapidly. The blood cells and the nerve cells suffer the most when vitamin B_{12} is in short supply. Vitamin B_{12} also aids in the development of red blood cells and nerve functions. Children should eat foods that encourage the production of vitamin B_{12} and these include whole grain cereals, soya products and organically grown vegetables.

Getting enough vitamin B_{12} should never be a rationale for feeding meat or dairy products to a child.

I recommend that babies be given *Bifido Bacterium Infantis culture* from birth (if not breast-fed) till 18 months. It can also be given to expectant and breast-feeding mothers. After 18 months you can give a combination of probiotics (natural bowel flora) ie *bifidobacterium* and *lactobacillus acidophilus.* "*Acidophilus provides a natural antibiotic, helps with assimilation of nutrients and manufactures B vitamins including B_{12}.*"
(*Source: Robbins, Joel – Health and Wellness Clinic, Inc.*)

I have used these guidelines in the care and feeding of my own grandchild, as well as many other children whose mothers sought my advice.

These children have improved not only in their behaviour but in classroom performance as well. Mothers have also remarked that their children don't have as many colds, ear infections, and tonsillitis as they had before.

Incorrect feeding has its most harmful effects during the years of growth. It is during this time that proper nutrition is most necessary. Nothing is more important for the health of our children than the nourishment they obtain from proper natural foods. This is the best medicine that you can give your children.

Nutrition, Behaviour and Emotions – Is there a connection?

What you eat will not only affect your weight and health, but your state of mind too

ALEXANDER SCHAUSS

Proper nutrition is not only the foundation for physical health, but also the prerequisite for emotional and mental wellbeing. What you eat definitely affects your behaviour patterns, for example, diet can prevent or promote delinquency and antisocial acts. While some foods contribute to your feeling of wellbeing and self-esteem and truly satisfy hunger, other foods may depress you and make you feel even hungrier.

Millions the world over are suffering from psychological disorders such as depression, mood swings, anxiety, suicidal tendencies, schizophrenia etc. These disorders are treated either through psychological counselling or drug therapy. Psychologists and psychiatrists are focusing totally on the mind of individuals and ignoring eating patterns. What you must realise is that your brains are fed by your blood and your blood is made up from the food you eat. A body that is properly cared for with good nutrition is able to withstand emotional and mental problems. In other words you have to feed the cells of your brain with nutrients from natural sources that are toxin free.

FOODS THAT AFFECT BEHAVIOUR AND CREATE DEFICIENCIES

- **Artificial sweeteners** have been reported to cause undesirable behavioural reactions.
- Many children today seem to have be-

haviioural and/or learning problems because of exposure to additives *in utero*. The mother's placenta is not a barrier but rather a sieve. **Alcohol, drugs,** and **cigarette smoke** can reach the foetus and impair its development.

Refined carbohydrates and **sugars, fast foods,** and **junk food** as well as **colourants** and **additives** all seem to contribute to hyperactivity, emotional disturbances, delinquency and outright crime. Foods such as **yeast, cow's milk, chocolate, cheese, coffee, wheat, corn** and **eggs** can also cause behavioural disorders. During my years of teaching I found that such disorders dropped significantly when all the above foods were eliminated from children's lunch boxes. For example, bed wetting (enuresis) stops when **dairy products** are discontinued. It could take 25 days or less.

- Complex carbohydrates which have been proven to be the primary nutrient needed for maintaining a healthy nervous system tend to be eliminated on a "lose weight" diet. Dieters often show signs of irritability, especially when they resort to foods that are low in calories, but high in artificial additives eg **diet cold drinks**. These drinks are worse than ordinary soft drinks because they contain up to 100 different chemicals as substitutes for calories, caffeine etc.

- Phosphoric acid from phosphates commonly found in sodas, meat, sausages and other processed foods, can produce hyperactive and aggressive behaviour.

HOW BAD ARE REFINED CARBOHYDRATES AND SUGARS?

Refined carbohydrates and sugars (the curse of the modern diet), eg candy, cakes, biscuits, ice cream, soft drinks, alcohol, coffee, white flour, white rice and pasta, do not really satisfy your appetite, hence the endless craving for more and more. They supply empty calories and are the very foods that play havoc with the blood sugar level, sending people into periods of depression or irritability. They seem to make calm children noisy and hyperactive and have been known to trigger schizoid behaviour.

Refined carbohydrates and sugars known as "nutrient destroyers" deplete the body of B vitamins; vitamin B complex is necessary to metabolise carbohydrates. When you eat refined sugar (sucrose) it passes directly into the intestines where it becomes predigested "glucose". It is absorbed into the blood, increasing the glucose level. The balance is now destroyed and you start manifesting mood swings. Your immune system is also affected. Vitamin B is removed or destroyed during the processing and refining of foods. Since the the body needs vitamin B to assimilate sugar, it starts to draw upon its reserves to help metabolise the sugar. Vitamin B is the "anti-stress" vitamin and if there is no vitamin B, you can't cope with stress. You now experience sleep disturbances, emotional outbursts, depression, chronic fatigue, failure to concentrate, abnormal sensations such as prickling or burning and excessive eating of junk food. This becomes a vicious circle and this is exactly how the stress/junk food cycle gets started. Refined carbohydrates are responsible for many diseases and, of course, obesity.

WHAT ABOUT IRON DEFICIENCIES AND BEHAVIOUR PATTERNS?

In the early 1970s paediatric researchers discovered evidence that some school children who displayed conduct disorder in class and also learning problems with science, maths, writing and languages were suffering from an iron deficiency. Eating foods high in **vitamin C** such as fresh fruit and vegetables facilitates the absorption of iron in the body. **Tannins** in tea and coffee can reduce iron absorption by 20% – 60% especially when consumed with meals.

Cadmium, a chemical found in water, also interferes with iron absorption. You should always use purified water. Nuts, whole grains, legumes, dried fruits, and apricots are all good sources of iron. Foods rich in copper, such as nuts, bananas, wheat germ, prunes, sesame seeds and mushrooms also increase iron absorption.

Another factor that contributes to hyperactivity, learning disorders and behaviour problems is **lead**, found in calcium supplements, for example, dolomite and bone meal. This is due to the soil and animal being exposed to lead pollution. If we eat a diet high in refined carbohydrates and low in raw fruit and vegetables we will have a bad reaction to lead (toxic fumes from cars).

WHAT HAPPENS TO THE BODY WHEN YOU EAT WHILE STRESSED?

Eating while under stress is actually one of the worst things you can do. When you are under stress, your digestive system is inhibited and this may result in indigestion.

I suggest that whenever you feel stressed, skip the next meal or do a short fast. This will allow the body to rebuild itself and strengthen the nervous system. A strong and healthy nervous system is our first line of defence against stress.

It has been found that **certain amino acids can promote a stress-free lifestyle**. Amino acids are chemical agents contained in protein. Once inside our bodies they change into "neurotransmitters" which send messages to the brain that can bring either positive information (your mood is now elevated), or negative information (you now feel depressed). One very important amino acid is **tryptophan**; it produces **serotonin**. If the level of serotonin in the brain falls too low, you can become depressed, aggressive and often have trouble sleeping.

Foods that contain **tryptophan** are bananas and pineapples. Another amino acid that affects moods in a positive way is **tyrosine** found in sesame seeds. Fresh fruit, raw vegetables, a moderate amount of nuts, seeds, avocados, sprouts, legumes and whole grains supply you with a super abundance of all the needed nutrients, as well as important minerals and trace elements to build strong nerves.

I have found through my counselling sessions, that the foods that definitely trigger depression and behaviour problems, and increase hunger are: cow's milk, refined sugars and starches, eggs, wheat, chocolate, pickled foods, alcohol, sour cream, aged cheese, beef, lobster, artificial colourants, Monosodium Glutamate (MSG) and other preservatives.

You must first educate yourselves about proper nutrition and then develop an awareness about the foods you put into your body. Unfortunately, advertising contributes to shifts in the choices of foods you believe you can and should consume.

There seems to be a lot of opposition, particularly from the giant food processing companies, to the existence of a link between what you eat and how it affects you. If they had to admit to the existence of such a link, sales of cola, sweets, and packets of chips would drop dramatically.

Your earliest memories of security go back to being fed by your mother. Thus eating definitely represents a way back to security.

However, what you have to accept is that you alone are responsible for your mental and emotional health. Individuals tend to blame the failure of interpersonal relationships or even complete emotional and mental breakdown on "outside factors" such as hidden stress, poor home environments etc. This allows them to shift the responsibility away from themselves to some other person or event. You have to develop a positive self-image. Many people indulge in self-destructive eating habits out of a desire to punish themselves for "not being good enough".

The best way to avoid behaviour and emotional problems is to follow a varied, balanced diet high in raw food, ie lots of fresh raw fruit, vegetables, avocados and a moderate amount of nuts and seeds (essential fatty acids).

Always remember to eat some raw food before you eat cooked food.

A healthy lifestyle, especially with regard to wholesome activities, balanced with exercise, adequate rest and sleep, plays a significant role in your ability to create a mental and emotional wellbeing within yourself. Please do not ignore these factors. They are just as important as your choice of food.

How to lose weight easily

The only successful weight loss programme is one that is in tune with an individual's nutritional needs and his/her physical and mental wellbeing

ROBERT S. MENDELSOHN

The public is continually bombarded with an abundance of "winning weight loss diets". The information I have to offer on losing weight provides a total programme of superior nutrition that supplies all the requisites for a healthy physiology; it will not deprive the body of any essential nutrients. By following this programme, your body will find its correct weight for your frame and redistribute the weight intelligently, based on its inner wisdom.

The diet of today's average man is unhealthy for a number of reasons. Not only does it contain excess proteins, fats, sugars and starch, but it is made up largely of refined and processed foods that have been artificially flavoured, coloured, preserved and adulterated. It is also eaten in haphazard, indigestible combinations. The emphasis in this book is on correct food combining.

I cannot guarantee how much you will lose but lose you will. How overweight you are depends on your sex and your activity schedule. It is safe to say that you can expect to lose between 4 to 8 kg by following this weight loss programme for 4 weeks. Your success is not only measured by the number of kilograms you lose but by the fact that your overall physical wellbeing will be healthier from eating healthier foods, and your emotional wellbeing will improve when you recognise the source of your overeating.

With increased weight, various forms of disease seem to evolve much earlier in life. People grow fat and diseased because of an inability to cope with situations that confront them and they then overeat to compensate for this inability.

People become conditioned to using foods as a catalyst to help them cope with difficult situations or as a substitute for love or because of boredom or anger. Certain foods are used as a drug by overeaters because they offer temporary relief, but they often end up making them feel worse than before. It is a vicious circle.

HELPFUL HINTS

- Sit down at a designated place, relax and really enjoy your meal.
- Eat slowly and chew your food well. If you feel you should stop eating - **STOP**. Don't wait until you're uncomfortable. This is the hardest part of dieting, but it is only difficult for a few minutes. Your appetite **will** go away and you will begin to feel satisfied several minutes after you've stopped eating. Any remaining appetite is a psychological appetite, not a physical one. A psychological appetite is to be ignored if you are to successfully lose weight and keep it off.

- If you find you tend to binge at night, I suggest you eat your heavier meal (protein) for supper as it takes longer to digest and will provide more satisfaction than a light meal. This will also help you not to eat just before bed – something you shouldn't do whether you are trying to lose weight or not.

Willpower is often greater in the morning and you don't seem to overdo the eating at that time of the day. For most people, willpower seems to lessen towards the evening, and most overeating is done at night. If you still find it difficult to resist eating later in the evening then go to bed early, even if you're not sleepy. This is very difficult but it's a lot easier to refrain from eating once you're in bed than while you're up. The fact that your willpower is not strong, is a sign that you have run low in energy and need rest. Pat yourself on the back while in bed because you are not going to get up and get more food. You have done well!

- Another suggestion I find very helpful is to brush your teeth after every meal. This gives a fresh, sweet-smelling taste in your mouth and actually does not encourage eating after a full meal.
- I do give you a variety of foods from which to choose. You don't have to eat all these foods in one day.
- You don't have to count calories on this diet.
- Do not take in too much unnecessary fluid. When tissues contain too much fluid, flabbiness takes the place of firmness.
- Weighing of your food is not necessary, except for proteins and fats.
- If you weigh yourself daily you are going to be disappointed and discouraged. I suggest you weigh yourself when you start the programme first thing in the morning, before you dress, and thereafter once a week. Do not forget to take your measurements as well. At first you will reduce rapidly, then you will reach a plateau for a time, after which you will begin to lose weight again. (Even when fasting, the rate of weight loss slows down after the first week.) If you ate food containing salt, or if you ate too much, or too late at night, this will be reflected by your weight the following morning. Losing weight is a gradual process. You **will** lose weight if you adhere to my recommendations (even though it takes time) and you will also be getting healthier at the same time.
- Remember, once you have lost the weight, maintaining your ideal weight requires the same good habits and practices that are necessary to lose weight.
- You must have an exercise programme. Often a diet fails because the importance of stimulating the metabolism with a regular programme of exercise has been overlooked.
- There **are** certain foods, however, that you should not eat while on this weight loss programme. These are:
  - **Red meat**
  - **Condiments**

Losing weight and using condiments do not go well together, as condiments can increase your appetite and this often leads to overeating.

Non caloric carbonated beverages
These drinks are loaded with sodium chloride (salt) as well as chemical sweeteners and often contain caffeine. People often fill up on these drinks instead of eating food which will give them better nutrients.

WHY PEOPLE PUT ON WEIGHT WHEN ON HOLIDAY

People eat a lot of refined high fat foods, especially during the holiday season. These kinds of foods are low in fibre, vitamin- and mineral-deficient and very high in calories. Thus weight gain is very apparent. The food eaten also contains sugar combined with fat and salt, a combination especially found in convenience foods. When you eat sugar, you unknowingly eat fat too, for example, cakes and biscuits are mixed with butter and sugar. A pattern of eating that incorporates fresh raw fruit and vegetables, whole grains, sprouts, a moderate amount of nuts and seeds, and avocados is far superior – the fibre remains intact and vitamins and minerals are not lost. These foods are not loaded with empty calories as they only contain 1 – 4% fat and no sodium chloride (salt). The conventional diet has 78% of its fat content hidden, ie the fat is cooked into foods during preparation and contains salt as well. This is the very reason why people on such a diet gain weight.

WHY DIET PILLS ARE NOT THE ANSWER TO LOSING WEIGHT

All kinds of diet pills are unhealthy and dangerous, and should never be used.

- **Appetite suppressants** – Amphetamines are the most widely used appetite suppressants. Long-term users find their moods are often characterised by intense feelings of persecution. These appetite suppressants are often mixed with barbiturates, bulk-forming agents (to prevent constipation) and thyroid hormones. Taking appetite suppressants may cause nervousness, restlessness, tremors, insomnia, cardiovascular disturbances (faster heartbeat), high blood pressure and gastro-intestinal disturbances. Susceptible people may develop a psychic dependence as well as a physical dependence on these drugs.

- **Thyroid hormones** are commonly prescribed for overweight people, with the intention of heating up the body's fires, to burn more food as fuel, and theoretically promote the lipolysis (breaking down) of fat. People with bad hearts should not take thyroid hormones. These kinds of hormones play havoc with your whole endocrine system.

- **Diuretics** are drugs that increase the flow of water from your body. Diuretics work by stimulating the kidneys to draw water from the blood and excrete it in the urine. Caffeine is a diuretic, which explains why it stimulates urination. The most commonly used chemicals in diuretics are the thiazides. These can dehydrate you and cause nausea, weakness and drowsiness. They also rid the body of potassium along with the water and can aggravate diabetes.

- People take **laxatives** thinking that they speed food through their intestines, so not all food will be absorbed, and that which is not excreted, will not turn to fat. These laxatives range from those which directly stimulate the nerves of the bowels, eg castor oil and mineral oil, to bulk-forming agents which fill the colon and make it contract. Laxatives taken indiscriminately and frequently, can affect not only your bowels but your entire body. Their use in time can totally destroy the nerve network of the bowels which in turn aggravates the normal functioning of the digestive system. When this type of nerve damage eventually occurs, the constipated individual is **addicted** to laxatives. The continual use of laxatives leaches organic minerals from the body and disturbs the normal rhythm of

170

the excretory organs which sooner or later rebel. People often start with mild laxatives and if these do not work, resort to stronger ones. They then find they have to take them on a regular basis in order to work their bowels.

In order to lose weight effectively and keep it off, you have to go on a sensible weight loss programme. The most ideal method for attaining your ideal weight is the same as that for attaining ideal health, ie lots of fresh raw fruit and vegetables, sprouts, a small amount of avocados, nuts or seeds, whole grains, legumes and a minimal amount of free-range chicken or fish (if you are not a vegetarian). The right kind of food is the only successful way to reach your goal weight and optimum health.

GUIDELINES WHILE ON THE WEIGHT LOSS PROGRAMME

- When eating concentrated foods such as nuts, seeds, whole grains, chicken and fish, only eat the amounts stipulated.
- Do not have more than 2 bananas per day. You can eat more of the subacid or acid fruit groups.
- Always wait 4 hours between meals; this gives the digestive system a chance to rest.
- Use only a small amount of unsalted butter.
- Do not eat dried fruit (sulphur dioxide free) on the same day as nuts or avocados.
- Do not eat nuts and avocados at the same meal nor on the same day.
- Eat only 1 protein meal per day and 1 type of protein at a meal.
- Do not have avocados with protein meals. (They can be eaten with starch meals.)
- If you are hypoglycaemic, do not have fresh fruit juices or fruit only at a meal. You must always add lettuce and/or celery to

these foods.
- Never drink with your meals. Wait 1 hour after fruit and 2 hours after other foods before drinking. You can drink $1/2$ hour before a meal; only drink purified/distilled water.

IF YOU ARE ON ANY FORM OF MEDICATION, PLEASE CONSULT YOUR PHYSICIAN BEFORE EMBARKING ON ANY DIET PROGRAMME

WEEK 1: Liquids only

First 3 Days: Drink only purified/distilled water.

Days 4 – 7: Drink fresh fruit juices. Use the recipes given on page 173.

A word of warning: Overeating after the first week is harmful. If you feel you do not have the discipline nor the desire to attempt a water and a juice fast, then start with WEEK 2. You will still lose weight. I do however feel that fasting is useful in helping to clear a previously distorted sense of taste.

During the fast:
- Blood pressure decreases. Excess fat and abnormal deposits are consumed as food, while the cells and tissues of vital organs are preserved.
- You can expect to lose not less than 3 kg during the first 3 days of fasting. Men tend to lose more than that.
- Drink only when thirsty. Drinking excessive amounts of water will not help you to lose more weight. Drink purified / distilled water at room temperature.
- Do not prepare juices ahead of time because they lose vitamins and minerals very quickly.
- Avoid doing **strenuous exercise** during the fast.
- If you wish to fast for only 2 days instead of 3, then skip day 3 and move on to day 4.
- All juices on the juice fast are interchange-

able, depending on the fresh fruits and vegetables in season.

• Do not fast on juices for more than 3 days.

• To get the best results, follow the programme.

WEEK 1 MENU PROGRAMME

	Morning	Noon	Evening
DAY 1	Distilled / purified water all day		
DAY 2	Distilled / purified water all day		
DAY 3	Distilled / purified water all day		
DAY 4	120 ml orange juice	180 ml tomato and celery juice (see recipe No. 5)	240 ml carrot vegetable juice (see recipe No. 2) and if you are very thirsty have 180 ml watermelon juice before bedtime *

After Day 4, the total juice intake in one day must not exceed 720 ml (under 1 litre). If you want some juice before bedtime, then cut down on your mealtime allowances.

	Morning	Noon	Evening
DAY 5	240 ml fruit drink (see recipe No. 9)	240 ml cucumber and tomato juice (see recipe No. 1)	240 ml vegetable juice (see recipe No. 3)
DAY 6	180 ml orange-pineapple juice (see recipe No. 4)	180 ml carrot vegetable juice (see recipe No. 2)	300 ml blended avocado salad (see recipe No. 6)
DAY 7	180 ml watermelon juice	240 ml vegetable juice (see recipe No. 3)	180 ml tomato and celery juice (see recipe No. 5) or banana drink (see recipe No. 8) *

JUICE FAST RECIPES

1 Cucumber and Tomato Juice
2 medium tomatoes
120 g cucumber

Blend in blender

2 Carrot Vegetable Juice
1/2 pepper, red or yellow
4 medium carrots
1/2 cucumber

Use a juice extractor

3 Vegetable Juice
3 medium carrots
3 stalks celery
2 butter lettuce leaves

Use a juice extractor

4 Orange-Pineapple Juice
2 peeled oranges
1 pineapple slice (medium thickness)

Blend in blender

5 Tomato and Celery Juice
2 medium tomatoes
3 stalks celery
parsley (optional)

Use a juice extractor

6 Blended Avocado Salad
1/2 avocado
1 tomato
1 red or yellow pepper
3 spinach or cabbage leaves

Use a juice extractor or blender

7 Celery and Apple Juice
2 small apples
3 stalks celery

Use a juice extractor

8 Banana Drink
2 medium bananas
small amount of distilled/purified water

Blend in blender

9 Fruit Drink
1/2 papaya (papino or pawpaw)
1 peeled orange
1 medium apple
1 pineapple slice (medium thickness)

Blend in blender

WEEK 2: INCLUDES FRESH FRUIT, RAW VEGETABLE SALADS AND *STEAMED NEUTRAL/GREEN VEGETABLES.*

This week consists of predominantly raw food. I have found through research and experience with my clients, that the more raw foods you eat the faster you will lose weight, as well as prevent degenerative diseases. As willpower is greater in the early part of the day I suggest you eat only 2 meals per day, ie lunch and supper. The first food that goes into your mouth at lunch time must be fruit.

You should not live on **Fruits only** for a period longer than one month. For special purposes such as dieting or before or after a fast, it is acceptable. During winter you can add 60 g of sulphur dioxide free dried fruit, correctly combined with other fruits. You can also add lettuce and/or celery to any fruit except melons. This will increase your calcium and iron intake. Keep the amount of sweet fruits lower than that of acid and subacid fruits because of the higher sugar content. This will help you to lose weight. If I have mentioned fruits which are not in season, then choose those fruits in season and remember to combine correctly.

DAYS 1 – 2: Eat only **Mono fruit meals** (eat 1 type of fruit at a meal). Eating like this will make you lose weight more quickly. You will find, however, that fresh raw fruit and vegetable meals simply do not produce the feeling of fullness you are accustomed to on a conventional diet. Therefore you must eat a substantial amount of the particular fruit specified for that meal.

DAYS 3 – 5: You can now add raw vegetables. You must eat a large tubful but **add no seasoning or spices**. A simple dressing of just lemon juice, or avocados blended with water or lemon juice or any of the following dressings may be added. Keep salads simple, using only 3 – 4 different vegetables

DAY 6: Add steamed neutral/green vegetables. No seasoning is allowed. You can, however, add 1 tablespoon of fresh lemon juice together with 2 tablespoons of cold-pressed oil. Do not add avocado if using the oil dressing. Limit the amount of steamed vegetables to less than 2 cups.

DRESSINGS:
Avocado-Tomato Dressing:
1 medium avocado, peeled
2 small tomatoes
3 tbsp celery juice

Blend in blender

Avocado-Pepper Dressing:
1 medium avocado, peeled
2 tbsp celery juice
1 red pepper

Blend in blender

Tomato Dressing:
2 medium tomatoes
1 red pepper
1 small avocado

Blend in blender

DAY 7: Mono fruit day.

WEEK 2 MENU PROGRAMME

	Morning	Noon	Evening
DAY 1	Watermelon	Watermelon	Peaches – lettuce and/or celery optional
DAY 2	Watermelon	1 small pineapple blended	Nectarines – lettuce and/or celery optional
DAY 3	Mixed melons	2 bananas and 250 g grapes	Large raw vegetable salad (any raw vegetables you like – no dressing)
DAY 4	No breakfast	12.30 large fruit salad correctly combined (use only 3 fruits)	Large raw vegetable salad – any dressing
DAY 5	250 g grapes	3 mangoes	Raw vegetable salad and 1/2 avocado
DAY 6	2 mangoes	6 ripe, firm tomatoes	1 large raw vegetable salad – any dressing plus steamed neutral vegetables. Avoid mildly starchy vegetables
DAY 7	Eat as many grapes as you want until you go to sleep – chew them well. (You can choose any other fruit but only 1 kind.)		

WEEK 3: INCLUDES FRESH FRUIT, RAW VEGETABLE SALADS, STEAMED NEUTRAL/GREEN VEGETABLES AND *PROTEIN*

Overindulgence in protein is dangerous for your body. The body is not capable of storing large amounts of protein; excess protein passes out via the kidneys, causing them to overwork. When more protein is eaten than needed, some is excreted unused, and that which is undigested tends to putrefy in the digestive tract and colon, resulting in foul stools and poisons in the bloodstream. When you eat a protein meal do not add oil or avocados. Fats inhibit digestion.

If you are trying to lose weight limit your daily intake of fat. Don't indulge in more than a dab of unsalted butter or eat more than 1/2 an avocado per day. The less fat you eat the more weight you will lose.

The following menus have been created for vegetarians. You can substitute 90 g fish or free-range chicken for your protein meal.

Avoid mildly starchy vegetables if you have a great deal of weight to lose. Remember, you can substitute the fruits in the fruit meals for any fruits you particularly desire.

If you do not want dressing with your salad you need not have it.

WEEK 3 MENU PROGRAMME

	Morning	Noon	Evening
DAY 1	Watermelon (eat till satisfied)	1 banana and some grapes	Raw vegetable salad, 60 g unsalted, unroasted nuts (no peanuts)
DAY 2	1/2 pineapple and 1 mango	Watermelon (eat till satisfied)	Raw vegetable salad and steamed neutral/green vegetables – add any recommended dressing if desired
DAY 3	2 nectarines and 1 peach	Grapes (eat till satisfied)	Raw vegetable salad, 60 g unsalted, unroasted nuts (no peanuts)
DAY 4	Any of the melons (eat till satisfied)	1 banana, 2 peaches	Raw vegetable salad, with any recommended dressing
DAY 5	Mangoes and grapes (eat till satisfied)	Nectarines and peaches (eat till satisfied)	Raw vegetable salad, with any recommended dressing and steamed neutral/green vegetables
DAY 6	1/2 pineapple and 2 peaches	Grapes (eat till satisfied)	Raw vegetable salad and 1/2 avocado
DAY 7	1 banana and 3 peaches	Watermelon (eat till satisfied)	Vegetable salad with any recommended dressing

WEEK 4: INCLUDES FRESH FRUIT, RAW VEGETABLE SALADS, STEAMED NEUTRAL/GREEN VEGETABLES, PROTEIN AND *STARCH*

- When adding starch to your diet, eat **less fruit** that day.
- Potatoes are not fattening if you eat them with neutral/green vegetables and limit the amount of butter (a dab).
- Indigestion and catarrh result from eating cooked starch and sugar together, for example bread.
- Tomatoes or lemon juice should not be included in a salad that is followed by a starch if you suffer from digestive problems.
- You can add dressing to your salads if you desire, but only use the dressings I recommend in this section.

WEEK 4 MENU PROGRAMME

	Morning	Noon	Evening
DAY 1	Papino (eat till satisfied)	Kiwi fruit and apples (eat till satisfied)	Raw vegetable salad (no tomatoes), 1 or 2 baked potatoes or sweet potatoes with a dab of unsalted butter
DAY 2	Strawberries and peaches (eat till satisfied)	Cherries (eat till satisfied)	Raw vegetable salad and steamed cauliflower
DAY 3	1 banana and 2 apples	Pears and kiwi fruit (eat till satisfied)	Raw vegetable salad, 120 g steamed beetroot/butternut/ pumpkin
DAY 4	$1/_2$ pineapple and pears	Papinos (eat till satisfied)	Raw vegetable salad, $1/_2$ avocado, 90 g cooked brown rice or 2 slices health bread. (You can put the $1/_2$ avocado from the salad on the bread if you wish.)

WEEK 4 MENU PROGRAMME (continued)

	Morning	Noon	Evening
DAY 5	2 apples	Kiwi fruit and pears (eat till satisfied)	Raw vegetable salad with 60 g nuts or 90 g free-range chicken or fish or 60 g unprocessed cheese (if you are not a vegetarian)
DAY 6	1 banana only or as many grapes as you want	Melon (eat till satisfied)	Raw vegetable salad, 2 steamed mealies or steamed broccoli
DAY 7	Papino (eat till satisfied)	Apples and kiwi fruit (eat till satisfied)	Raw vegetable salad and 60 g unsalted, unroasted nuts eg cashews

Principal Source: Shelton H.M., Willard J., & Oswald J.A. – The Original Natural Hygiene Weightloss Diet Book.

Good diets end sooner or later, and for their effects to be lasting, they must be followed by a continued healthful eating pattern. If you did not reach your goal at the end of the 4 week programme, follow my Maintenance Programme for one week and then begin the weight loss programme again.

The answer to permanent weight control and a long healthy "sickness free" life is that you definitely have to base your diet on an abundance of fresh fruit and raw vegetables, some nuts and seeds, sprouts, a reasonable amount of cooked whole grains, steamed vegetables and legumes. These foods are the most powerful foods for controlling weight. Most people can still eat all they want and stay slim and healthy after they have finished the initial weight loss programme, provided they continue with my Maintenance Programme.

178

PART 6

General Information and Questions Regularly Asked during My Counselling Sessions

GENERAL INFORMATION

- People who are **anaemic or deficient in folic acid** must avoid the following:
  - Chemotherapeutic agents
  - Oral contraceptive pills
  - Alcohol
  - Drugs used to lower blood cholesterol
  - Antiseptic agents
  - Drugs used for ulcerative colitis
  - Antacids
  - Modern anti-ulcer drugs.

  The above can interfere with the absorption, utilisation and storage of folic acid.
  - Disorders of the stomach and small intestine, eg coeliac disease and Crohn's disease may lead to folic acid deficiency as a result of malabsorption of nutrients.

  Early symptoms of folic acid deficiency may include tiredness, irritability and loss of appetite.

  Folic acid is found in dark green, leafy vegetables, legumes, wheat germ and all fresh, raw fruit.

- If you tend to suffer from **blood clots** you should avoid smoking, birth control pills, hormones and the eating of high fat foods. Exercise is a very important part of the health programme I recommend.

- If you enjoy **bread** (even health bread) you should be aware of the following:

  Most bread contains yeast and this creates fermentation in the gastrointestinal tract which irritates the intestine. If you are going to eat it, it should be toasted. The browning process changes the starch into dextrin. This makes it more easily digested and partially destroys the fermentation of the yeast. White bread causes constipation as well as nervous disorders. You should also not eat bread that has been enriched with vitamins. Chemicals are also used in the bleaching process and all this is injurious to the delicate membranous lining of the gastrointestinal tract. My advice is to try and eat bread that is yeast and gluten free. Enquire at health stores.

- **Cold drinks** contain refined white sugar (about 5 teaspoons per 240 ml serving). The only difference between ordinary and diet cold drinks is that artificial sweeteners are used and these can be cancer producing. Some cold drinks also contain caffeine. When cold drinks are taken with food, it leads to fermentation instead of good digestion. There are many carbonated waters on the market, which although not ideal (because of the high salt content and inorganic minerals), are far better than cold drinks.

- **Carob** is an excellent substitute for chocolate. Carob is naturally sweet, rich in B vitamins and tastes just like chocolate (without the caffeine and dairy products which cause a great many problems). Carob is a fruit which normally grows in the Mediterranean area. Chocolate contains refined white sugar as well as dairy products, which definitely put a damper on a weight loss programme.

- **Flaxseed/linseed oil** is the best cold-pressed oil to use if you suffer from inflammatory conditions, eg arthritis, bursitis, etc.

- **Frozen is better than canned** if fresh is not available. Frozen foods, other than vegetables, are not ideal because they contain hidden salt, sugar and fat. The canning process requires the food to be cooked at high temperatures which decrease the vitamin and nutrient content. Canned foods are also cooked with chemicals, preservatives and salt, and contain aluminium or tin, which is leached from the inner surface of the can itself.

- **Gallstones and kidney stones** can be autolysed (broken down) on a totally raw food diet. It is best to consult a nutritional counsellor.
- My clients continually ask me about **guar gum** which is found in cereals. Guar gum is a vegetable gum made from the guar plant. It is used as a stabiliser or thickener and is not very well digested.
- **Irradiation** is a new method of food preservation. It serves as a substitute for chemical food additives and is used to control insects, delay fruit ripening and inhibit vegetable sprouting. In South Africa there is no law forcing irradiated foods to be labelled. The foods that may be subjected to irradiation are fresh fruit, spices, mushrooms, onion, garlic and a variety of meats and fish. According to *Bell, Alswang and Phillips*, 5 000 tons of food a year are irradiated (or radurised as it is sometimes called) in South Africa. South Africa has 5 irradiation plants situated in Tzaneen, Pelindaba, Isando, Cape Town and Durban. As consumers you should be aware that the long-term effects of eating irradiated foods have not been studied sufficiently and although you may be given assurances on the safety of irradiation, there is no guarantee of what the long-term generic results will be.
- **Sleep** is very important in maintaining health. Most people need 9 – 10 hours of good quality sleep per 24 hour period to keep well. With less sleep than this, you will accumulate wear and tear, resulting in degenerative disease as well as a compromised immune system which can bring about an accumulation of cancer cells.
  You may feel fine on less sleep, but you must never reach a stage of exhaustion.

If you find it difficult to fall asleep at night you must look at increasing your exercise schedule which aids in eliminating stress. Excess sugar, including fruit sugar, can disturb sleep patterns in some people. Drinking coffee during the latter part of the day can also result in insomnia.

- **Unsalted butter** is preferable to margarine. Margarine is a fat processed by hydrogenation, and should be avoided. When any oil is heated, it becomes denatured and forms harmful heat degradation by-products called "free radicals". Free radicals are not easily processed by the body and can be responsible for circulatory problems. My suggestion is to buy unsalted butter from a reputable health shop.
- If your child is **hyperactive** you will find a great improvement in the behaviour of the child if placed on a diet free of artificial colourants and flavourants, preservatives, especially Monosodium Glutamate (MSG), and caffeine-containing products (chocolate).
- **Lactose intolerant** indicates that you do not have the enzyme lactase to digest the lactose (sugar) in milk. Lactose may be used as a sweetener or binder in foodstuffs and medications.
  A deficiency of the enzyme lactase results in symptoms such as diarrhoea, a bloated feeling, flatulence and malabsorption of nutrients.
- **Uric acid** is a substance found in the blood and urine that is formed in the body as a waste product of protein metabolism. It results from a high dietary intake of animal products (meat and dairy) as well as coffee, salt and legumes. Excess uric acid can lead to gout, arthritis and back pain.

GENERAL QUESTIONS

Q *Do you believe in colonic irrigation and enemas?*

A I find these very exhausting to the body and wasting of nerve energy. They deplete the body of electrolytes and calcium. You have to look at the cause of constipation. If you keep resorting to these unnatural methods, the colon becomes lazy and will soon atrophy. The above treatments can be of benefit in certain situations. Consult a nutritional counsellor.

Q *How do I overcome vitamin deficiencies?*

A Your first step is to do everything you can to improve your health by improving your eating pattern and lifestyle. Many people have overcome deficiencies after a long fast. During a fast, the body actually repairs itself. Certain normal body functions that are not working properly are renewed after a fast. This results in a more efficient organism, which is then able to utilise food nutrients more efficiently.

Q *Many vegetarians enjoy tamari, miso and soya sauce. Are they as healthy as they are made out to be?*

A All these foods are high in sodium. One tablespoon of tamari contains more sodium than is healthy. You have to have a favourable ratio of potassium to sodium, as this is important in maintaining normal blood pressure. These foods must be used sparingly, especially by those who have problems with their heart, kidneys, blood pressure and fluid retention. Enquire at health stores for foods low in sodium.

Q *Why is it important to consult a nutritional counsellor?*

A When you are dealing with something as valuable as your health, you don't want to do too much of your learning by trial and error. Reading all the books on health is often not enough for most people, as everything that is known is not always written. There is nothing like experience to develop the confidence and/or reduce the stress experienced when trying something unconventional. Friends and family might call this approach radical but under a qualified nutritional counsellor you are assured of the safety of the procedure, and the potential benefits are maximised. In order to become good stewards of health, you need to be well educated in Natural Hygiene and its principles and practices. To achieve this, we need the best qualified teachers available.

Q *What do you think of taking medication when one has flu, a headache etc? Do you believe in immunisation?*

A Drugs (medication) are not the solution to the illness (the symptoms you are suffering). Illness is the effort of the body to restore normality. By halting this process, the medication may further aggravate the condition. Such treatments stop the body's attempts to restore normality and allow cellular waste to further accumulate in the body. One factor contributing to any illness is the excessive retention of cellular waste products in the body. Treatments may give symptomatic relief, but they do not address the underlying cause. Symptomatic treatment can establish a cycle in which a deteriorating condition can result in the increased use or dependence on medication as time goes by. If you are not feeling well, I suggest that you abstain from eating concentrated foods (meat, fish, chicken, dairy, nuts, avocados etc). Just eat fruit, or better still, drink distilled/purified water till you feel better. Always consult a nutritional counsellor.

Immunisation is probably one of the main causes of immune system disorders. Auto-immune illnesses are probably the epidemic of our times, as a large percentage of the population suffers from at least one of these illnesses. According to *Robert Mendelsohn "There is a growing suspicion that immunisation against relatively harmless 'childhood diseases' may be responsible for the dramatic increase in auto-immune diseases, since mass inoculations were introduced".*
(Source: Mendelsohn, Robert S. – Confessions of a Medical Heretic)

Q How do we lose important minerals from our body?

A If you eat excessive amounts of protein, especially in the form of animal products, you can seriously damage your health. Excess proteins are broken down in the liver and excreted through the kidneys as urea. Urea has a diuretic action which causes the kidneys to work harder and excrete more water. Along with the water, minerals are lost in the urine, especially calcium. You now develop a negative calcium balance even if calcium supplements are taken. This means that more calcium is lost in the urine than is absorbed. This deficit must be made up from the body stores of calcium which are found primarily in the bones. If this is done regularly you will eventually get osteoporosis. You have to reduce the animal protein content of your diet because the body excretes calcium via the urine to neutralise the toxins found in these foods, in order to restore a positive calcium balance. The calcium lost through eating excessive protein in the form of flesh, dairy products, eggs etc ends up in the urine and this results in high levels of calcium in the kidneys, which can cause painful stones. *Dr John McDougall says "You have to return to a diet of mostly fresh fruit, raw vegetables, a moderate amount of nuts, seeds, sprouts, avocados, legumes and grains to prevent a negative calcium balance."* (Source: McDougall, John and Mary – The McDougall Plan)

Q Why is exercise so important? I thought that if you ate correctly you didn't have to worry about physical activity.

A Exercise is an important factor in reducing the risk of heart disease. It increases good cholesterol-HDL (a lipoprotein associated with the decreased probability of developing atherosclerosis) and lowers bad cholesterol-LDL (a lipoprotein associated with the increased probability of developing atherosclerosis and raising triglycerides). Exercise can also lower blood pressure and help you to lose weight. A brisk walk 5 days a week for at least 45 minutes does wonders for the body. Vigorous exercise creates the release of endorphins. Endorphins attach themselves to specific receptor sites in the brain which contribute to reversing stress, lifting depression and enhancing sleep. Exercise works better than tranquillisers and has no undesirable side effects. Always choose an exercise you enjoy and do it regularly.

Q I'm a body builder and not very fond of meat. I have been told to eat animal products to ensure my protein requirements. Can you please advise me?

A Proper weight gain really comes from the enhancement of muscular activity and eating correctly. Overeating on animal protein will not cause weight gain. On the contrary, this can cause lots of problems. The sugars in fruits are excellent for building and maintaining adequate fat reserves. Remember, more calories must be eaten than expended, to build up fat reserves and these are supplied by eating dates, raisins and bananas etc. Nuts, fresh fruits and vegetables are rich in proteins, minerals, vitamins and fats. I advise you to eat a variety of plant foods, whole grains and legumes included. If in doubt consult a nutritional counsellor.

Q *I'm nearly 90 and my wife is 95. We live on the conventional S.A. diet, including a great deal of meat, which in your opinion is not so healthy, as well as smoke and drink alcohol. I have never been ill, though my wife has been ill all her life. My father lived to over a 100 and really didn't know the first thing about "diet". We have experienced some form of stress in our lives, which certainly doesn't contribute to good health, longevity or happiness. Do you consider us exceptional? Is it purely accidental? Is it a miracle? How do you explain this situation?*

A There are so many variables involved, that without more detailed information about your lifestyle and what other foods you included in your diet, it is difficult to make an intelligent comment. Firstly, you have inherited good genes. You chose the right parents! In your youth, there were fewer chemical additives in food and fewer poisonous pesticides to contaminate the soil. People lived more natural lives. As our internal and external environments became more polluted, our constitution and our genetic endowments started to break down. This fact is constantly coming to light in experiments done on animals.

Animals may survive a deficient diet apparently without harm, but their "offspring", after several generations, become deformed or sterile.

The same is true for humans. The deformities usually become evident only in the 2nd and 3rd generations. You didn't mention what type of illnesses your wife has suffered from during her life. If her illnesses were acute, inflammatory crises, such as colds, flu, all the "itises" etc, her body is manifesting vitality and her illnesses were the body's effort to reduce the toxic load. But if there is degenerative disease, be it arthritis, diabetes etc she is paying for errors in her lifestyle. In either case, your conventional diet has been producing its effects on your wife. Maybe your day of reckoning is just further away. Remember, every cause has its effect. You obviously have a strong genetic tendency that enables you to withstand the abuse of the wrong foods for longer periods of time, before disease is apparent. We all have different genetic weaknesses, and we are all susceptible to certain diseases. Nutrition is such a powerful regulator of disease incidence, that when an optimal diet is consumed throughout life, genetics will have little effect in contributing to the development of the common causes of death we see in society today.

Q *I travel a great deal to the States, and suffer from terrible jet lag. How can I prevent this?*

A The day before the flight you should eat raw foods only, ie fruits, vegetables, salads and nuts/seeds or avocados. On the day of the flight, either fast (drink purified water only) or eat as much fresh fruit as you want on the plane. This helps your digestive

185

system prepare for the change in mealtimes at the end of your journey. When you arrive at your destination, continue eating raw foods till you go to sleep that evening. The day after, you can go back to the maintenance programme. If you follow my recommendations, you will sleep well at night, and if you are on business you will be able to work productively as well. Try it – it works!

QUESTIONS ABOUT WEIGHT LOSS AND WEIGHT GAIN

Q *I feel I am carbohydrate sensitive, because I just can't lose weight eating fruits and vegetables. What do you think of the popular high protein diets? Can the sugar in fruit cause too much insulin to be released, causing fat to be stored or immobilised? Does eating a lot of fruit cause excessively high levels of insulin in the body?*

A Eating fruit does not cause an excessive rise in insulin. Excessive fat consumed and fat on the body are the main reasons for the body being forced to produce abnormal levels of insulin. I do not recommend a diet of fruit only. Vegetables should form a major component of your diet, with fruits and grains supplying a lesser amount of calories. Beans (legumes), nuts and seeds can be added in small amounts, if you are not significantly overweight. High protein, carbohydrate restricted diets do cause weight loss, but they also cause ketosis; this means that the body can't find enough carbohydrates to properly run its machinery, so it looks for another emergency fuel that can be utilised in times of crises or fasting, and that fuel is ketones. Ketones are fat breakdown products that the cells can use as an alternative fuel, rather than carbohydrates. When ketosis occurs, the acidity in the bloodstream increases. You can measure this increase by checking your urine by means of keto-sticks. If you eat in this way for a prolonged period of time, the elimination of the excess protein which can't be stored in the body, and all the acids created as a result of protein metabolism, will cause the kidneys to overwork, and in time kidney damage will occur. As the acids are washed out through the kidneys, many minerals that are stored in the bones, especially calcium, are also washed out and so lost. High protein diets are linked to the development of serious diseases such as cancer, heart disease, osteoporosis, rheumatoid arthritis, lupus, renal disease and kidney stones etc. We are not biologically adapted to eat a high protein diet. Put simply: when our diet contains more protein than we need, the liver attempts to break down the excess and excretes it in the form of urea via the kidneys. People with advanced liver disease should not eat animal products. There are other toxins besides urea, that are breakdown products of protein metabolism. Uric acid and other potentially harmful nitrogenous wastes, including ammonia, increase in our bloodstream when we eat excessive protein. Vegetable proteins, however, generate less ammonia. When the eating of animal protein is initially stopped, the body will attempt to eliminate toxins with corresponding painful symptoms of headaches, feelings of mental fatigue and irritability. Animal-based foods are almost 100% fat, high in protein and devoid of fibre. They contain none of the protective anti-oxidant nutrients that protect against heart disease and cancer.

Scientists have discovered that animal-based foods, ie high protein foods may contribute to cancer, especially colon, prostate, and breast cancer as well as heart attacks. The answer to permanent weight control and a long healthy life, free from chronic diseases, is to base your diet on more raw fruit and vegetables, whole grains, legumes, and a moderate amount of avocados, nuts and seeds; in other words a high plant-based diet. These foods are also the most powerful foods for controlling weight and you could eat them in abundance and still stay slim and healthy.

Q *I'm always on a diet. I have been to a number of dieticians, hoping I will receive the answer to my weight problems. You are my last resort. What advice can you give me?*

A My counselling sessions with people who are overweight and obsessed with dieting, have revealed that these people are always in a state of depression and self-hate. Food looms as the major issue in their lives. I will give you some tips which should help you in planning your eating pattern.

- Try to fast one day a week and drink only purified water on that day. This should be your first objective in losing weight.
- Plan ahead – write down what you intend eating on each specific day.
- Keep a food journal of what you actually do eat on that day.
- Try and have a few raw food days.
- Avoid oily foods initially, like cold-pressed oil, tahini sauce, avocados and nut butters.
- Go easy on sweet fruit and avoid dried fruit initially.
- Keep meals very simple. Now and again eat mono fruit meals.
- Practise food combining.
- Eat only when hungry. Listen to your body and stop eating when you have had enough.

- Most importantly, don't punish yourself with guilt when you are not perfect. This encourages continual overeating of the wrong foods.
- Always keep in contact with a support group or nutritional counsellor.
  Besides food there are other factors that will encourage weight loss. You have to have adequate rest and sleep, emotional poise, self mastery, creative pursuits and meaningful work. If you follow my recommendations with the support of a nutritional counsellor, you should start losing weight.

Q *I am a vegetarian eating lots of fruit and vegetables, grains and avocados and a moderate amount of nuts and seeds, but I am still experiencing drastic weight loss and I really want to gain weight. Please point me in the right direction.*

A Strict raw vegetarian diets tend to keep you slim. There are, however, other factors to consider if you are not gaining weight.

- Inefficient digestion and/or absorption can make it difficult to gain weight or even maintain weight. Fasting has been very successful in resolving various digestive problems.
- You should add more calorie-dense foods to your meals at both lunch and supper, eg whole grains, legumes, whole grain pastas and breads. I suggest you have two different kinds of starches at a meal, eg mealies and bread. Don't fill up on coarse, fibrous foods eg raw celery, cabbage and butter lettuce etc. They are very wholesome, but are known as negative calorie foods. Rather fill up on whole grains etc. Eat more sweet fruits, eg bananas and papinos than acid fruits, eg citrus fruit and pineapples.

Dried fruits are high in calories but can cause wind. In order to prevent this, I suggest you soak them first in purified water overnight.

Nuts are high in calories, protein, vitamins and minerals, but they are also very oily and high in fat. Limit your intake to $1/2$ cup every other day.

- Add more weight training to your fitness schedule and cut down on aerobic activities.
- Check your vitamin B_{12} levels.
- You must make sure you are getting sufficient rest and sleep and try to reduce stress. Consult a nutritional counsellor.

Q *I have been following the pattern of eating you advocate and have lost weight, which I am thrilled about. A week ago I reached a plateau and since then my weight has not budged. Please advise me what to do now as I still want to lose more weight.*

A I am sure that besides the initial weight loss, you are also feeling much better. Your body is a highly intelligent organism and it only works on priorities.

You have reached a plateau because there is still repair work to be done internally. When this has been accomplished, the body will return to the task of losing more weight. Your body will decide what weight it wants to be. You must continue to feed yourself correctly and your body will do the rest.

A quick way to facilitate further weight loss is to go on a fast for at least 3 days, drinking only purified water. I would prefer you, however, to do this under supervision. You can consult a nutritional counsellor who will offer you other options.

QUESTIONS RELATING TO THE HORMONAL SYSTEM

Q *I have reached menopause and have been advised to take Hormone Replacement Therapy (HRT). I am experiencing hot flushes and I find this very unpleasant. Have you any suggestions?*

A As women go through menopause their ovaries produce less oestrogen. The body, however, still continues to produce a small amount indefinitely in the fat cells, adrenal glands, muscles, liver and brain. *"There are also certain estrogenic compounds, phytoestrogens (plant estrogens) such as genistein which binds to estrogen receptors in the breast or endometrium, 'locking out' the bad estrogens associated with disease. In addition, these phytoestrogens provide a natural and gentle source of estrogen as women's levels drop during menopause."* (Source: Campbell, T. Colin – The China Project)

Plant oestrogens can be found in many foods; soya beans are one of the main sources of these hormones. According to *Christine Cox "Eating a daily cup of soybeans may provide roughly the equivalent of 1 tablet of Primarin, a widely prescribed estrogen for menopausal women. Another intriguing source of plant hormones is the Mexican wild yam, Dioscorea villosa. This root – not to be confused with our popular supermarket variety – contains hormone-like substances that may convert to estrogens in the body."* (Source: Cox, Christine – The Magic of Phytoestrogens – New Century Nutrition Volume 2 No. 8, August 1996). Research studies claim that it may be progesterone women need. Most HRT formulas contain synthetic progesterone (progestin). This is very different from natural progesterone. *Dioscorea villosa*, mentioned above, is the source of phytoprogesterone. In the USA, a highly sophisticated enzyme process has been developed which converts diosgenin (extracted from the root) into phyto-progesterone.

Women on high fat diets, leading unhealthy lifestyles, often have a lot more symptoms associated with menopause eg hot flushes. Women following the programme of eating I recommend, as well as including other non-nutritive factors in their lifestyle, go through menopause with fewer hot flushes, and less irritability, moodiness and vaginal dryness. When you are exercising regularly, you are better able to handle hormonal swings. Sunshine is also very important as it enables the body to produce vitamin D which helps in the absorption of calcium. I have found that the following foods definitely upset the hormonal system:

- **animal products** such as meat, fish, chicken, eggs, cheese, milk and yoghurt
- **stimulants**, such as caffeine found in colas, tea, coffee and chocolate
- **artificial sweeteners** and **refined sugar**
- **vinegar** and **alcohol**.

Essential fatty acids found in nuts, seeds, avocados, olives in brine, yellow mealies and cold-pressed oils help the hormonal system to function optimally. If a woman goes through menopause without many symptoms, it means that her body is still producing adequate amounts of oestrogen to meet her needs. With regard to your hot flushes, I suggest a supervised fast at a health hydro or a fasting clinic. You will then find that the hot flushes will reduce considerably or even disappear. If it is not possible for you to fast at a fasting clinic, change your eating habits; eat a high raw food diet, combine foods correctly, and exercise. This will definitely reduce the

incidence of hot flushes. According to some medical doctors, the best thing to do is to have very hot baths every time you have a hot flush and "flush it away". Try it! It works! The most sensible approach, however, is to change your eating habits. Before opting for hormone replacement therapy, find out as much as you can about alternative methods. Consult a nutritional counsellor.

Q *I have terrible menstrual cramps during my periods. They are also very heavy. The doctor has told me that I also have fibroids and ovarian cysts. What do you suggest I do to lessen the menstrual cramps and how can I get rid of fibroids etc. I have also been battling to fall pregnant. How important is a correct eating pattern?*

A I have found through my counselling sessions that dairy products are definitely associated with menstrual cramps and heavy periods. Once I remove these foods, much lighter periods and fewer menstrual cramps are experienced. Fibroids and ovarian cysts are also caused by consuming dairy products, ie cheese, ice cream, butter or milk. Infertility can result from the Fallopian tubes being blocked by mucus due to excessive consumption of dairy products. Many disorders of the reproductive system, eg vaginal discharges and vaginal infections seem to be linked to dairy products. Consult a nutritional counsellor for guidance regarding a correct eating plan.

HOW THE BODY ACTS ON THE FOOD YOU EAT
Q *What foods provide the appropriate nutrients required by the body?*
A The nutrients required by the body are

made up of vitamins, minerals, proteins, fats, water and fibre, as well as enough concentrated foods to meet your energy needs. The foods I recommend supply the body with the right nutrients. They are fresh fruits, raw vegetables, especially green, yellow and cruciferous vegetables, such as kale, cabbage, cauliflower and broccoli. Cruciferous vegetables top the list as potential cancer inhibitors; they contain anti-oxidants. You must also include a moderate amount of seeds, nuts and legumes as well as carbohydrates, ie potatoes, whole grains etc. You should take in at least 10 – 15% protein from plant-based foods. These foods contain the least amount of toxins and are high in fibre. Foods that lack dietary fibre are refined carbohydrates such as white flour products, and animal protein. These foods may encourage diseases such as diverticulitis, bowel cancer, constipation, piles, appendicitis, high blood pressure and heart disease.

Q I am all in favour of a raw diet. Can I live on totally raw food for ever? Are there any problems if I follow this pattern of eating and how do I know if I am getting enough calories?

A Some people can live healthfully for long periods on uncooked foods. But not all of us can or feel obligated to try to do so. Let me point out certain pitfalls regarding the eating of certain raw foods.

If you eat a large amount of nuts you will be taking in too much fat and protein, and this is not desirable. You should eat only a $1/2$ cup of nuts 3 times a week. You can eat a lot on a raw diet and still lose weight. If this concerns you, you should eat a more calorie-sufficient diet, otherwise you might start to binge on unhealthy foods. Cooked starchy vegetables provide a concentrated source of readily available calories that can often be lacking in an "only raw diet", especially if you are not eating a variety of raw foods. If this applies to you, I suggest you eat a variety of steamed neutral and starch vegetables on alternate days and on the other days, eat only raw food.

When people are not getting enough calories, they manifest symptoms which include:

- progressive weight loss
- weakness and fatigue
- constant feeling of cold
- symptoms of nervous irritability
- increased susceptibility to infections, particularly fungal (yeast) infections
- problems with hair and skin
- brittle and cracking nails
- problems with teeth and bleeding gums
- digestive problems such as gas, bloating and diarrhoea.

If you feel great on a totally raw diet, provided you are eating a variety of foods, then stay with it. It is the most ideal approach to optimum health.

Q I have been told to drink 8 glasses of water daily to help me lose weight. I really dislike water. Do I have to drink this amount?

A The "8-glasses-a-day advocates" contend that water "flushes" toxins from the body. This idea is totally false. The body is entirely self-cleansing. Thirst will tell us when and how much water to drink. Water is necessary only when we are thirsty. We overwork our kidneys if we consume water beyond the demands of thirst. Most thirst results from pathological (disease producing) practices and is not normal. For example, people who ingest excess salt have an abnormally high water need. Most foods on the conventional diet are pre-salted, so even people who do not add salt to their food consume rather large amounts of this substance. All the sodium we need is found in its usable, healthful, organic form in fresh fruits, vegetables, nuts and seeds. The more salt that is ingested the greater the body's requirements for water. Water holds salt in solution, thus diluting it and reducing its irritating and damaging effects on cells and tissues. Other condiments and seasonings such as pepper, ginger, cinnamon, onions, and garlic etc also occasion thirst for the same reason salt does. Soya sauces, miso, and kelp are also high in salt and occasion great thirst. The correct diet is water sufficient. The pure water of fruit and vegetables is far better than the water supplied by the water systems in our cities. The only time you may experience thirst if eating properly, is during periods of fasting, vigorous activity or exposure to heat. The rule is: drink as thirst demands.

Q Do you think that correct food combining is very important?

A I have found through my counselling sessions that many people have developed bad eating habits and often need to make dramatic changes in their eating patterns to gain the benefits of health. **Food combining** offers you a new pattern of eating. This helps you make the transition to a healthier diet. Diet and nutrition are only part of the concept of Natural Hygiene. Neither food in general, nor food combining, in particular, is the primary focus of Natural Hygiene. I have found, however, that for those people who are not yet willing or able to adopt the dietary recommendations I propose,

which are mainly raw fruit and vegetables, some whole grains, a moderate amount of nuts, seeds, avocados and legumes, then food combining may just make that significant difference. Those who have used the food combining rules have definitely enjoyed enormous benefits. They find they eat simpler meals and they actually don't overeat. Those people who still want to eat their meat, fish, poultry, eggs and dairy products will find if they combine correctly they will eat less of these foods.

By combining correctly you will also help to keep your weight down. I feel that food combining is not that important for people who are eating raw meals only. Food combining is, however, absolutely essential in the immediate post-fasting period and when digestive difficulties are present.

Q I have heard that if you add bran to your food or eat cereal containing bran it will help constipation. Is this true?

A The only food that will help constipation is high-fibre food, such as fresh raw fruit and vegetables. Bran prevents the absorption of nutrients such as iron and calcium. If you are anaemic, you should not use it. Bran has sharp points which irritate the colon as it moves through the intestinal tract. Fruit does not do this. Bran is a waste product of milling and grain processing and does not break down in the body. Do you still want to take it? I am not in favour of using laxatives for constipation either. These cause the colon to atrophy.

Constipation is caused by eating an abundance of animal as well as refined products, which are all devoid of fibre. Exercise and eating the correct foods will prevent constipation.

Q Why do we crave certain foods ?

A Cravings are expressions of temporary body imbalances and needs. They are normal and an accepted part of the physiological adjustment to an improved diet. These cravings are temporary, and will disappear altogether as soon as your body is able to derive optimum nourishment from the food you are eating. Try not to fall into the clutches of the guilt trip. It has a totally negative effect on your health and creates a whole chain reaction of conflicts, tensions and oppositions for your body to deal with, at a time when it needs all its energies for healing and cleansing. Eating the food you crave can have positive overall effects, especially if you take only a small quantity and go about it in the right way. It can, for instance, give you the opportunity to clear your head of the old cobwebs of food memories that hang around to haunt you. You can also derive positive benefits from giving in to a craving by using it as a learning experience. Set out to see how the body will react to a small amount of the "unhealthy" food you crave. Instead of a binge mentality, adopt an experimental attitude. Observe carefully how you feel. Note the symptoms and signs of distress eg, eating yoghurt when you have been on a well-established non-dairy food diet will make you feel "heavy" and congested. A slice of baked bread on a live-food diet can immediately upset your digestion.

If, now and then you eat something less vital and nourishing than you are accustomed to, it can serve the important purpose of bringing you to the full realisation that simple, light foods are what your body will automatically come to select, when given the choice.

Q What do you think of commercial juices and frozen concentrates?

A People who enjoy juices should preferably use only pure fruit and vegetable juices prepared at home using a juice extractor. Commercial juices and frozen concentrates are heated (pasteurised) and acid-forming in the bloodstream. If you are going to drink such juices, my suggestion is to dilute them.

Q You keep emphasising that it is very important to eat raw green vegetables ie lettuce, celery, cabbage, broccoli etc. I really don't enjoy vegetables. I much prefer eating fruit. Can I still maintain optimum health without eating vegetables?

A Green vegetables, when eaten raw, contain a rich source of chlorophyll which has almost the same molecular structure as the haemoglobin molecules of human blood. Chlorophyll can offset the effects of environmental pollutants. If you are looking for permission to skip eating vegetables, I am afraid I am going to disappoint you. Fruit alone does not constitute an adequate long-term diet, although it is digested rapidly and does not burden the body. Vegetables are the best source of minerals, including macro-minerals (calcium and magnesium) and microminerals (zinc and copper), and I do insist you definitely include these in your pattern of eating. I find people do not eat a sufficient variety of vegetables consistently every day, especially nutrient-dense vegetables such as broccoli, kale, spinach and cabbage.

Q Is fruit juice better than fresh fruit?

A Most of the fibre has been removed through juicing, as well as pectins, bioflavonoids, and other important nutrients contained in the wholefood. My suggestion is, if you like a smooth texture, rather purée whole fruits. Fresh fruit juices, however, are very important on a juice fast and after breaking a fast.

Q *What are the benefits of a vegetarian diet?*

A vegetarian diet has been advocated by philosophers such as Plato and Nietzsche, political leaders such as Benjamin Franklin and Gandhi, and modern pop icons such as Paul McCartney. A multitude of studies have proven the health benefits of a vegetarian diet to be remarkable. "Vegetarian" is defined as avoiding all animal flesh including fish and poultry. Vegetarians who avoid flesh but do eat animal products such as cheese, milk, and eggs are called lacto-ovo vegetarians (ovo = eggs; lacto = milk, cheese etc). People who avoid all animal products are called vegans.

Breast cancer rates are dramatically lower in countries such as China, that follow plant-based diets. High fat diets encourage the body's production of oestrogens, in particular, oestradiol. *"Increased levels of this sex hormone have been linked to uterine, breast and ovarian cancer."* (*Source: Barnard, Neal D. – Cancer and Your Immune System – Nutrition Advocate, October 1995*)

The process of breaking down the lactose (milk sugar) into galactose evidently could damage the ovaries. Blood analysis of vegetarians reveals a higher level of natural killer cells (specialised white blood cells), that attack cancer cells. Vegetarian diets may also help in the prevention of heart disease. Animal products are the main source of saturated fat and cholesterol in the diet.

Animal products contain no fibre and fibre helps reduce cholesterol levels. Heart diets that include animal products are much less effective in slowing the process of atherosclerosis – hardening of the arteries. A low-fat, high-fibre, plant-based diet combined with stress reduction techniques, smoking cessation and exercise could actually help reverse atherosclerosis. Two weeks on a vegetarian diet can significantly reduce high blood pressure.

Adult Onset Diabetes can be controlled through a vegetarian diet along with regular exercise. Vegetarian diets are low in fat, and high in fibre and complex carbohydrates. They allow insulin to work more effectively. The diabetic can easily regulate his glucose levels on such a diet, and eventually can often reduce the amounts of insulin used.

Vegetarian diets have been shown to reduce the risk of kidney stones and gallstones. Diets high in protein, especially animal protein, cause the body to excrete more calcium oxalate and uric acid crystals. These 3 substances are the main components of urinary tract stones. For many of the same reasons, vegetarians are at a lower risk of developing osteoporosis. Osteoporosis is definitely less common in nations that eat a predominantly vegetarian diet.

It appears that our best option for health is a plant-based diet. In 1985, a Swedish study demonstrated that asthmatics who practised a vegan diet for a full year without consuming dairy products showed a marked decrease in their need for medication and in the frequency and severity of asthma attacks. Although "vegetarian children" may grow more slowly, and reach puberty somewhat later, they live substantially longer than "meat eaters".

Q *Why do you keep insisting that we cut down on eating excess protein especially in the form of animal products.*

A I have found that those who overeat on proteins also eat them in incompatible combinations, which creates a putrefactive colonic environment. While the bowel wall guards against the entry of toxins into the body, colitis, bowel cancer, haemorrhoids and numerous other diseases can result from a chronic putrefactive condition of the colon.

Q *What are the effects, besides tooth decay, that people might suffer from eating refined sugars on a daily basis?*

A Ordinary white sugar is an intestinal irritant and causes the stomach to produce large quantities of mucus to protect itself. Mucus combines with hydrochloric acid and thus retards digestion. Sugar not only promotes tooth decay, but also lowers the immune system resistance. It may lead to elevated cholesterol, vascular and coronary heart disease, atherosclerosis, hypertension, diabetes and obesity. Sugar makes people fat because it is made up of empty calories; this causes you to overeat to obtain the needed nutrients, and excess simple carbohydrates are converted into fats which add on weight.

Eating the correct combination of fruits helps you eliminate the craving for sweets. The sugar in fruit supplies the body with the nutrients it craves. It also supplies fibre and bulk. This satisfies, whereas refined sugar is without fibre and even after eating a lot of it, you often still feel hungry.

Refined sugar, eaten in any form, eg convenience foods, candy etc, ferments in the colon causing the formation of acetic acid, and alcohol which is harmful to the body. The continued and regular consumption of sweets and chocolates brings about an eventual breakdown of stamina and a lack of resistance to disease. When sugar and milk are added to cereals, rapid fermentation results. If you are very fond of sweet foods, rather choose fruits, dried fruits or carob. Overeating on healthy foods is also not ideal, especially when snacking, but it is better than overeating on unhealthy foods.

Q *Do you think it is important to include dairy products in children's diets?*

A The only time we should have milk is when we are infants, nursing at our mother's breast. Dairy products need not be included in children's diets as they get older. Rather present children with a wider variety of raw and cooked vegetables (leafy greens), unrefined starches, grains, sweet potatoes, lentils, beans, seeds, nuts, tofu and soya milk. This will give them a wider variety of vitamins and minerals and increase the caloric density of their diet in a balanced, constructive fashion. Children should eat lots of bananas, fresh fruits, avocados etc. Low gluten grain varieties such as brown rice and millet should also be eaten. Children should get 10 – 20 minutes a day of sun exposure to the face and arms to promote the manufacture of vitamin D. This helps the absorption of calcium, which in turn prevents bones from weakening. Children who eat the foods I recommend have a much higher degree of health than children raised on the conventional animal protein diet.

Remember that without dairy fat in your blood, you become lean and healthier. The absence of dairy fat also minimises the chances of heart attacks, clogged arteries, some cancers and other diseases.

Q *Is honey better than sugar?*

A I prefer **raw** honey to sugar. Commercially produced honey is pasteurised (heated), resulting in the loss of vitamins and enzymes (which help digestion).

You can purchase raw honey from health stores. Do not give honey to infants aged 9 months or younger because honey contains bacteria that can cause botulism which is a dangerous condition. Use raw honey very sparingly. It is a good transitional food to help you come off sugar and artificial sweeteners.

Q *Do you allow "olives" on your diet?*

A Olives are a fat and should not be eaten at the same meal as avocados, nuts or animal protein. They should really be eaten in their natural dried state, which is very difficult to find. Be careful of olives that are canned, bottled or pickled. In this form they are very indigestible. If you do enjoy olives, buy them in brine (not in oil) and eat them sparingly.

Q *I enjoy stir-fried vegetables. I fry them in some olive oil. Now and again I will have fried fish. How bad is this for you, if it is not done regularly?*

A Unfortunately, eating fried foods does not do us any good. When fats are heated, even unsaturated vegetable oils (cold pressed), a lot of free radicals are generated, such as acrolein and acrolic acid. These are deadly carcinogens. Rather stir-fry in some boiling water and when ready to serve, add some cold-pressed oil. Grill fish and when ready to serve, melt some butter over it. At least you are not heating the fat at a high temperature.

Q *Why do you prefer brown rice to white rice?*

A White rice has had the hull removed. The hull is the source of most of the nutrients (B complex vitamins). Brown rice has the hull, thus the vitamins are intact.

SYMPTOMS THAT MAY BE EXPERIENCED WHILE FOLLOWING MY RECOMMENDATIONS

Q *Please will you explain what happens to the body if exceptions to the diet are made while following your recommendations.*

A You will experience problems, not necessarily immediately or soon after the less healthful meal, but after you get back on the pure diet. Remember, your body has become much more vital since your change over to a healthier pattern of eating. It is just like that of a baby now. For example, if you give a child even a small glass of whisky it will react. The child's immune system has a high vitality. The reason why some adults can go on eating the wrong foods with no reaction, is that the body has become so weak over the years, it hasn't the vitality to react as it should. Be aware that the body will go into shock one day. You can't get away with a bad eating pattern forever.

Once your body is no longer burdened with the energy-draining task of digesting unnatural foods, it speedily rids itself of the decomposed materials (the garbage). In addition, room must now be made in the digestive tract and bowels for new (even less harmful) waste. Thus waste material from previous meals is quickly voided,

195

hence diarrhoea (loose stools), gas and bloating etc are experienced. There are several ways to handle the discomfort when returning to the ideal dietary foods. If you have eaten cooked foods, wrong combinations or processed foods on occasion, just get back on your optimum diet and bear the discomforts. This is the price you pay for your indiscretions and it is not due to eating fruit. Depending on the extent of your indiscretions, within a few days you should be back to feeling well again.

Skip a meal or two after you have cheated. This will reduce or eliminate the discomfort that results from indulgence in less wholesome foods.

The best solution is to **STOP** the consumption of these processed foods and stick to fresh **fruit only** throughout the day till you go to sleep. You can add butter lettuce and/or celery to your fruit meals.

Q *Whenever I go onto fruits only I always feel bloated. Why? It is the most uncomfortable feeling. How will I ever be able to follow your recommended pattern of eating?*

A First of all fruit assists the body in cleansing toxic materials (wastes) from the lining of the stomach. Thus it is best to eat fruit on an empty stomach. If this bloated feeling still occurs it is because wastes are stirred up by the fruit, which then ferments and causes a bloated feeling. Eventually, toxic residue will be totally cleansed from the stomach and bloating will not occur – but that's in the long term. I have found that if you add lettuce and celery to your fruit meals, they seem to reduce the interaction between the toxic residue and the fruit.

Never eat fruit with or after a conventional meal as this retards digestion. The absorption of fruit sugars will be held up in the stomach and fermentation will result causing gas (wind). It is not fruits that cause the digestive problems, but the unwholesome foods previously eaten.

Q *I have tried the plant-based wholefood diet you recommended, but I had to go back to my regular diet because my periodic headaches worsened. What should I do now?*

A Have no fear – this is all very encouraging. Please don't revert back to your old diet. People initially experience severe symptoms when changing over to a healthy diet. These symptoms resolve themselves within the first 2 weeks of starting the diet. From then on, people generally feel better and have more energy. The fact that changing your diet caused the headaches to worsen points out how necessary it was for you to improve your diet. The intense headaches brought on temporarily by dietary change are part of the progression towards recovery.

I would like you to keep these points in mind.

• When something harmful is removed from your system such as heroin, alcohol, cigarettes or caffeine, withdrawal symptoms usually occur, especially headaches.

• The average diet consumed by most South Africans is a low-fibre diet and the digestive tract of the typical person is unaccustomed to the high fibre and water content their stools contain, as a result of an improved diet. There are going to be changes in bowel movements. Your stools now contain more weight, which allows them to pass through the digestive tract at a faster rate. The peristaltic waves that propel the food have to adjust to a new type of stool. It can take 2 weeks or longer for this adjustment to take place. You might experience diarrhoea.

- Retained proteinaceous wastes are also eliminated when you change to a low protein, low fat diet. Fat cells are also broken down and the toxins stored in the fat cells are released into the bloodstream. The body is now in a position to "clean house" more effectively.

The symptoms experienced are the temporary result of this detoxification. My advice to you is: do not let temporary discomfort lead you to abandon your new eating habits. Healing cannot be accomplished overnight. You must eat slowly and chew vegetables very well. A few leaves of lettuce added to each meal could help you initially perhaps, rather than a big raw salad before each cooked meal.

THE FOODS AND OTHER FACTORS THAT AGGRAVATE DISEASES

Q *My husband is on medication for high cholesterol and high triglycerides. He has been following mainly a vegetarian diet without medication. He has lost weight but his cholesterol and triglyceride levels have not come down. The doctor has put him back on medication. Would an extended fast be his answer? What would you suggest to lower his cholesterol? His blood pressure is normal to low.*

A High (bad) cholesterol (LDL) and low (good) cholesterol (HDL) with high triglyceride levels are both risk factors for early cardiac death. A **total vegetarian diet** rather than a mainly vegetarian diet is of great importance. Cholesterol is produced in the liver and cells of animals. My advice to your husband is: initially, avoid animal

products totally. In time you could choose free-range chickens and fish only, because they are low in total fat. Do not eat the skin of the chicken. You should also avoid smoked, fried and cured foods such as sausages, biltong and cheese. These foods definitely produce a great deal of plaque in your arteries. People assume that low fat dairy products, skinless chicken, fish and eggs are healthful foods. Even small amounts of these foods can prevent disease reversal from taking place. It is not just the fat in the food but the animal protein itself that has a significant effect on raising serum cholesterol levels. *Dr T. Colin Campbell* suggests that animal protein is more problematic in the diet and disease relationship than is total fat. A combination of sugar and animal fat raises the fatty substances in the blood to a higher level than either substance on its own. The low cholesterol benefits of plant foods can be sabotaged by an excessive intake of sugar, especially chocolate. Sugar plays a key role in both cholesterol and triglyceride levels. Triglycerides increase in your bloodstream when you eat excessive carbohydrates in the form of refined products such as white flour, white sugar and alcohol. Often a person's triglyceride levels actually rise when he/she eventually adopts a vegetarian diet and starts losing weight. As you lose weight the fat comes out of the fat cells and into the blood, to be removed from the body. After the first 6 months on the diet, the level will then begin to fall and keep falling. A prolonged supervised fast will definitely lower your husband's short-term cardiac risk, although it will not dramatically lower his cholesterol level.

An interesting phenomenon that is observed in fasting clients who have atherosclerotic plaque in their blood vessels, is that their cholesterol level actually rises on the fast. They lose weight and release cholesterol into the bloodstream. More important than the level of cholesterol or triglycerides is the weight loss that occurs. My advice to your husband is: eat a diet of natural plant foods, take regular exercise, lose the excess weight and don't be overly concerned about the short-term blood test results.

An increased cholesterol level for a short period of time is not important and may actually represent reversal of the atherosclerotic plaque, provided you are following my recommendations. A point I would like to mention is that when individuals are brought up on a high cholesterol diet and adopt a very low or zero cholesterol diet, they will have higher levels than those raised on low cholesterol diets.

The liver remembers the cholesterol level it is accustomed to, and will produce the extra cholesterol it needs to maintain the level at which it has been for years. However, after many years of dietary change, perhaps even 10 years, the liver slowly begins to lose this nasty habit. I repeat, stick with the healthiest diet, ie an abundance of fresh vegetables and fruit, and do not be discouraged even if you do not see good short-term results. These foods play a cumulative role in serum cholesterol control.

SOME IMPORTANT FACTS ABOUT CHOLESTEROL

Cholesterol is vital for health. It helps to make bile acids for digestion. Vitamin C is an important link in the conversion of cholesterol into valuable bile acids. Thus it is very important to eat lots of fresh fruit and raw vegetables (high in vitamin C). Cholesterol is the culprit that clogs the arteries but not all cholesterol is created equal.

There is bad cholesterol (LDL) and good cholesterol (HDL). The ratios between these two forms of cholesterol are more important than the actual level of cholesterol. If you lower your cholesterol ratio by only 10% your heart attack risk is lowered by 20%. The rate of aging of your arteries also slows down. As arteries age, sludge (plaque) is deposited in the artery walls.

This plaque is mostly cholesterol and as it builds up, the artery openings narrow. As the blood flow to the heart is restricted, you will experience shortness of breath and sometimes chest pains. In order to keep the arteries free of cholesterol build-up, you not only have to reduce saturated fats and high cholesterol food in your diet, you also have to stop smoking, include exercise in your lifestyle, lose weight and eat an abundance of fresh fruit and vegetables. By doing the above, you will reduce the chance of a blood clot forming in one of the arteries.

WHAT IS THE DIFFERENCE BETWEEN LDL AND HDL?

Low Density Lipoprotein (LDL) takes cholesterol from the liver to the arteries and deposits it there. Our level of this particular type of cholesterol must be as low as possible.

High Density Lipoprotein (HDL) takes cholesterol from the arteries for excretion. We need as much HDL as possible.

The ratio of total cholesterol to HDL is the best predictor of heart disease and is more important than total cholesterol. Heart attacks are often seen in people with fairly low total cholesterol levels and not in people with high total cholesterol levels.

How to work out your cholesterol

Divide your HDL into your total cholesterol.

Client A	
total cholesterol	250
HDL	50
ratio	5

Client B	
total cholesterol	200
HDL	20
ratio	10

Client A has much higher total cholesterol than Client B. He should be at greater risk of a heart attack, but is not. Client B who has lower total cholesterol is at greater risk of a heart attack. The major difference is the ratio. Studies have shown that people with low total cholesterol levels but high ratios are the ones who are susceptible to cardiac arrest. I suggest you test your full lipid profile – this is the total analysis of the fats in your blood, including HDL and LDL cholesterol, and triglycerides etc. If you do not know your levels, get them checked now by a good laboratory.

FOODS TO AVOID

Avoid all foods containing saturated fats, ie all meats including cold meats, poultry, eggs, sausages, milk, cheese, butter and yoghurt. You should also avoid ice cream and potato chips. Fat, however, is essential for the absorption of fat soluble vitamins A, D, E and K. The right fats are essential fatty acids and these are found in avocados, nuts, cold-pressed oils and olives in brine. Without the presence of fat and bile, the vitamins A, D, E and K cannot be carried across the intestinal wall into the blood. If you combine your food correctly, you automatically reduce the consumption of fats. You must cut out sugar (as in refined carbohydrates) because sugar increases the absorption of fats and raises blood fat levels. Alcohol has a similar effect. The liver converts both the sugar and alcohol into saturated blood fat. Only animal foods contribute to dietary cholesterol. Plant foods like fruit and vegetables, avocados, grains and legumes do not. Excess consumption of cholesterol and fats can continue for a long time before it actually results in disease. Hence you are unaware of how hardened your arteries are, until you are actually ill.

Q I have gallstones and have been advised to have an operation. I really don't want to do this. Can I get rid of the gallstones by changing my way of eating?

A Initially, you will have to be very radical in your eating pattern. I suggest you cut out animal protein totally, and include an abundance of fresh fruit, raw vegetables, sprouts, a very limited amount of avocados, unsalted, unroasted nuts and seeds, and a few steamed vegetables and grains, now and again. Gallstones result from diets rich in processed fats and spreads, as well as the consumption of excess animal protein. Consult a nutritional counsellor who will advise you on a correct programme of eating. I feel a fast will get rid of the gallstones very quickly, but this has to be done under supervision.

Q I have been following your programme of eating for the last eight years. I am still suffering from constipation. I really thought that by adopting the correct pattern of eating, this would be a thing of the past.

A It really is unusual for someone eating a mostly raw plant food diet to be troubled with constipation. You might try eating more grapes, apples and plums and fewer bananas. Raw fruits and vegetables have much more fibre than cooked food. There are different kinds of fibre and for some people the fibre in grains (such as brown rice) does more to support good bowel action than the fibre in fruits and vegetables, believe it or not. So try eating brown rice if you are not already doing so. You could try eating psyllium husks which can be purchased from a health store. These may give you some relief. If you are doing everything you can, in so far as diet and exercise are concerned, maybe you need to look at other areas of your life. Are you getting enough rest and sleep? Are you psychologically poised and balanced? The mind has a great effect upon the whole digestive system. Stress increases tension in the visceral muscles including those of the colon. Learning how to relax and release tension may be more important in your case than any further dietary changes. Anyone who has battled with constipation for a lifetime, cannot expect any "quick fix" solution. The most important thing is always to remove the causes. Consult a nutritional counsellor who will offer other alternatives.

Q *I am a chronic **migraine** sufferer. Do you have any suggestions I might follow regarding an eating pattern? Are there any foods that trigger a migraine attack?*

A I feel that stress-related tension, nutritional and digestive irritants, intestinal toxaemia, and spinal distortion are the major factors that influence the intensity, duration, and frequency of migraine headaches. Irritants like nicotine, caffeine (chocolate, coffee and tea), hard cheese, yeast foods, artificial sweeteners, foods high in additives, organ meats such as liver, alcohol, milk and eggs can act as triggers for a large percentage of migraine headaches. The protein poisoning and acid irritation associated with the conventional diet which is high in animal protein, fat, salt, and refined sugar, all contribute to intestinal toxaemia and allergic-type responses which can trigger migraine headaches. Many of these common triggers of migraine headaches are powerful stimulants, which usually result in profound rebound exhaustion and depression when they are eliminated. I am also in great favour of a short fast under the care of a medical doctor versed in Natural Hygiene. This professional support will often help guide you through withdrawal symptoms, as well as other difficult periods in the recovery process.

Q *What is **asthma**? Are there any foods I should avoid? If I follow your pattern of eating, is there a chance I can get rid of my asthma and be weaned off medication?*

A Asthma is an allergy-related disease and is characterised by coughing, wheezing and shortness of breath. Inferior nutrition and other negative lifestyle factors promote asthma. It is particularly aggravated by animal foods, especially dairy foods and eggs. Beer also tends to close up the chest. Other common dietary allergens include gluten (the protein component found in wheat, rye, barley and oats), corn and citrus fruit. Some of the factors that could be associated with the development of asthma are the lack of breast-feeding in infants, premature weaning from breast milk and premature introduction of food other than breast milk to infants. When choosing foods, don't choose refined sugars and grains, or processed foods. Avoid adding lots of salt to your food.

Animal products are high in protein and sodium and this has the effect of reducing the uptake of cellular waste and retarding the self-cleansing abilities of each cell. The foods I recommend contain essential phytonutrients (plant-derived nutrients). These foods are: green and yellow vegetables, leafy green vegetables and fresh fruits. These foods help the body to function optimally. You must also increase the amount of sleep you generally have, as this will give the body the opportunity to heal the immune system which has become abnormally sensitive to environmental and dietary allergens.

I also suggest a supervised fast for those resistant cases of asthma. It must be done under supervision. Allergies generally lessen or disappear on a fast, as the person's health improves.

I would like to add that symptomatic treatment can establish a cycle, where an ever worsening condition results in the increased use of, and dependence on medication, as time goes on. Unfortunately, most doctors never seem to connect symptoms with the person's nutritional state, or overall immune function. The very fact that you have an asthmatic condition which is not improving, is an indication that you urgently need to change your usual pattern of eating.

Q *My doctor says I am very allergic. Can you tell me more about* **allergies?**

A Many people suffer from allergies. The number one allergen is milk, followed by chocolate and wheat:

- By the age of 3 we have lost the enzymes lactase and rennin. Without these enzymes the body can't digest the lactose (sugar in the milk) or casein (protein in the milk).

- Chocolate contains theobromine, a poisonous alkaloid.
- Wheat contains phytic acid and gluten. These are found in grains, and are non-metabolisable by humans.
- Many people also have difficulty in breaking down the protein and fat contained in nuts.

I find that when allergic people fast for approximately 7 – 21 days, their body's defensive mechanisms usually normalise. Allergies disappear and do not reappear unless the body becomes toxic due to waste that it is unable to eliminate. After the fast, you must follow a predominantly raw diet for some time, consisting primarily of fresh fruits and raw vegetables. You must exercise and get adequate sleep. Many people are allergic to pollen and develop symptoms such as runny noses, and sinus congestion. I have found through my counselling sessions that a healthy body is better able to deal with environmental irritants such as dust and pollen, than an unhealthy body.

Q *I have been reading Dr William Howard Hay's book on Food Combining and he says all diseases are the result of acid-alkaline imbalances. Do you agree?*

A I feel that the S.A. diet is a predominantly acid-forming diet and this definitely upsets your acid-alkaline balance. You can correct acidity by fasting or eating mono fruit meals for a certain period of time. Within a day or two of going on a proper eating plan, the acidity conditions are corrected. I suggest you don't use antacids for heartburn; they don't solve the problem. It is the raw fruits and vegetables eaten in correct combinations, that quickly restore the acid-alkaline balance. Celery and figs are some of the foods rich in alkaline salts. I have found that it actually takes 9 alkaline meals (3 days) to correct an acid-alkaline imbalance.

Q *My mother has terrible **arthritis**. What causes it? What foods should she avoid?*

A Arthritis is inflammation of the joints. My research has shown that diet is a major factor. In cultures where people eat very small quantities of animal fat and protein, there is a much lower incidence of all kinds of arthritis.

I can offer the following advice to your mother: you must combine your foods correctly, otherwise an accumulation of acid end products can occur, once the food is metabolised. You have to avoid proteins which cause inflammation such as dairy products, meats, soya, eggs and wheat. You should eat a plant-based diet made up of fresh fruits and vegetables as well as nuts, whole grains and legumes. These foods are low in fat, low in protein and high in fibre. Initially, you should avoid citrus fruits. Avoid refined carbohydrates and sugar (cakes and biscuits), onions and garlic. An effective strategy for inflamed joints is a brief 1 – 3 day fast on pure water (180 ml of pure water to be taken hourly) or vegetable juices (fresh carrot, or carrot, beet and apple). Both are extremely effective in "cooling off" hot joints. You really should include the least "joint" offending foods and these are brown rice, potatoes, sweet potatoes, green and yellow vegetables and non-citrus fruits. A natural anti-inflammatory is flaxseed (linseed) oil. Add one tablespoon of this oil daily to your salad – never cook with it. Fats can make inflammatory arthritis flare up, so beware of fried foods and always read labels to guard against hidden fats. If you follow my recommendations for 5 – 14 days, you will more than likely find your joints much improved, and usually pain free. Avoid free radical generators, such as tobacco smoke, alcohol, caffeine, processed foods and stress. Try to get more rest, sleep and sunshine and indulge in a mild form of exercise, which will improve posture and body mechanics. All of these changes will make you feel better. Consult a nutritional counsellor if you need guidance.

Q *Is **low blood pressure** harmful to health? What are the causes of low blood pressure? How can low blood pressure be restored to its normal level?*

A As long as you feel well and energetic, it does not matter if your blood pressure is low. The most important thing would be to rule out a serious underlying condition; this you must discuss with your doctor. Diets low in calories, and rich in garlic and onions can cause low blood pressure. Low blood pressure in itself is not harmful to health. The worst thing that can happen is that you can faint. A dietary adjustment may be all that is necessary to correct it. I suggest you see a nutritional counsellor.

Q *I keep getting **yeast infections** (**candida**). What can I do to prevent these infections?*

A Candida typically refers to a yeast-like fungus, candida albicans. Everybody has candida in their bodies, because it is part of the normal flora of the mouth, skin, intestinal tract and genital tract (vagina). This fungus is kept in balance by the normal bacterial flora of the body and healthy endocrine (immune) systems.

If you have candida, you should avoid the following:

- sweet fruits, dried fruits and all forms of sugar (syrups and honey etc)
- yeasty foods, such as marmite, bread, yeast extracts and spreads
- fermented foods, such as wine, beer, alcohol, yoghurt, miso, all kinds of vinegar, pickled foods, buttermilk, and sour cream
- frozen or concentrated orange juice and citrus fruit, grapes, grape juice, raisins and overripe fruit
- grains with a high gluten content (wheat, oats, rye and barley)
- all foods containing Monosodium Glutamate (MSG)
- garlic, because it kills off residue bacteria in the gut that help keep candida in check
- smoked meats and fish, sausages, corned beef, hot dogs and hamburgers
- chemicals and stimulants, chocolate, caffeine and nicotine abuse
- animal products (flesh and dairy).

The correct eating plan and correct lifestyle definitely support a healthy gut ecology and inhibit the potential for candida growth. Eat an abundance of green leafy vegetables, a small amount of subacid fruit and berries, legumes, nuts, sweet potatoes and low gluten grains such as millet and brown rice, while you have the problem.

Other factors which damage the healthy flora of the body and weaken the immune system are: antibiotic abuse, the use of corticosteroids, oral contraceptives, chemotherapy or irradiation, stress, lack of rest and sleep, and strenuous exercise.

All the above cause the fungus to multiply, resulting in the infection known as candidiasis. This infection may involve various parts of the body, including the ears, nose, gastrointestinal tract and reproductive organs. As a result, candidiasis may be associated with a variety of symptoms (gas, abdominal distension, vaginitis, bladder infections, muscle and joint pain, etc).

The conventional treatment of candidiasis is to condemn all fruit eating. This seems rather extreme to me. I can see the point in prohibiting certain fruits or perhaps even limiting them, but I don't think it is necessary to eliminate all fruits from the diet completely. I do insist that you eat more vegetables than fruit. If you are concerned about your problem, consult a nutritional counsellor. Fasting under supervision is an invaluable approach in dealing with this infection. This also gives your endocrine (immune) system a chance to rest and recover. In stubborn cases of candida, I have often suggested probiotics. These products definitely help in balancing your gut ecology.

*Q I have been diagnosed as having **chronic fatigue syndrome (yuppie flu)**. I am confused between the medical approach and the more natural approach to the problem.*

A The causes of fatigue may include various nutritional factors and emotional stresses, as well as inadequate sleep. Other symptoms may contribute to this condition; please discuss this with your doctor. I feel that when the causes are removed and a programme of superior nutrition is undertaken, renewed health becomes possible. In order to do this successfully, all contributing factors must be considered and evaluated. I have found through my counselling sessions that the diet of most people suffering from chronic fatigue needs to be changed.

Not only is their diet lacking in essential nutrients and phytochemicals but their lifestyle also involves too much exercise, stress etc, and this places a burden on the normal functioning of the immune system. The typical diet that most people consume is high in fats, processed foods and animal products. These are damaging enough by themselves, but they are made more harmful through contamination (especially the animal products) with petrochemicals, hormones and antibiotics. This type of diet definitely contributes to immune system dysfunction, making people more prone to infections and allergies. Chronic fatigue could be a symptom of this suppressed immune state. Sleep is very crucial in restoring the body to normality. People suffering from chronic fatigue may require more than 10 hours of good quality sleep each night for some time, to maximise their chance of recovery. Many of these people have a strong dependence on stimulants such as coffee, tea, colas and sweets. Although these products may offer some temporary relief, the constant use of a stimulant is detrimental to the individual and interferes with his eventual recovery from this cycle of fatigue. Although discontinuation of these toxic substances seems to result in even more fatigue and more immune system dysfunction, it is absolutely necessary for potential recovery. I have sent many clients suffering from this syndrome to a fasting clinic with incredible results.

Q *I have **diabetes** and have been told that reducing my fat intake is very important for my condition. What have you to say about this?*
A You must initially consider adopting an optimal diet and lifestyle. A strict vegetarian diet and regular exercise can have a significant positive impact for diabetics. An optimal vegetarian diet is one consisting of fresh fruit, vegetables, grains and legumes. You have to lower your fat intake. Even a little extra fat on your body will raise your insulin requirements. Diabetes greatly accelerates the development of atherosclerosis and cardiovascular diseases. Eat lots of green vegetables, potatoes, whole grains (such as brown rice, millet and polenta) and legumes. These foods help to maintain stable blood glucose levels. You should avoid fatty foods, such as animal products (meat and dairy foods) and go very easy on avocados and nuts. I suggest either a small avocado or $^1/_2$ cup of unsalted, unroasted nuts/seeds only three times a week.

Avoid dried fruit and eat only one sweet fruit a day. You can eat as much fruit as you want from the other fruit groups. Limit your intake of fruit juices and avoid the use of diabetic candies containing sorbitol, as high amounts of this substance could increase the risk of cataract formation. Refined and highly processed foods, convenience foods that are high in refined carbohydrates, salt and other additives should all be avoided. The acceptable sugar for diabetics is fructose. This sugar requires no insulin for metabolism. Use fructose in moderation. Avoid margarine and use unsalted butter sparingly. Limit your intake of cold-pressed oils such as olive oil. Avoid caffeine (tea, coffee and coke) as it upsets the blood sugar level by forcing the pancreas to secrete insulin. The low protein content of this particular diet protects the kidneys, a factor which is of the utmost importance for the diabetic. Every nutrient that has been shown to have a favourable effect on glucose control is present in fresh fruits and vegetables, as well as the other foods mentioned. If you follow my programme, you will definitely keep the diabetes under control.

Q *I am suffering from* **eczema.** *I have tried a range of treatments including cortisone. I have avoided dairy products but have still found no relief. What do you suggest?*

A Eczema is a distressing skin disease often associated with asthma. The skin is inflamed and the itch often initiates scratching. The term eczema is derived from the Greek *ekzema, from ek – out + zein to boil.* Scratching and rubbing of the irritated areas does not contribute towards recovery; creams, applications and internal medication does not remove the cause of eczema. In my experience, fasting is the most effective method, followed by a carefully supervised feeding programme and lifestyle change. I have found that dairy foods and grains are often a source of aggravation to the eczema sufferer. Sunshine and fresh air are important. Finally, the emotional aspect should also be investigated. This is very important. Please consult a nutritional counsellor.

Q *I have been told I suffer from* **hypoglycaemia.** *What can I do to prevent it? Does eating fruit aggravate a hypoglycaemic condition?*

A Hypoglycaemia means low blood sugar. The bloodstream contains too little glucose and there is too much insulin secretion. Symptoms such as weakness, fatigue, headaches, abdominal pain, anxiety, rapid heartbeat, mental confusion, clouded vision and shaking are often experienced. These symptoms often appear 3 – 4 hours after eating, especially when eating has been delayed or a meal has been skipped. If there is not sufficient amounts of utilisable sugar in the blood to satisfy the needs of the brain, an alarm goes off. This alarm manifests itself in the symptoms of low blood sugar. The conventional treatment is to give frequent meals of high protein foods. This will cause the symptoms to abate, by diverting the energy to the stomach to digest the food. It only offers temporary relief and ensures the prolonged existence of the problem, leading to more frequent eating. I am not in favour of this. There is a far more rational approach that can eliminate frequent meals and the hypoglycaemia. Symptoms such as migraine and tension headaches, and other symptoms of hypoglycaemia, are all a result of retained proteinaceous and nitrogenous wastes due to the consumption of protein foods. Consuming concentrated sugars is also stressful on the system and generates wide swings in blood sugar levels, depleting the body of nutritional reserves needed for optimal immune and endocrine system functioning. It is absolutely imperative that the right kind of sugar be introduced into the bloodstream. Any kind of processed sugar will only make the condition worse. The ideal kind of sugar is the sugar found in fresh fruit. The sugar in fruit is called fructose. Inside the body it turns to glucose faster than any other carbohydrate. You have to eat fruit correctly, ie on an empty stomach and correctly combined. As the sugar is in its natural state, it will pass swiftly through the stomach and be absorbed into the bloodstream within an hour. As odd as it may seem, fruit is actually the most effective and efficient way of overcoming the problem of hypoglycaemia. The energy-usurping, acid-producing nature of the South African diet is certainly consistent with creating low blood sugar. I will give you some positive steps on how to handle your low blood sugar.

- Abstain from foods that contain refined carbohydrates and simple sugars such as chocolates, sweets, cakes and biscuits. Eat high-fibre foods such as fresh fruit, vegetables, and starchy vegetables such as potatoes, whole grains and legumes. All these foods have their sugar bound in fibre, which causes the sugar to be absorbed into the bloodstream more slowly.
- Avoid all soft drinks, coffee, tea, artificially flavoured foods and food additives. Avoid alcohol, as this aggravates hypoglycaemia and also results in withdrawal symptoms, which are exacerbated during periods of low blood sugar.
- You could eat a small amount of protein plant food, such as nuts and seeds, with each meal for the first month, especially if you stop eating animal protein. This will minimise the initial symptoms of withdrawal from an animal protein based diet. If you **do** eat animal protein, you must cut it down to twice a week.

If you conform to these guidelines you should find that symptoms of hypoglycaemia will disappear. If you do, however, still get uncomfortable symptoms before a meal, you should consider a short fast under qualified supervision to resolve the condition.

Q I have noticed that even though I am combining my foods correctly I still have indigestion as well as increased gas. Are there certain foods that cause more gas than others?

A The main determinants of indigestion and gas formation (flatulence) are: what, when and how you eat. A vegetarian diet causes more flatulence by nature because of colonic bacterial action on the indigestible high fibre content of the diet ie fresh fruit and vegetables. This is normal. Gas is produced by bacteria in the digestive tract, and by undigested material not breaking down completely. I must point out, however, that if you are not accustomed to eating large quantities of fresh fruit and vegetables, you should increase the quantity of these foods gradually. In time the body will develop the necessary bacterial flora needed for their digestion. Rather start by adding more steamed vegetables to your diet than eating only raw foods. The following guidelines will definitely improve digestive efficiency and eliminate excess gas.

- Eat within your digestive capacities. Do not overeat.
- Chew your food thoroughly. Many intestinal and digestive problems, including abdominal cramps and possibly appendicitis, stem from bolting down your food, with insufficient chewing. This applies especially to fibrous foods.
- Never drink any form of liquid with your meals.
- Do not eat concentrated foods (other than fruit) between meals.
- Avoid all carbonated beverages.
- Avoid legumes initially. The bloated feeling results from hemicellulose, a sugar contained in the beans.
- Avoid all concentrated sugars, including fruit juice, dried fruit and refined carbohydrates.
- Nuts and seeds must be chewed very well and eaten in small quantities. Preferably grind nuts.
- Onions and garlic contain mustard oil (an

irritant to the digestive tract) which causes gas. The formation of gas, however, is partially reduced by cooking.

- Spices in general can irritate the digestive tract.
- Some healthy foods cause more gas than others eg raw broccoli, cauliflower and cabbage contain oils which produce gas. These oils are mostly evaporated when cooked. Broccoli, cauliflower and cabbage must be chewed very well if eaten raw, because they are much harder to digest than other vegetables.

When you first make dietary changes, your body needs time to make adjustments, in order to digest the new type of food efficiently. In time, if you eat a predominantly wholefood, plant-based diet and you discontinue your previous eating habits, which definitely lead to indigestion anyway, your ability to process a high-fibre diet will increase, and gas production decrease. The intestinal bacteria will change and become used to the new food mixture. Gastric reflux and hiatus hernia are also digestive problems. The advice I have given above serves equally well for these conditions too. You must simplify your eating pattern. Avoid animal fats and proteins; they are the most difficult foods to digest. Eliminate coffee and carbonated drinks. Reduce the amount of food eaten at a meal and don't forget to combine your foods correctly. Always eat in a quiet, relaxed environment and never eat when tired, angry or stressed. Never go to sleep on a full stomach; you should allow at least three hours before retiring. You will definitely notice an improvement in your digestive problems, as well as a reduction in gas.

*Q I am concerned that I will get **osteoporosis**. I am a vegan and do not eat any dairy products, which I am told will help prevent osteoporosis. How do you feel about this? I am also not taking oestrogen therapy nor calcium tablets.*

A Contrary to medical opinion, osteoporosis is not the result of decreased oestrogen production, but the result of a lifetime of wrong eating and living practices. A diet containing too many acid-forming foods, and too few fresh fruits and raw vegetables is deficient in calcium and other alkaline minerals. The conventional diet has a toxic effect on the body. The body is thus forced to borrow calcium from the bones, to maintain a normal acid-alkaline balance. This would not be so bad, if we rarely indulged in the wrong foods and the normal alkaline-forming diet was our main diet. The body would then be able to return the alkaline minerals to the bone and would not deplete our skeletal structure of alkaline minerals. The conventional diet, which is acid forming, results in a chronic loss of alkaline nutrients, essential for strong bones. We can hold onto the calcium in our bones, by avoiding the foods that encourage the kidneys to lose calcium via the urine.

Calcium robbing thieves are:

- Animal proteins such as chicken, fish, red meat, dairy products and soya products (plant protein) should not be taken in excess.
- Foods rich in sodium such as dairy products, pickles, cold meats and biltong.
- Caffeine – just one cup of coffee a day can cause lower bone density, especially after menopause is reached.
- Soft drinks with phosphoric acid.
- Certain vegetables – cooked spinach and parsley contain oxalates which bind with

calcium. Eat only twice a week.

- Grains contain phytates, which also bind with calcium. Eat only twice a week.
- Cigarette smoke (nicotine).
- Refined sugars found in cakes, biscuits, sweets etc.
- Insufficient exercise. You have to avoid a sedentary lifestyle. You must do some form of exercise, such as a brisk 20 minute walk, at least 4 times a week or an exercise against gravity such as stair climbing, carrying parcels, or using hand weights.
- Too much stress. Try to minimise stress in your life and find ways to deal with it creatively.

There is no conclusive evidence that calcium supplements have a substantial effect in preventing osteoporosis. Bones require more than just calcium supplements. Vitamin K, magnesium, natural progesterone and trace minerals such as boron are all essential for strong bones. Foods especially rich in these nutrients are dark green leafy vegetables and seeds, such as sesame seeds (tahini sauce). You must also get plenty of rest and sleep, as well as sunshine at the right time of day. These are very important factors in your lifestyle.

Q *I have **psoriasis**. Are there certain foods I should avoid?*

A Psoriasis is a chronic, recurrent skin disease. Factors which may precipitate the disease include injury to the skin, acute infections and more commonly and significantly, psycho-emotional upsets. Again, fasting under proper supervision enables the body to cope with this inflammatory condition and also enhances the immune system. You should avoid animal foods, refined and processed foods and also maintain a low fat diet. Choose foods that are low on the food chain ie fresh fruits, vegetables, whole grains, legumes and a moderate amount of nuts, seeds etc.

Q *I have a **spastic colon**. Can I follow a totally raw diet? I enjoy lots of fresh fruits and raw vegetables.*

A I feel that the nutritional approach has to be modified in your case. You have to include more steamed and cooked whole grains, to allow the reactive tissues of the stomach and bowel to accommodate the increased roughage and fibre. It might even be necessary to purée vegetables and fruits. Caffeine, refined sugar and alcohol can provoke irritation and inflammation. It is essential to avoid these foods. The condition may improve if you avoid gluten found in whole-wheat bread, cereals and pasta. There may, of course, be other factors, such as stress. It would be advisable to consult a nutritional counsellor.

Q *I have **ulcerative colitis** and experience multiple bowel movements (10 — 14 bowel movements a day). I do not seem to tolerate raw fruits, vegetables, nuts and high-fibre foods. I feel I need to eat foods that slow down the small intestine transit time, but still provide adequate nutrition. I need some nutritional guidelines regarding the programme you advocate.*

A The application of the principles I recommend, requires a great deal of care in your particular case. You cannot eat an abundance of only raw fruits, vegetables and nuts. You need to eat a variety of soft, less fibrous, natural foods such as steamed vegetables, potatoes, sweet potatoes, carrot juice, banana and avocados. Millet is a grain that could be well tolerated. In cases such as yours, I sometimes make use of tofu (a legume made from the soya bean curd). I would suggest you see a nutritional counsellor who could supervise a pattern of eating suitable for your needs.

Q *I have been diagnosed as having* **multiple sclerosis.** *Do you think "diet" will help me?*

A I have come across many MS patients in my counselling practice and I have found that when they avoid high fat foods (all forms of animal products, ie meat, chicken, eggs and dairy), their condition improves and they have fewer attacks. MS patients should also avoid wheat and foods containing gluten, such as oats, rye, barley, pasta and couscous, as well as foods containing preservatives. It would be advisable to consult a nutritional counsellor.

Q *Can diet prevent* **cancer?**

A *"Foods are extraordinary allies in our personal war on cancer."*
(Source: Barnard, Neal D. – Cancer and Your Immune System - Nutrition Advocate, October 1995)

Cancer doesn't just happen. It takes time to develop. As there has been no cure for cancer as yet, we have to look at alternative methods. There is definitely an urgency for you to look at the kind of foods you are consuming, as well as the kind of lifestyle you are leading. This information I gleaned from the research I have been doing, as well as from the medical doctors I met abroad. The National Cancer Institute in the US estimates that at least 35% of cancers are linked to diet. The cancers which seem to be diet-related are: cancer of the digestive tract (oesophagus, stomach, colon, liver and pancreas), breast and prostate cancer. Certain foods may increase the amount of hormones in the body, which

in turn can increase the risk of cancer.

The most common forms of cancer are linked to your sex hormones, ie cancer of the breast, uterus, ovaries and prostate. High fat diets increase the level of oestrogen, the female sex hormone in the blood. It is now known that many breast tumours are fuelled by oestrogen. Oestrogens are normal and essential hormones for both men and women. The more oestrogen there is, the greater the driving force behind some kinds of breast cancer. On high fat diets, oestrogen levels increase; on low fat diets they decrease. We have to choose more plant-based foods as these contain a good source of fibre, as well as powerful anti-cancer substances, such as vitamin C and beta carotene. Fibre is essential for the normal excretion of sex hormones. Fibre has the wonderful property of diluting and neutralising the effect of dietary fat. Animal fats, such as meat, cheese, butter, and milk, preserved and processed foods, alcohol and salt, seem to increase our cancer risk. A vegetarian diet based on fresh raw fruit and vegetables, whole grains and legumes is the most powerful diet for health, but this power is often eroded if milk, cheese and other dairy products are consumed. Heated vegetable oils can also affect oestrogen levels and increase the production of cancer-causing free radicals. It is therefore no good replacing fried chicken with fried onion rings.

How much fat is too much? *The National Cancer Institute's* guidelines show that fat intake should constitute no more than 30% of the total calorie intake. According to *Neal Barnard* this is too high to be of any significant benefit. He suggests that fat intake should be approximately 10% of the total calorie intake. Some foods also contain carcinogens as well as increasing the production of free radicals. *Dr T. Colin Campbell* claims that the most relevant carcinogen of all is an animal based diet, due to both the presence of cancer promoting agents, and the absence of protective agents found in plants. You must eat an abundance of fresh fruit and raw vegetables, especially orange and green vegetables, as well as a variety of whole grains. It is also very important that you try and eat unsprayed, organically grown fruits and vegetables. Reduction of cancer risk through diet does not depend on any single factor, but requires an overall change in your total eating pattern. To obtain lifelong benefit it is important that you consider implementing all these guidelines. You must also not forget about the non-nutritive factors, such as fresh air, sunshine, adequate sleep, exercise and emotional health and wellbeing.

FACTORS THAT CAUSE CANCER

Dietary factors	35 – 70%
Tobacco	30%
Alcohol	3%
Radiation	3%
Medication	2%
Air and water pollution	1 – 5%

(Source: Campbell, T. Colin – Nutrition Advocate, October 1995)

In today's busy world, it is sometimes difficult to find the time to prepare and eat all of the needed vegetables.

*BARLEYGREEN™ is a 21st century product that provides a convenient way to increase your daily intake of organic vegetables. BARLEYGREEN™ is a wholefood concentrate produced in the powdered form of the pure natural juice of organically grown young barley leaves. This powerful food contains all the nutrients and phytochemicals as well as minerals, vitamins, enzymes and amino acids necessary for a healthy, balanced diet.

BARLEYGREEN™ has a high alkalising effect which helps keep the ratio between acidity and alkalinity in our body fluids balanced, thus creating healthy cells, to boost the immune system.

BARLEYGREEN™ is a product for the whole family that is easily digested, readily absorbed, and will give the family the benefits of good nutrition in a convenient form.

*AIM / BARLEYGREEN™

Conclusion

Health is not a priority for most people in the course of their daily lives, and only surfaces when health problems emerge

JOAN AUSTOKER

It is a long, hard road to health. Is it worth the struggle and sacrifice? Only we are responsible for the kind of life we want to have. We can help ourselves, our children and our friends adopt better eating habits that we can live with, so that we can live free from the fear of heart disease, strokes, diabetes and many other serious illnesses.

People often suffer from the same diseases as their parents did. It is no good putting the cause of disease down to hereditary factors but rather the same cooking methods, tastes and lifestyle – that is why we succumb to the same diseases. I have found through my counselling sessions that if the programme I recommend is consistently followed for 3 months, it will definitely bring about positive changes.

By changing to a more plant-based diet and living a better lifestyle by incorporating exercise, fresh air, sunshine and sleep, and looking after your emotional health and wellbeing, your body will be able to defend itself against any of the influences that threaten its existence. We are what we eat. *Dr John McDougall* maintains that knowing the cause of our diseases is the first step towards prevention and treatment. Health is not a commodity which can be purchased with money, but an asset to be gained by sheer hard work.

In this book I have given you the tools to take responsibility for your health. I have given you a plan to work with and a direction to follow. This will enable you to reinstate your natural healing power. In order to ensure a life of wellbeing all the powers of body, mind and soul must be brought to bear. I will strive to keep abreast of new scientific information and to make this information available to you in future editions of this book. If you eat and live correctly, your bodies will function properly, giving you no pains, no aches, no illnesses, or weaknesses. You will live in peace and harmony with your digestive system. The long-term rewards of improving your diet will also give you: increased vitality, improved sleep, more energy, regular and soft bowel movements, lower cholesterol, a healthy heart, lower cancer risks and stronger bones.

If you fail to recognise the absolute necessity of a correct diet and lifestyle, you may well be living with the consequences right now. You have to avoid the dietary causes of illness. The question is : what will you do with this information? You have a choice, and that choice will determine to a large extent the length and quality of your life. Living in the era of knowledge, you have to become an independent thinker and a person of action. Remember, it takes education, a strong personality and tremendous effort on your part to overcome the social roadblocks to health.

Through my research I have come up with the following scientific information.

Dr. Peter D'Adamo (The Eat Right Diet - Dr. Peter D'Adamo with Catherine Whitney) an American naturopath, has discovered scientific evidence that blood type is a significant factor in determining the effectiveness of your diet, your susceptibility to illness as well as your ability to help kick those last hard-to-lose kilograms. He maintains a chemical reaction occurs between your blood and the foods you eat.

Lectins, abundant and diverse proteins found in foods have agglutinating properties that affect your blood and which may cause a variety of problems. Equally a food which may be harmful to the cells of one blood type may be beneficial to the cells of another. The key to losing weight and avoiding acute and degenerative diseases is to avoid the lectins that agglutinate your particular cells.

There are 4 blood types - A B AB and O

BLOOD TYPE A - basically vegetarians

BLOOD TYPE AB - a rare blood group - can eat a mixed diet in moderation

BLOOD TYPE B - can eat a wide variety of foods

BLOOD TYPE O - thrive on a high protein diet, limiting grains, beans and legumes

Dr. Peter D'Adamo maintains when you use the individual characteristics of your blood type as a guide for eating and living, you will be healthier, reach your ideal weight and slow down the process of aging.

I have successfully used Dr. D'Adamo's principles as an additional tool in my counselling armoury.

REMEMBER . . .

IT'S NEVER TOO LATE TO CHANGE!

I hope that this book has provided you with more than just a broad outline of information.

If you wish to further your knowledge of natural health and nutritional science then I suggest you do the following courses:

- Feeling fit ... for Life Natural Hygiene Course, an internationally recognised correspondence Nutritional Course (with certification).
- The Health, Nutrition and Lifestyle Education Course (with certification) which covers a 10-week period.

Write for further information to the author at: P.O. Box 64171, Highlands North 2037, Johannesburg, South Africa. Kindly enclose a self addressed stamped envelope. You can also contact me on my website http://www.healthseekers.co.za. I also have an E-mail address - celene@healthseekers.co.za.

214

Select Bibliography

This Bibliography is a list of most of the sources consulted by the author in the course of preparing this book. It includes suggestions for further reading.
Abbreviations:
        n.d. = no date of publication in book
        n.p. = no place of publication in book
        no pub. = no name of publisher in book

ABRAMOWSKI, O.L.M. Fruits Can Heal You. Westville, Natal: Nutritional and Natural Health Publications, 1981.

ABRAMOWSKI, O.L.M. Fruitarian Diet and Physical Rejuvenation. Wethersfield, Connecticut: Omangod Press, 1973.

ALLEN, Hannah. The Happy Truth About Protein. Manchaca, Texas: Health Excellence Systems, 1986.

ALLEN, Hannah. Homemaker's Guide to Foods For Pleasure and Health and Handbook for Hygienic Living. Tampa, Florida: Natural Hygiene Press, 1976.

ANDERSON, Henry. Helping Hand: 8 Day Diet Programs. Pacific Palisades, California: Publius Publishing and Productions, 1986.

APPLETON, Nancy. Lick the Sugar Habit. 1st ed. New York: Avery Publishing Group, 1985.
ATTWOOD, Charles R. Dr Attwood's Low-Fat Prescription For Kids. Harmondsworth, Middlesex: Penguin Books, 1995.

AUSTOKER, Joan. Cancer Prevention in Primary Care. London: B.M.J. Publishing Group, 1995.

AVERY, Phyllis. The Garden of Eden Raw Fruit and Vegetable Recipes. Vista, California: Hygeia Publishing, 1992.

BAKER, Arthur. Awakening Our Self Healing Body: a Solution to the Health Care Crisis. Los Angeles, California: Self-Health Care Systems, 1994.

BALCH, James F. and BALCH, Phyllis A. Prescription For Nutritional Healing. New York: Avery Publishing Group, 1993.

BARNARD, Neal D. The Power of Your Plate. Summertown, Tennessee: Book Publishing Co., 1990.

BELL, Alice and others. Good For You! The A-Z of Healthy Eating, by Alice Bell, Gail Alswang and John Phillips. Cape Town: Don Nelson, 1993.

BETHEL, May. The Healing Power of Natural Foods. North Hollywood, California: Wilshire Book Co., 1978.

BIDWELL, Victoria. Health Seeker's Yearbook, 1990. Freemont, California: Get Well, Stay Well, America, 1990.

BIDWELL, Victoria. The Salt Conspiracy. Freemont, California: Get Well, Stay Well,

America, 1986. Reprinted 1990.

BIELER, Henry G. Food is Your Best Medicine. London: Neville Spearman, 1968. Reprinted 1974.

BRANDT, Johanna. The Grape Cure. Pietersburg, South Africa: Kellermann (Distributor), 1948.

BROWN, Harold R. The Fast Way To Health and Vigour. Johannesburg: Health Life Publishers, 1973.

BUDD, Martin L. Low Blood Sugar: How to Understand and Overcome Hypoglycaemia. 3rd ed. London: Thorsons, 1995. First published in 1981. 2nd ed. 1984.

CAMPBELL, T. Colin. Diet, Lifestyle and Mortality in China: a Study of the Characteristics of 65 Chinese Countries. Cornell: Cornell University Press and People's Medical Publishing House, 1990.

CAMPBELL, T. Colin. New Century Nutrition. New York: New Century Nutrition, July 1995 – November 1996.

CHAITOW, Boris R. My Healing Secrets. Bradford, Holsworthy, North Devon: Health Science Press, n.d.

CHAITOW, Boris R. My Way For a Healthier Life. Stellenbosch, South Africa: High Rustenburg Hydro, [1994?].

CHAITOW, Leon and TRENEV, Natasha. Probiotics. London: Thorsons, 1990.

CHARMAINE, Susan E. The Complete Raw

Juice Therapy. Wellingborough, Northamptonshire: Thorsons, 1977. Reprinted 1980.

COLBIN, Annemarie. Food and Healing. New York: Ballantine, 1968.

COLGAN, Michael. The New Nutrition: Medicine For the Millenium. Encinitas, California: C.I. Publications, 1994.

D'ADAMO,.Peter. The Eat Right Diet. Century Books Limited 1998.

DIAMOND, Harvey and DIAMOND, Marilyn. Fit For Life. London: Transworld Publishers, 1987. (Bantam Books)

DIAMOND, Harvey and DIAMOND, Marilyn. Fit For Life II: Living Health, The Complete Health Programme. London: Transworld Publishers, 1988. Reprinted 1995. (Bantam Books)

DOUGLASS, J., RASGON, I. M., FLEISS, P. M., et al. Effects of a Raw Food Diet on Hyper-tension and Obesity: Southern Medical Journal, 1985.

DUFTY, William. Sugar Blues. New York: Warner Books, 1975.

ESSER, William L. Dictionary of Natural Foods. Bridgeport, Connecticut: Natural Hygiene Press, 1983.

Fit Food For Humanity. Bridgeport, Connecticut: Natural Hygiene Press, 1982.

Food Intolerance Databank. Johannesburg: Association For Dietetics in Southern Africa, 1996.

FRY, T.C. Correspondence Course: Natural Hygiene, Nutrition and Health Sciences. Austin, Texas: Life Science Institute, n.d.
Note: The Course, essentially the same as the original formulated by T.C. Fry, has been taken over by Feeling Fit... For Life.

FRY, T.C and SHELTON, Herbert M. Correct Food Combining For Easy Digestion and Wonderful Health. Manchaca, Texas: Health Excellence, n.d.

FUHRMAN, Joel. Fasting and Eating For Health: a Medical Doctor's Program For Conquering Disease. New York: St Martin's Press, 1995.

GRANT, Doris and JOICE, Jean. Food Combining For Health. London: Thorsons, 1984.

GRANT, Ellen. Sexual Chemistry: Understanding Our Hormones, the Pill and HRT. London: Cedar Publishing, 1994. (Mandarin Paperbacks)

GUYTON, Arthur C. Guidance Text Book of Medical Physiology.
7th ed. N.P.: Saunders Publishing, 1981.

HANSSEN, Maurice E. The New E For Additives. London: Thorsons, 1987.

HAY, W.H. A New Health Era. London: Harrap, 1934.

HEALTH SCIENCE: the Journal of the American Natural Hygiene Society. Tampa, Florida: The Society, January/February 1996.

HERITAGE, Ford. Composition and Facts About Foods. Mokelumne Hill, California: The Author, 1968. Reprinted 1971.

HOFFMAN, Jay Milton. The Missing Link in the Medical Curriculum: a Ready Reference Guide to Nutrition and Health. 2nd ed. Valley Centre, California: Professional Publishing Co., 1982. Reprinted 1984. First published in 1981.

HOLFORD, Patrick. Family Nutrition Workbook. Wellingborough, Northampton-shire: Thorsons, 1988.

HONIBALL, Essie. I Live on Fruit. Pretoria: Makro Books, 1981.

HOWELL, Edward. Enzyme Nutrition. Wayne, New Jersey: Avery Publishing Group, 1985.

HUGGINS, Hal A. It's All in Your Head: Diseases Caused by Silver-Mercury Fillings. n.p.: Life Sciences Press, 1989.

HURD, F. and HURD, Rosalie. A Good Cook: Ten Talents. 2nd ed. Chisholm, Minnesota: The Authors, 1985. First published in 1968.

IMMERMAN, Alan. Health Unlimited. Happy Camp, California: Naturegraph Publishers, 1989.

JENSEN, Bernard. Foods That Heal. New York: Avery Publishing Group, 1993.

KENTON, Leslie. Ageless Aging. London: Arrow Books, 1989. First published in 1985.

KENTON, Leslie. The Biogenic Diet. London: Arrow Books, 1986. Reprinted 1987, 1988.

KENTON, Leslie. Passage to Power: Natural Menopause Revolution. London: Ebury Press, 1995. Reprinted Vermilion Books, 1996.

KENTON, Leslie. Raw Energy. London: Arrow Books, 1984. Reprinted 1987.

KINE, Zane R. Sunlight. Penryn, California: World Health Publishing, 1980.

KLAPER, Michael. Pregnancy, Children and the Vegan Diet. Paia, Maui, Hawaii, n.d.

KLAPER, Michael. Vegan Nutrition: Pure and Simple. Paia, Maui, Hawaii, n.d.

KULVINSKAS, Viktoras P. Nutritional Evaluation of Sprouts and Grasses. Fairfield, Iowa: 21st Century Publications, n.d. Cover title: Sprouts For the Love of Every Body.

LAURA, Ronald S. and ASHTON, John F. 101 Vital Tips For a Healthy Lifestyle. Sydney, Australia: Angus and Robertson, 1993.

LEE, John. Natural Progesterone. Burwash Common, East Sussex: Nutrition Line, 1996.

LEE, William H. The Friendly Bacteria. New Canaan, Connecticut: Keats Publishing Co., 1988.

McDOUGALL, John A. McDougall's Medicine: a Challenging Second Opinion. Clinton, New Jersey: New Win Publishing, 1985.

McDOUGALL, John A. and McDOUGALL, Mary A. The McDougall Plan. Clinton, New Jersey: New Win Publishing, 1983.

McGRAW, James R. editor. Dick Gregory's Natural Diet For Folks Who Eat: Cooking With Mother Nature. New York: Harper and Row, 1974.

McMAHON, Peggy O'Mara. Mothering: Special Edition: Immunizations. Santa Fe, New Mexico: Mothering Magazine, 1987.

MANDY, Neville. The Keys to Disease-Free Living. Volume One Johannesburg: Natural Health Foundation, 1995.

MANDY, Neville. Nature's Way: The Lifestyle For Life. Johannesburg: Talitha Cumi Publishing Group, 1989.

MARIEB, Elaine. Human Anatomy and Physiology. Holyoke, Massachusetts: Benjamin Currings, 1989.

MEEK, Jennifer. How To Boost Your Immune System. London: ION Press (Institute For Optimum Nutrition), 1988.

MENDELSOHN, Robert S. Confessions of a Medical Heretic. Chicago: Contemporary Books, 1979.

MENDELSOHN, Robert S. How to Raise a Healthy Child...in Spite of Your Doctor. New York: Ballantine Books, 1992.

MEYER, B. J. Fruit For Thought. Pretoria: HAUM, 1979

MILLER, Bruce B. The 4 Week Cholesterol Cure. Dallas, Texas: Bruce Miller Enterprises, 1992.

MILLSTONE, Erik and ABRAHAM, John. Additives: a Guide for Everyone. Harmondsworth, Middlesex: Penguin Books, n.d.

NELSON, Dennis. Food Combining Simplified. n.p.: no pub., 1983.

NELSON, Dennis. Maximizing Your Nutrition. Santa Cruz, California: no pub., 1988.

NOLFI, Kristine and FRY, T.C. The Miracle of Living Foods and the Curse of Cooking. Manchaca, Texas: Health Excellence Systems, 1991.

NUTRITION ADVOCATE. Vol.1, 1995- Vol.2, 1996. Ithaca, New York: New Century Tradition. Monthly.

OSWALD, Jean A. and SHELTON, Herbert M. Fasting For the Health of It. Franklin, Wisconsin: Franklin Books, 1983. Reprinted 1989.

PARHAM, Vistara. What's Wrong With Eating Meat? 2nd ed. Northampton, Massachusetts: Sisters Universal Publishing Co., 1981. First published in 1979.

POTTENGER, Francis M. Jr. Pottenger's Cats: a Study in Nutrition. La Mesa, California: Price Pottenger Nutrition Foundation, 1983.

ROBBINS, Joel. Eating for Health and Wellness. Tulsa, Vitality Unlimited. n.d.

ROBBINS, Joel. Pregnancy, Childbirth and Children's Diet. Colonia, New Jersey: Vitality Unlimited, n.d.

SCHARFFENBERG, John. Problems With Meat. Santa Barbara, California: Woodbridge Press Publishing Co., 1989.

SCHAUSS, A.G. Nutrition and Behaviour. USA: Keats 1988.

SCOTT, Caryl Vaughan. Whole Energy. Johannesburg: Harry C. Pouyoukas Publishers, 1985

SHELTON, Herbert M. Correct Food Combining For Easy Digestion and Wonderful Health. Manchaca, Texas: Health Excellence, n.d.

SHELTON, Herbert M. Fasting Can Save Your Life. 2nd ed. Tampa, Florida: 1978. Reprinted 1991. First published in 1964.

SHELTON, Herbert M. Food Combining Made Easy. San Antonio, Texas: Willow Publishing, 1987. Reprinted 1992. First published in 1982.

SHELTON, Herbert M. Human Life Its Philosophy and Laws: An Exposition of the Principles and Practices of Orthopathy. Mokelumne Hill, California: Health Research, 1979.

SHELTON, Herbert M. Hygienic Care of Children. Bridgeport, Connecticut: Natural Hygiene Press, 1970. Reprinted 1981.

SHELTON, Herbert. M. The Science and Fine Art of Fasting. 5th ed. Tampa, Florida: American Natural Hygiene Society, 1978. Reprinted 1993. First published 1934.

SHELTON, Herbert M. Superior Nutrition. San Antonio, Texas: Willow Publishing, 1987.

SIDHWA, Keki R. Medical Drugs on Trial? Verdict "Guilty!" Chicago, Illinois: Natural Hygiene Press, 1976.

SIDHWA, Keki R. The Quintessence of Natural Living for Health and Happiness. London: British Natural Hygiene Society, 1994.

SINDEN, André. Health Won. 2nd ed. Erasmia, South Africa: Abraham Kruger, 1994. First published in 1993.

STEWART, Maryon. Beat the Menopause Without HRT. Great Britain: Headline Book Publishing, 1995.

TAUB, Edward A. The Wellness Rx. Eaglewood Cliffs, New Jersey: Prentice Hall, 1994.

TAYLOR, Renee. Hunza Health Secrets for Long Life and Happiness. Keats Publishing, 1994.

TROP, Jack Dunn. Please Don't Smoke in Our Home. Tampa, Florida: American Natural Hygiene Society, 1976.

UNITED STATES. DEPARTMENT OF AGRICULTURE. Composition of Foods. Washington: The Department, 1975. (Agricultural Handbook No.8)

VEITH, Walter. Diet and Health: New Scientific Perspectives. n.p.: Southern Publishing Association, [1993?]

WALKER, Norman W. Colon Health. Phoenix, Arizona: O'Sullivan Woodside, 1979.

WALKER, Norman W. The Vegetarian Guide to Diet and Salad. Phoenix, Arizona: O'Sullivan Woodside, 1940. Reprinted 1979.

WEIL, Andrew. Spontaneous Healing. London: Little Brown, 1995.

WEITZ, Martin. Health Shock: a Guide to Ineffective and Hazardous Medical Treatment. London: David & Charles Publishers Limited, 1980.

WHAT DOCTORS DON'T TELL YOU. Edited by Lynne McTaggart. London: Wallace Press, 1979-1996.

WIGMORE, Ann. The Sprouting Book. Wayne, New Jersey: Avery Publishing Group, 1986.

WINGATE, Peter. Penguin Medical Encyclopedia. 2nd ed. Harmondsworth, Middlesex: Penguin Books, 1976. Reprinted 1982.

Recipe Index

Index

factors in 3
related to milk consumption 74-77
role of certain foods in 197-210
diseases, degenerative
causes 5-6
diuretics 35-36, 82, 170
Douglass, Dr J. 54
drugs 9
calcium inhibitors 34
effect during pregnancy 165
recreational 82-84

eating habits
changes in 89
diet plans 91-92, 100-102
guidelines 90-91
rules 99-100
eating plans, for breaking of a fast 154-155
eating plans, transitional 91-92
eczema
factors causing 52
relief of symptoms 205
eggplant 19
nutrient composition 46
protein content 27
eggs 23, 48, 70, 90, 165
effect on behaviour 167
problems concerning the consumption of 73, 200
protein content 27
elderberries
nutrient composition 46
elements, life-sustaining 7
elimination diet
use of fruit in 16
elimination organs 3, 6
emulsifiers 51
endive 20
nutrient composition 46
vitamin content 40
endorphins 184
enemas 183

enzyme pool 56
enzymes 7, 53
Esser, Dr William. L. 15
exercise, importance in correct lifestyle 9-10, 184, 189

fasting 5
benefits of 150-151, 189, 197-198
definition 149
diet programme 171-173
effect on the body 150
for relief of allergies 201
for relief of arthritis 202
for relief of asthma 201
for relief of eczema 205
for relief of high blood pressure 197
for relief of gallstones 199
guidelines 149-150
guidelines for ending 154-155
preparations for 153
professional supervision during 152-153
prohibitions on 151-152
role in lowering high cholesterol levels 197
rules for 152-153
short-term 153-154
weight loss 187-188

fats
combination chart 63
cooked 55
effect on digestion 57
effect on menopausal women 189
harmful 199, 204, 207, 209-210
heated 38
saturated 38, 199
unsaturated 38-39
vegetable 38
see also animal fats
fatty acids 7, 38-39, 189, 199
fennel 19
figs 17
calcium content 35

232